PRAISE F

"We can only aspire to the curios[...] [...]n
Emily Pennington's *Feral* despite the boulders and storms life might
have tumbled at her."
—Nick Offerman, author of *Where the Deer and the Antelope Play* and
Paddle Your Own Canoe

"Emily peels back the superficial layers of van life with unflinching
honesty to reveal the beautifully frustrating reality that is life on the
road, while also gifting readers with important epiphanies set in our
beloved national parks. This is a must read for anyone who values
public land, our environment, and compelling storytelling."
—Craig Grossi, author of *Craig & Fred* and *Second Chances*

"Please read Emily Pennington's brilliantly written story about her year
visiting our national parks. It is filled with the savage beauty, historical
depth, and existential joy nature has to share with all of us. Do not miss
this extraordinary adventure."
—Lyn Lear, Emmy-nominated filmmaker and environmental activist

"Self-improvement, but also connection. The rush of new challenges,
but also the tranquility of quiet moments. Emily Pennington travels
for all the right reasons, and we're so lucky she's brought us along on
the adventure of a lifetime."
—Sebastian Modak, editor-at-large at Lonely Planet and
former *New York Times* 52 Places Traveler

"Emily's vivid memoir is for anyone seeking what could be, rather than accepting what is. Her national park journey is a testament to life-changing relationships, finding oneself, and the transformative power of the outdoors."

—Heather Balogh Rochfort, adventure journalist and author of *Women Who Hike*

"Emily was facing major obstacles as she set out on a huge adventure to visit every US national park, from a breakup to the onset of COVID-19. In an awesome *Eat, Pray, Love* approach to the natural world, she sets out on the adventure of a lifetime, dodging grizzly bears and hiking in some of the world's remotest places. There's no one I'd rather go on this journey with."

—Mary Turner, deputy editor, *Outside* magazine

"Emily Pennington knows America's park system better than most people know their own backyards—it is a privilege to get an intimate glimpse of how that relationship has shaped her."

—Megan Spurrell, senior editor at *Condé Nast Traveler*

"On paper, a plan to visit all sixty-two US national parks in one year sounds like a fun trip—what makes *Feral* an adventure story worth reading, though, is everything that wasn't in the plan."

—Brendan Leonard, author of *The Camping Life* and *Sixty Meters to Anywhere*

"A timely travel memoir that melds together stories of our national park system and the author's life. This is a book about themes that touch us all: exploration, discovery, and home. Packed with vivid details and brutal honesty, to read *Feral* is to know Emily."

—Abigail Wise, digital managing director, *Outside* magazine

FERAL

Losing Myself and Finding My Way in America's National Parks

EMILY PENNINGTON

Little
a

Published by Little A, New York

www.apub.com

Amazon, the Amazon logo, and Little A are trademarks of Amazon.com, Inc., or its affiliates.

ISBN-13: 9781542039710 (hardcover)
ISBN-13: 9781542039703 (paperback)
ISBN-13: 9781542039727 (digital)

Cover design by Kimberly Glyder

Cover image: ©Bill45 / Shutterstock

Map credit: Jacy Zuckerbrow

Interior photos courtesy of the author

Printed in the United States of America

First edition

For the void chasers and the void embracers.

For anyone who has ever wanted to throw a hand grenade into their humdrum life.

For all the defenders of wilderness, near and far.

When you come out of the storm, you won't be the same person who walked in.

That's what this storm's all about.

—Haruki Murakami

Instructions for living a life:

Pay attention.

Be astonished.

Tell about it.

—Mary Oliver

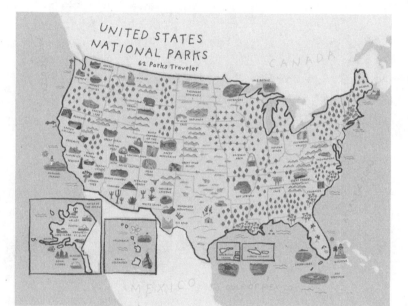

AUTHOR'S NOTE

I feel it's important to note at the beginning of this book that the history of America's national parks (and public lands in general) is one riddled with violence, displacement, and the erasure of countless Native cultures. For much of my journey, I was traveling on lands that were essentially stolen from Indigenous peoples who had lived there since time immemorial. When possible and where it was relevant to the story, I have done my best to highlight some of this rich underlying narrative. I would also like to mention that this is, of course, a mere drop in the bucket when it comes to unearthing and celebrating important Tribal history and achieving any sort of racial equity within the parks. It's an important and timely conversation, and our work has only just begun.

Prologue

Even as I was sinking, the earth was rising. The stubborn, glaciated hulk of Mount Blackburn loomed imperiously on the edge of the Alaskan horizon, staring me down like a god. Awash in alpenglow as if lit from within, its 16,390-foot summit felt hilariously out of place in the scene I inhabited, slouched over a pockmarked picnic table watching the words fall from my mouth and into the vacuum between me and the man I had loved for the last two years.

"I think we should break up."

Adam's deep hazel eyes rioted back from across the table. They twitched for a moment, then squinted as a yellowjacket landed on his forearm. His face twisted into something resembling agreement as he nodded, knocking my ego onto the sandy riverbank below. I couldn't believe it. My adventure-loving dreamboat. My cuddle cult leader. The only person crazy enough to almost marry me. And now he'd be gone from my future forever.

On a mounting list of worst-case scenarios, it was one I hadn't planned for when I set off to visit every US national park seven months earlier. Before the trip, a churning list of potential pitfalls had run at a steady pace in my mind: grizzly bears in Yellowstone, plane crashes in the remote Arctic, flat tires in Death Valley, hurricanes in Florida. But nowhere on the list had I scrawled: "Losing my home and my family. Letting them go." At the onset of my journey, I was a tangle of red hair and a cheeky grin hell-bent on one thing and one thing only: getting through the adventure alive.

That goal was why I had started saving up three years prior, taking my time to build out a used minivan to live in; research a serpentine route that would waste a lot of gas money but intersect each of the parks at their peak season to avoid snow, heat, and road closures; and secure a decent nest egg before quitting my office job and swan diving into the fray. I had $30,000 to my name, more money than I'd ever seen in my life. If everything went according to plan, I would blow it all on a glorious rumspringa to learn more about my country's wilderness—and my own.

Adam took a sip from his water bottle as a yellowjacket began to gnaw at his earlobe, and I violently smacked dozens of the little demons from the air in front of my eyelashes. I blew my nose into the woolen sleeve of my thermal, fighting back tears as another striped yellow asshole landed on my neck, its body vibrating my nerves to war.

Full of rage and confusion, I kept my eyes fixed on the sharp edges of the landscape, skin on fire, stomach boiling, rib cage vacant and jagged. I stepped sideways into a surrealistic melted-clock painting of my own making, and the world swirled around me. Mountains of impossible proportions. The dying light now bathing the serrated curves of the Kennicott Glacier in bright coral. The void ripped open to spill bees onto our faces.

My relationship is over. My love is no longer my love, and my home is no longer my home. I belong nowhere.

Yet somehow, this wasn't even close to the worst thing that would happen to me that year.

A spiky Joshua tree towers over me in Joshua Tree National Park, California.

Chapter 1

Wilderness Pablum

Gray sheets rippled as Adam crawled his hand across my belly, unearthed my naked hip bone, and gently kissed me on the neck. Half-awake, I curled my warm body into his and burrowed under the covers, praying to make the moment last longer. We were months away from that pivotal day at a picnic table in Alaska, and wrapped in the comforts of home and hearth, I felt silly to be leaving the love of my life to catapult myself, for the better part of a year, across a few lines that someone else had drawn on a map. I nibbled at Adam's rib cage, as though silently bargaining for more time. Soon, he would leave for work. The dimple-cheeked man who had been my weekend-adventure companion for the last year and a half was staying behind on the first leg of my trip. It was time to strike out on my own.

"Do you feel ready?" Adam asked, his earnestness filling the room.

"Not a bit."

"I'm sure you'll figure it out when you get on the road. You always do."

He pulled me in and kissed me deeply, his eyes tremendous and almost pixie-like as he pulled back, curious what the creature who lived in his bed might do next.

"Happy trails."

I spent the next hour rolling around, lingering in our sheets to ready my mind for the challenge of actually leaving. Sure, sleeping in a van while traveling the country like a wandering bodhisattva in search of personal transformation might conjure up romantic images of Kerouac and Steinbeck, but when faced with the stark reality of abandoning my plush mattress to live in a car, eating takeout and peeing into a water bottle, I was in less of a hurry to leave.

My plan to visit every national park had existed for years before I met Adam, which was why I had decided to start the adventure alone. After a decade of being chained to my executive assistant desk, I had grown weary of spending my waking hours managing the lives of other, more successful people. Besides, I was never any good at staying put. From the moment I finished college, I fought like hell for jobs I didn't want, did the bare minimum to keep my colleagues happy, secretly researched international flights or far-flung trails from my work computer, quit to build out a van or literally join the circus, and then repeated the cycle. By the time I was thirty-two and had quit my job for good, my résumé's timeline was a swiss cheese of inexplicable sabbaticals and wilderness wanderings. I always felt too big for my skin suit, bursting at the seams from all the wild animal energy swirling around in my veins. I was a maelstrom of unfulfilled desires. A dirtbag in a pantsuit. A cheetah tied to a stake.

There was the matter of my mental health, too. Four years prior, when the deaths of two close friends, an ego-smashing job search, and a bad breakup had left me depressed and suicidal for the first time in my life, the national parks had provided a refuge from which to build myself back up. Like John Muir and Terry Tempest Williams before me, I fled to the outdoors every possible weekend to strengthen my body and soul, prostrating at the feet of the one thing in life I held sacred: mountains. I didn't much care that my healing sanctuary often battered me with hail and wind and falling rocks; I was giddy with a newfound obsession that drew out my innate strength. I was beginning to define myself, free of the confines of city or man, and learning how it felt to stand tall on my own two feet. If I was to fully inhabit my life moving forward, I reasoned, I would need to break away from the daily rhythm of Los Angeles and uncover who I was deep down, separate from partner and profession. The parks didn't care if I was beautiful or bookish or well mannered. They only cared if I was competent.

I wanted to know if this fresh ballast was going to last, so I did the only logical thing I could think of. I started planning a yearlong escape into the American wilds.

I spent three years saving all my extra money for the trip, giving up my West Hollywood bungalow for an apartment shared with two equally thrifty friends, forgoing restaurants in favor of groceries, and working nights as a journalist on the rare occasions that anyone bought my magazine pitches. Though the National Park Service manages more than four hundred units of protected land, I wanted a goal that was affordable and feasible within my twelve-month timeline, so I settled on the sixty-two congressionally designated "national parks" that existed at the time. The trip would cost around $30,000, I reckoned, but hitting my target budget would mean holding fast to an allowance of $1,500 per month, plus a few odd plane tickets to reach Hawai'i, the US Virgin Islands, and the colossus to the north, Alaska.

Thirty thousand dollars seemed like a lot of money at first, given that I would travel and live rent-free in my minivan, staying with friends where I could and stopping only once a week to write and shower in a cheap motel, but when I considered the staggering number of miles I'd need to drive between the parks, my gas budget was often going to be over $600 each month—the same as rent for a place outside New York or Los Angeles. Once I added in the fact that the eight Alaskan parks would cost me nearly $10,000 to visit, between the car rentals and bush planes I'd need to charter to move around, $30,000 started to feel like a pittance. Still, I continued to plan, to save, as the years and months ticked by. I had a road map. I was going to change my life, and I'd make the sacrifices necessary in order to immerse myself completely. In a last-minute burst of luck, I managed to sell my upcoming park dispatches for publication on *Outside* Online, which increased my budget by a few thousand dollars, but I was still operating at a huge loss. If I failed, I had little additional savings to fall back on.

People tend to think big adventures happen only to big people, yet there I was on that unassuming Tuesday, feeling tiny as ever. My meticulous research was full of holes. No matter how much I'd prepared, the frustrating truth was that I had no idea what I was doing. No one ever told me that big adventures start in living rooms. They start in bleary-eyed morning conversations over pancakes. They start in modest coffee shops with old friends. They start struggling over an Excel spreadsheet. When something beckons from deep inside, it will creep into the most mundane corners of your life, tug at the edges of your heart, and quietly whisper, "It's time to go."

I threw the duvet back over my head and procrastinated on my phone for thirty minutes. Then I took a deep breath and leveled with myself.

Look. You don't have to scale a mountain or stare down a grizzly bear right this second. All you have to do is take the first step. And right now, the first step is getting into your van, putting on some music, and driving to Joshua Tree. It's time to go.

And that's exactly what I did.

⚜

My adventure chariot sat quietly in our driveway, baking in the pervasive California sunshine and blanketed in a fine coat of Los Angeles smog. Since my nickname for the last eight years had been Gremlin (I shouldn't eat after midnight, and yes, I bite), it seemed only fitting to dub my trusty steed Gizmo, a nod to both her complex machinery and her unpredictable temperament.

Gizmo was far from a model-esque, Instagram-ready adventuremobile. She was lightly dented and completely gutted, a 2015 Ford Transit Connect that I had rescued two years earlier from one of those sad lots on the side of the road that buys cars at auction, hoping to flip them at a profit. At three years old, she was already wiser and crankier than her age might suggest; her previous owner had managed to rack up 96,115 miles in her short lifespan.

She was unruly too. A few years prior, on a weekend romp in Sequoia, her transmission completely went out while I wound past colossal trees and fading sunset views of Moro Rock. As my anxiety soared, I slammed my foot down, alternating between the gas pedal and brake in a desperate attempt to get her to kick into gear. Gizmo rolled downhill at a crawl, Subarus full of hungry, tree-hugging families riding her bumper all the way into the small mountain town of Three Rivers, where, after an embarrassingly slow lurch forward from a red traffic light, she took a two-hour nap in the parking lot of a restaurant.

Heart in throat, panicked, and near tears, I pulled up an educational YouTube video on my phone aimed at teaching children how a transmission works. A 1950s-style male voiceover crooned over black-and-white footage of gears gyrating. I hated that I had grown so reliant on technology whose inner workings were a complete mystery to me. The van might as well have run on fairy dust. My companion on the trip stared, dumbstruck, as I watched the video in the driver's seat. I knew we'd be lucky if Gizmo survived the long drive back to LA.

Piles of cash and a rebuilt transmission later, my relationship with Gizmo was solidified. Wanting to ritualize my moment of embarkation, I stepped out of the house and into the sunlight, my water bottle in one hand and a bundle of sage in the other. I lit the sage and watched as flames crawled upward, then turned to pulsating embers. My nostrils filled with sweet, herbaceous smoke. Leaning into the cramped bedroom quarters of the minivan, I swirled the smoldering leaves around her embroidered bohemian fabrics, thick wool blanket, and midnight-blue curtains, conjuring up my best attempt at graceful sorcery, blessing the space. If there ever was a moment for reverence, this was it. My entire life had been simmered down into a small vehicle, and I was about to hop in and drive.

One of my oldest friends, Jack, had helped me construct a bed platform and line the doors with hand-stained wood in Gizmo's rear cargo area. An old-school burner and Berkeley hippie at heart, he was confident that the traditional cabin-style two-by-four paneling on most van build-outs was not going to be as fun as lining the walls and ceiling with motley textiles I had picked up on my travels abroad to India and Thailand.

"Fabric's just so much easier to work with," he assured me. "Plus, you know, it'll be so much more comfortable if you do, like, drugs."

Since then, I had worked hard to turn Gizmo into a road trip–ready marvel. Though she was hardly more than a full-sized mattress in the back of a two-seater cab, I had outfitted her with as many creature comforts as I could fit inside her molded steel walls.

There were five long, flat, clear plastic bins that slid under the bed and held my everyday possessions: one for clothing, one for dry food and pantry items, one for shoes, one for tools and electronics, and one for kitchen essentials. My vanity had been reduced to five shirts, three pairs of pants, three sports bras, eight pairs of socks, and ten pairs of underwear. I had two jackets and two sets of thermals for the freezing nights I was sure to encounter. I'd splurged on a fancy cooler that melted my ice only ever so slightly slower than the next leading brand. If I wanted to cook a meal, I would have to rely on my cigarette lighter, water-boiling kettle, single-burner propane stove, aluminum pot, nonstick frying pan, and two sets of plastic plates, bowls, and utensils. Hanging behind the passenger seat was a two-tiered toiletry bag crammed full with my toothbrush, toothpaste, acne medicine, Band-Aids, hairbrush, lotion, solid shampoo and conditioner, and enough ibuprofen to kill a horse. Ford had designed a narrow shelf above the two seats up front, and I used it for items I might need in a pinch—pee funnel, water bottle, baby wipes, and a national parks guidebook. In the far back, behind the last of the plastic bins, I'd managed to squeeze a fold-up camping table against the side wall. Between the edge of the bed and the rear doors sat a seven-gallon water container and a portable power station attached to a solar panel that I'd Velcro-sealed to the roof so I could charge my laptop, phone, camera, and vibrator on the go. I wanted my year in the van to feel like roughing it, but not too rough.

Up top were a roof rack and a rigid, charcoal-colored plastic box that served as an attic for all my camping equipment. It was filled to the brim with a tent, a down sleeping bag, three backpacks of differing sizes, an inflatable mattress pad, a bear canister, crampons, an ice axe, a helmet, climbing gear, two fold-up camping chairs, a shovel, fire starters, trekking poles, a tiny backpacking stove, a bear bell, a first-aid kit, a water-purifying device, dehydrated meals, and loads of extra sunscreen and bug spray.

⚜

It's amazing how often our bodies know just what to do. The mind may lock us into inaction, but set loose to move, play, and discover, a body will make magic happen every time. The corporeal can shape-shift a tired mind into presence.

Saged and ready, I was nervous to finally be on the road after years of planning and buildup. I sat my hips onto the driver's-side seat and turned the key in Gizmo's ignition. Tears welled up in my eyes as I backed out of the driveway to embark on a three-day test run in Joshua Tree, the first park of the year. Though leaving home was a task I had completed hundreds of times before, this moment signified me willingly grabbing the steering wheel of my own life and spinning doughnuts at the feet of the Fates, weighting the unknown with intention. I set a course east.

Two and a half hours away from Los Angeles, beyond cardboard suburbs cloaked in smog, past the peeling paint of dismal 1970s strip malls, across a parched California desert littered with windmills the size of skyscrapers, I arrived at Joshua Tree, a wonderland of enormous monzogranite boulders and many-armed Seussian trees.

Legend has it that in the mid-1800s, after fatigued Mormon immigrants first crossed the Colorado River, they were hungry for a sign of good fortune while traversing this arid landscape. As they looked out and saw the spiky octopus limbs of thousands of head-high yucca plants, they interpreted the shapes as the silhouette of their prophet, Joshua, arms skyward, beckoning them to the promised land.

I wished I had the fortitude that a saintly apparition could bring as I nervously laced up my boots and stepped out onto my first trail of the yearlong voyage. What I lacked in divine swagger, I made up for in years of repetitive motion. Hiking had been my main source of therapy for half a decade, an excuse to commune with the dirt when overwhelmed and city-sore. I was anxious about hiking alone in an unfamiliar place, sure, but what trounced that fear was the muscle memory that my feet could carry me into an entirely different state of being. My hiking boots were a blade that cut through nerves.

The Boy Scout Trail is mostly flat and nestled into the pinyon-juniper belt that parades across much of Joshua Tree's high desert landscape. *What a perfect warm-up hike for my mushy, post-drive mind,* I mused.

To my right, the park's famous Wonderland of Rocks sprouted up and out of the ground like the fingers of some long-buried giantess, and as I tramped along the gravel walkway, I couldn't help but crane my neck skyward toward the myriad of thorny, green-afroed trees that dotted the landscape in every direction. Just off trail, I noticed a boulder garden low enough to hoist myself onto, and I scrambled hand over foot to reach a ledge seventy feet off the ground so that I could watch the dying light. I could see for miles. The crumbled remains of hundred-million-year-old igneous rock seemed to stretch on to where the snowcapped peak of Mount San Jacinto towered on the horizon.

The sunset that evening was spectacular. Delicate cirrus clouds paraded across the heavens, lit up in a radical neon-pink glow. The sky was made of rainbow sherbet. *What a way to start the trip,* I thought, as I watched the tangerine egg yolk of the sun dip below the horizon. A cottontail hopped by, and though it was only my first day on the road, I felt as though I had traversed a million miles to get to this precise moment. My solitude. My self-reliance. A year in the wild.

I waltzed back to the van, head high above the clouds as the delicate first stars began winking into view. I found a dusty, free campsite on a dry lake bed to the north of the park, situated the van, and came back down to earth when I stared into my cooler. My dinner options didn't seem to fit the otherworldly sights I had just encountered.

I settled on spicy bean burritos with a side of carrot sticks because my mother always said that dinner doesn't count without a vegetable. When your home is essentially a mattress with a cooler and a battery pack on wheels, you have to cobble together meals that at least play at being nutritious. Add in the fact that it gets dark at 5:00 p.m. and rapidly cools to subfreezing temperatures at the height of winter, and even the most seasoned camper will find themselves grabbing any protein-rich food that's fast and filling before cocooning themselves in their sleeping bag.

Tortillas, cheese, and soy milk were my saviors, their quick satiation essential when discomfort wrecked an otherwise ordinary evening. Night felt radically different in the wild, all unknown creaks and shrieks in the dark. Though I was parked in a legal area that was packed with full-time RVers, I felt uneasy. Despite my desire to live a more hermetic lifestyle and commune with nature, I stilled myself by pulling out my phone and watching a Netflix show, the ultimate millennial salve. I fell asleep early.

The night was cold, and I spent it tossing and turning against the yodeling clatter of coyotes. Gizmo had a myriad of creature comforts, but she didn't possess a stand-alone heater. If I wanted to warm up my bedroom, I had to run the engine and blast warm air through the front vents.

I woke to twenty-eight-degree weather and piled on extra layers of clothing until I resembled a marshmallow. Eager to hit the park's Cholla Cactus Garden by sunrise, I needed to hustle. I drove down a winding desert road in the pitch black, past ghostly groves of Joshua trees and a glaring marigold stripe of sun that was beginning to puncture a cluster of low-hanging clouds. When I arrived at the cactus garden, everything was awash in rose-colored light. Puckered flower pods protruded here and there from the teddy-bear cholla, a cactus so enveloped in miniature spines that it almost appears fuzzy and soft. Despite being starved for affection on the open road, I looked but did not touch. The sun blinked open its fiery cyclopic eye, and the thorny edges of the cacti lit up as though each one had an aura that suddenly glowed.

But reality called, and I drove around for an hour, desperately seeking a bathroom. The poetry of van life is twofold—half jaw-dropping encounters with earth's natural wonders, half trying to figure out how to manage unwieldy bodily functions.

On excursions, I often felt my body was like a newly adopted puppy, with a laundry list of hungers and urges that needed to be satiated if balance was to be restored. Like a pet, I'd take myself for walks and pee breaks and make myself dinner before I started chewing on my own shoes out of boredom. I'd plop myself onto a bed to recharge for eight hours every night. So that morning, just when I thought I was ready for my planned seven-mile hike out to an abandoned gold mine in the middle of the desert, my digestive system put a wrench in my plans. Driving through the middle of a desolate landscape, with no discernible shrubs or trees to hide my bare ass behind, I was in trouble.

I had to lurch Gizmo into a handicapped space at a nearby climbing crag and run behind a cactus.

Urgent needs met, I made it to Lost Horse Mine in time for lunch. I couldn't help but wonder how it must have felt to be one of the original thirty-five men who worked and lived in that bleak expanse of dust and silence. At the height of the operation, from 1894 to 1931, the mine had produced ten thousand ounces of gold and sixteen thousand ounces of silver, roughly $18 million in today's currency, but only a handful of men ever saw the profits. The rest worked grueling jobs like chopping wood and maintaining tunnels, cut off from civilization.

The wind flung an actual tumbleweed across the parched landscape, and I picked at my cuticles to stave off the unease of my mind's static. It was too quiet for comfort. Even with a car, an iPhone, and a credit card, my enthusiasm for alone time was already waning on my second day in. I loved spending time in the outdoors on weekends, but with the full force of a year of dirt and discomfort and bugs staring me down, I suddenly wasn't so sure. *Why the hell am I here? What do I hope to learn from living in the national parks for a year? Will I watch myself become stronger and more self-sufficient or flounder in the wake of my loneliness?* I meandered around the rest of the trail, feeling wistful for my city life and grateful that I had a honky-tonk bar to visit.

⁕

Pappy and Harriet's has been the stuff of Pioneertown legend for the last forty years, so it's no wonder that the place was already packed at 6:00 p.m., when I rolled up to the distressed, log cabin–style facade. The inside was full of desert hipsters and old-school locals—lacy kimono–wearing pixies and horse folk alike slamming back ice-cold PBRs. A gilded bald eagle soared above walls nailed with a tapestry of vintage license plates boasting slogans like "EVL WICH" and "MS KTEER."

Behind the bar was a sepia-stained bust of the late Pappy himself, a shaggy-haired mountain man complete with a suede fedora.

More wayward child than minxy barfly, I walked up to the only free stool and ordered a beer. There was an older man in an ill-fitting T-shirt leaning against an empty seatback, and I prayed that he'd let me sit down and eat.

"Excuse me," I said coyly. "Do you mind if I sit here and order some food before the band starts?"

"Sure thing! Sit on up here, missy. Them young folks sure done made it crowded on a Thursday night these days."

I ordered the ribs, and the man introduced himself as Pete. He had a lady friend sitting at his side whom he introduced as Mary. She had frizzy, bleached-blonde hair and a really sweet drunk mom energy. I liked her immediately. I told them about my project; about my boyfriend, Adam, who was home and wouldn't join full-time until summer; and about my decked-out minivan.

"Oh dear," Mary murmured between vodka tonics. "I would never let my daughter run around on her own like that. Where do you sleep? Don't you get scared? There's people running around out here at night."

Before I had a chance to answer, the band struck up, and I was catapulted back in time to the late 1960s. The lead singer was a fierce twentysomething with dark, wavy hair and a smile that radiated out from her face like a floodlight. She had the soul of Janis Joplin and the polished panache of an Instagram style icon. They kicked into an upbeat, twangy country tune, and the crowd rushed onto the dance floor. The scene was a melting pot of Converse-wearing toddlers, felt-hat yuppies, and ranch hands, and I danced for what felt like hours, a moment of connected bliss amid the solitude.

But on the drive back, I couldn't shake what Mary had said. For the first time, it occurred to me that perhaps my assumption that I could sleep safely in a car for a year was one of incredible privilege and naivete. Despite my having memorized nearly every page of Cheryl Strayed's *Wild* and clocking hundreds of miles on backcountry trails, maybe I wasn't as fluent in adventure as I'd initially believed. I tossed and turned in my blankets and couldn't quite seem to get comfortable. Sleep came in fits and starts.

Backpacking in the Grand Canyon, Arizona

Chapter 2

WESTWARD EXPANSION

The next day, I drove. I drove back across eastern California and its collage of dusty sameness. I drove through the Inland Empire, a sprawling mess spilling out of Los Angeles. I drove past familiar streets and palm trees, ultimately landing back at my own front door. But somehow, home felt different. The promise of domestic stability had been severed from me, at least for a while, and I began to hover above my former life like some detached, free-floating entity.

The next night, Adam threw me a formal "going away" party, though I'd already left, and I wandered through the space repeating practiced anecdotes about what it means to be a woman alone in the wild, and how I planned to use my spiritual practice to stare down the anxiety monsters when they inevitably arose. But part of me was still out on the road, and I was eager to rejoin it.

I woke early the following morning and sped out of the city on a smog-scented ribbon of highway. The plan was to meet my friend Cameron in the mountains just out of town and caravan five hours north to Pinnacles National Park for two days of hiking and rock climbing. By the time I caught up to him at Pyramid Lake, he looked like he could cry at any moment.

"You okay?" I asked. Though he was always a little dark and sardonic, the kid was going through a lot, I knew, even by his standards. He'd been struggling with a potential breakup and a dying father way out on the East Coast.

"Yeah . . . yeah. It's good to see you. I need a hug."

I pulled him in close for a good thirty seconds before we untangled and commenced with the long drive north, me in Gizmo and him following in his own van. Central California walloped me with its developed agriculture, all irrigated tracts, political dust-bowl billboards, and fields full of cattle ready for slaughter. Getting gas in Coalinga reminded me how so much of the country lives—fried food, dented pickups, and trailers housing produce pickers etched like bricks into the town's center. Los Angeles's maze of organic grocers and vegan gelaterias is not the status quo.

We entered the park under the black of night and snuck into a campsite without paying, since we couldn't find the fee station in the darkness. The cold turned my fingers white and my nose numb, and before long, I retired to my wool blanket and heated mattress pad to rest.

❦

"So the climb we want to do is over here." Cameron pointed to his map in the brilliant morning light as I sipped my coffee groggily. "Guess what side of the park we're on?" he asked.

"Umm . . . the exact opposite side?"

"Yeah."

"Fuck. FUCK. Fuck. Are we going to hike the extra miles with the rope and all of our gear?" I whined, already regretting our decision to go climbing.

"Yep."

". . . Okay, fine."

We wandered around camp, waiting for the sun to rise and the temperature to get above a goosebump-inducing forty-five degrees. Rock climbing with numb fingers and toes is a surefire way to either fall, second-guess every move you make, curse the day you were born, or all three simultaneously. So we waited.

When it was time to go, Cameron coiled up his rope, counted his carabiners and quickdraws, and clipped his climbing shoes to the outside of his bag while I made peanut butter sandwiches and laced up my hiking boots. We stomped our way across the park, paralleling a gently burbling creek, scrambling down into the maw of Balconies Cave, and hiking up and into the pinnacles themselves, towering spires of lichen-encrusted rock that soared above us.

Following the map, Cameron took a sharp left after the cave, lugging his lumpish pack through an increasingly steep series of boulders. The trail petered out, and I found myself crawling up a steep, grassy slope on hands and knees, exhausted and confused.

"I think we're lost," I offered, breathless.

"Yeah. I don't know. Maybe. Probably."

"We need to eat lunch. I'm going to freak out if I don't get some calories into my body."

The sandwiches helped. I took a deep breath and a second look at the map, reread the instructions, and hung my head in my hands.

"Dude," I whined, "we turned off too soon."

By this point it was early evening, and the sun had already begun to paint the surrounding mountains a honeyed shade of orange. We hopped back onto the main trail for a quarter mile, made it to the base of the first climb, a breezy 120-foot pitch called Costanoan, and roped up. Cameron took the lead while I belayed from below, funneling the woven rope through my fingers, and as he reached the top and built out an anchor to clip into, the weather was once again turning brisk. I couldn't feel my toes through the thin rubber of my climbing shoes as I started up the wall. Plus, this rock had seen a lot more moisture than the desert boulders I was accustomed to; it was freckled with moss and lichen, slippery and untrustworthy. I made it to the top, but I was kvetching the whole way.

"I'm kind of done," I grumbled.

"I'm kind of done too."

We rappelled down as the sunset intensified, our humble canyon of volcanic breccia illuminated in amber. On the hike back to the vans, Cameron leveled with me.

"I think I'm just going to head out tonight."

"Wait, what?"

"Yeah, I think if I leave now, I can make it halfway to LA and then maybe set up a date with that girl before flying home to my dad later in the week."

"You're just going to leave me alone in the dark in the freezing weather? And not eat dinner first? That sucks, man."

Disgruntled as I was, I couldn't do a thing about it. This trip was mine to bear. I begrudgingly said my goodbyes, and then I was on my own again. I cooked dinner at a park picnic area before looking for a free place to camp, warming my hands over the propane stove as I laid out the necessary fixings for a cheer-myself-up quesadilla. When I turned toward the van to put the shredded cheese back into the cooler, I noticed I wasn't alone.

There's a raccoon on my goddamn pillow.

I could see my breath illuminated by the van's headlights in the inky black of night as I stooped over a wooden picnic table, guarding my bounty. Compared to the wilderness that surrounded me—moss-laden trees, crags, creeks choked with poison oak—my small stove and LED lights must have seemed like the apex of high society to the forest's locals. It's no wonder I had uninvited dinner guests.

Still, I screamed. My heart leaped into my throat, and I lurched toward the unattended vehicle with the confidence of an unruly toddler, howling a convincing, "No! Bad raccoon! Go away!" As if the greedy little trash panda understood English. He ran up a nearby tree as I slammed the sliding door shut and returned to my frying pan, only to find a second pair of beady eyes, hungry and expectant, staring back at me from the opposite end of the table. Killing the flame, I nixed my plans for eating under the stars and sulked as I shoved a tortilla into my mouth from the driver's-side seat.

⌇

In my youth I spent two summers with my grandparents in Sweden—an only child and latchkey kid able to roam the old-growth forests of Scandinavia at will as long as I was home in time for supper. I often spent my afternoons traipsing along lakeshores, lounging on lichen-speckled boulders, and wondering which stumps faeries made their homes in. The world, as far as I was concerned, was awash in hidden wonders.

As a diehard optimist, I've found that managing my own expectations in the face of the less-than-stellar realities that the world serves up can be a constant struggle. When I grew up, I believed that my surroundings were uniquely magical and full of small miracles, even when explained by science. But my parents split before I was born, and my dad—an addict with mounting money problems and drug abuse issues—wasn't around for most of my childhood. He'd occasionally show up for the odd holiday or weekend hangout, then disappear back into the dust.

My father was an unreliable role model, to say the least. My mother, a hardworking immigrant who believed that good grades and extracurricular activities were my ticket out of the poverty she had faced in her early twenties. Raised in a suburban home outside Houston, I spent my summers looping circles around cul-de-sacs with my bicycle and trying not to turn my towhead green in the heavily chlorinated community pool. But with my mom working long hours and no steady male figure in the picture, my childhood never felt as settled or idyllic as the lives of the kids around me. I spent a lot of time home alone, watching reruns and microwaving chicken tenders when I wasn't finishing my homework. It was the perfect recipe for a child who hoped for the best but often felt abandoned.

One of the things I was most curious about on my year of exploration was that lingering sense of loneliness and abandonment. I wanted to understand it better, to face it as though I were my own parent, lovingly and calmly sitting with it and understanding what it had to teach me. If I was alone, I wanted to trust that it wouldn't kill me. If I was anxious, I wanted to soothe the feral child.

A week before I left on my big trip, I'd attended a meditation retreat at Deer Park Monastery, a friendly Buddhist enclave in the lineage of Zen Master Thich Nhat Hanh. My goal was to consciously transition from the office world that had been my constant companion for years to the silence and solitude I expected to find on the road.

At the retreat, practitioners woke at 5:00 a.m. and quietly began a morning ritual of mindful meditation, eating, working, and walking before a lunch break and a series of spiritual lectures. "In mindfulness, one is not only restful and happy but alert and awake," teaches Hanh. "Meditation is not evasion; it is a serene encounter with reality." When tasked with nothing else but to simply and consciously go about my day, I felt a hint of newfound peace rise within me. I fell so in love with this friendly, soulful hamlet that, on the final day of the immersion, I took part in a ceremony to receive the Five Mindfulness Trainings— reverence for life, true happiness, true love, loving speech and deep listening, and nourishment and healing—and was given a dharma name: Creative Healing of the Heart. It was a moniker I dreamed of living up to.

In the Sallatha Sutta, the Buddha speaks about the concept of the second arrow. The story goes that when an arrow strikes your body, you will feel pain. When a second arrow comes and strikes you in that same spot, the pain will be magnified ten times. The Buddha explains that the majority of the pain we feel in life is the product of this second arrow, not the first. When we stop to lament, or worry, or protest, or grow fearful, we are willingly driving a second arrow into a pain point that already exists, and though we may want to believe that we are calming ourselves down with cathartic outbursts of anger, or sorrow, or panic, the truth is that we're only multiplying our hurt. Adding pain to an already stressful situation by heaping an emotion or expectation onto it does nothing to solve the issue or heal our wounds. In times of emotional upheaval, the second arrow comes from our inability to let go.

⌘

The closest free campsite I could find that night was an hour's drive away. I set off in the darkness on a winding road through cow pastures and dilapidated ranch houses. A white pickup truck roared past me, headlights blazing a blinding white swath through the trees. *Am I about to be assaulted by Proud Boys drinking Miller Lite?* Mary's words of warning were pinging around in my brain. I refocused and parked near a placard marking site number two, frost already clinging to the surrounding shrubs. Lying in bed, I gazed up at the fabric-covered ceiling my friend Jack and I had glued together two years prior. There was the sparkling quilt embroidered in emerald green that I'd swooned over on a trip to India many years ago, sensing that it possessed good magic and would someday occupy an important place in my life.

But now, as I tossed and turned alone and the temperature dropped, the pull of my nerves and my fear of unknown creatures lurking just outside the van door clobbered any goodwill the tapestry offered. I couldn't help it. I hurtled a second arrow directly into my chest. The fact that I didn't have cell service only worsened my state. Every little sound pricked me awake. Every new thought was a hellion pummeling my sense of safety.

Someone will wake me in the night with a shotgun. I am going to be followed by the truck people and murdered and raped. I will be kidnapped and taken to a place where bears will eat me and hillbillies will tap-dance on my grave. This is stupid. Thisisstupid. Thisisstupid.

I rummaged through my first-aid stash, took half a Xanax, and passed out.

⚜

Morning came, and the world was awash in color. Tiny frost crystals sparkled on the oak trees that surrounded my campsite, and I lingered in bed, eating oatmeal and drinking coffee, waiting for the road to thaw. It seemed ridiculous that I had been so afraid of this hillside campground only hours before; everything was so beautiful, soaked in yellow light. If I was to survive a year in the wilderness, it seemed, I would need to accept that each day had two radically different sides: a light-filled expanse in which anything was possible and a frigid waiting game of darkness and slumber. It wasn't personal; it just was. Only specialized animals were nocturnal, and I, sadly, was not one of them. I vowed to let myself do whatever was necessary to stay calm and get a good night's sleep as the year progressed. If that meant skipping a sunset to find a safe campsite, so be it.

When I felt ready to drive, I cruised down the mountain road blaring Simon & Garfunkel, feeling grateful that the evening's sinister vibe had all been in my head. *I am in fabulous central California! In the winter! And it's sunny!*

After parking the van in a small lot at Old Pinnacles Trailhead, I felt eager to hear the familiar crunch of my boots against the earth, the clack-clack-clacking of my trekking poles like a heartbeat that could bring equilibrium to my own. I filled my backpack with crackers, cheese, and protein bars, forgot my sunscreen, ran back to the van to grab my sunscreen, and started walking. The plan was to link up the

High Peaks Trail, the Steep and Narrow section, the Rim Trail to Bear Gulch Reservoir, Bear Gulch Cave, and Moses Spring, capping it off with a little hike along Chalone Creek. An all-day romp around the entirety of the park.

Quail scuttled across the trail as unseen warblers called out from bush to bush along the fifteen-hundred-foot ascent that marked the beginning of my day. In all my years of tramping around Southern California, I had never noticed such a variety of birds on a single hike before. They fluttered around the low-lying chaparral, belting out their high-pitched trills as I walked. By the time I got to the higher-altitude Steep and Narrow area, I was sporting a massive grin. I ascended dozens of near-vertical stone steps that had been cut into the massive rock formations by 1930s trail crews. These park improvements, a product of Roosevelt's New Deal, are everywhere, if one knows where to look, and stumbling upon them was a fun Easter egg in any park visit.

I switchbacked down, down, down toward Bear Gulch Cave, kicking dust off my shoes as I practically galloped downhill and entered the eerie, boulder-strewn tunnels. Due to hibernating bats, much of the cave had been closed off, so I left as soon as I arrived and kept on walking.

I have a poet friend who says that, for him, woodpeckers symbolize love. I've never quite understood why, but whenever he hears one on a trail, he won't give up until he's located and identified it. Is it a pileated or a ladder-backed? He is relentless in his search for this kind of reverent affirmation in the wild. I've watched this forty-five-year-old man leap over downed trees and push through blackberry bushes to get to a small red-and-black bird and exclaim, "Ah, ladder-backed!" with a grin on his face that could swallow an ocean.

So it was with enormous glee that I rounded a corner near the Bear Gulch Nature Center to find not one but five acorn woodpeckers hopping across the tree bark in search of a meal. My mouth pulled into a toothy, childlike grin as I watched them scamper about from oak to oak. I felt like the universe was winking at me after my uneasy night spent solo. Feet on earth, I practically flew down the last few miles of the trail, my gravity and mood restored. Maybe this kind of careful attention was what I needed to recognize my place in all things. Maybe alone wasn't so lonely after all.

But I had a date with Adam for park number three, Death Valley. I made it back through my planned loop hike and hopped into Gizmo to speed off across the pastoral hillsides, shaking the balmy late-afternoon heat from my skin. Despite my solo revelation, I was ready for company.

The next morning I woke with a horrific head cold, my skull an overripe melon of snot. Tossing and turning with a balletic grace so as not to wake my slumbering boyfriend, I had slept maybe four hours in total. I felt entombed in my own body, pressure building like an underwater balloon. And yet, there was a schedule to keep. The tiny dictator living inside my mind knew that parks still needed to be seen.

"Adam . . . I feel like ass. Can you help pack up the van?"

Adam playfully smacked my butt as he rose out of bed, donning a pair of jet-black hiking pants, a periwinkle T-shirt, and a fuzzy blue Patagonia jacket that made him look like Cookie Monster on a diet. Say what you will about his fashion sense, but the man's immune system was rock solid. Over a year and a half of dating, I had caught nearly every illness known to humankind, including an ear infection, a stomach bug in Nepal, and a particularly attractive stretch of two colds and a flu in under eight weeks. Adam, on the other hand, threw up once in Arizona. If staying peaceful and well under stressful conditions were a horse race, my odds would be on him.

A full ten years older than I was, Adam was quieter and better versed in his mindfulness practice, remaining calm and centered in the face of the busy modern world. He had the uncanny ability to shake off a migraine; show up to his day job at a virtual reality company; complete a series of repetitive, mind-numbing computer tasks for eight hours; sit through traffic; and still manage to cook dinner for us before collapsing onto the couch to watch TV.

I was more the fun-loving, type A extrovert with a big heart and bigger dreams, who mapped out all of our adventures while working as an executive assistant and moonlighting as a wannabe writer. Regardless of our outward personality differences, Adam was always down for any shenanigan I proposed, whether it be a 17,769-foot walking pass on the Annapurna Circuit; an overnight backpacking trek to a series of muddy, secluded hot springs in the Sierra Nevada; or saying "I love you" for the first time in the belly of a mosh pit. He wasn't as wilderness savvy as I was, but it didn't matter. Whenever I got a hankering to escape Los Angeles, I planned and Adam followed.

This year felt different, though. I had been preparing for my national parks trip since well before we met, after a string of back-to-back relationships left me gutted. I reckoned that learning how to be alone for a year might do me some good. Meeting Adam threw a wrench into the whole idea, but I wanted to make it work. I wanted to have it all—the solitude and the stability of a partner. I wanted to fling myself onto the road for twelve months, jettisoned by curiosity and self-exploration rather than heartbreak or divorce, as so many of my adventure role models had done.·

And Adam wanted to join when he could, so when I awoke the first morning of our weekend in Death Valley fearing my nose might explode off my face in a symphony of snot, I was grateful he actually liked cooking so that I could hobble around in my pajamas, pretending to pack while he made eggs.

We sped across Highway 395, the relentlessly cheerful timbre of Jonathan Van Ness's audiobook *Over the Top* serenading us as our churning tires spun toward the Panamint Mountain Range. Chaparral and the occasional alpine conifer gave way to a barren expanse of huge berms speckled with the occasional cactus or creosote bush. Because I'm a devotee of lush mountainside forests, the desert has always struck me as inherently lonely. Its rows upon rows of mountains, in which nothing appears to live, leave uneasy pangs in my stomach. As we veered into the western entrance of the park, the waste only intensified. Death Valley is an arid wonderland, as if the god of rocks got bored one day and frivolously slammed together seemingly contradictory geology, neglecting to add the ingredients for organic life. Coarse rhyolitic lava flows hugged granitic intrusions. To my left were a series of enormous sand dunes. To my right, the turnoff for Mosaic Canyon. Van Ness's effervescent tone made me giggle through my sneezes as Adam steered the van toward the latter.

Desolation and fabulous queens. I couldn't think of a more polar-opposite pairing.

Parked and suited up in our outdoor uniforms of backpacks, boots, and trekking poles, the two of us set off on a gravel path toward the canyon's gaping mouth. Once we were inside, the light began to shift into extravagant honeys and buttermilks. The walls narrowed, and I traced my hands across cool, flash flood–polished marble and the rougher, more colorful breccia that lay just beyond. This mosaic breccia, created when clusters of smaller stones are cemented in place by a different type of rock, is what gives the popular canyon its name. When the sun hits it just right, the canyon appears to glow.

Adam shuffled his feet up a near-vertical dry fall, boots sliding against slick marble as he ascended. I couldn't contain my smile as we clambered up the steep walls, laughing whenever one of us made a wrong move and nearly fell face-first into the rock. In spite of a head that felt like an anvil, I was floored by the unexpected beauty of the hike. The canyon's walls narrowed, and soon we were squeezing through slot canyons freckled with a collage of pebbles. When we neared the final obstacle of the trek, a twenty-five-foot amphitheater of rock with no way to climb out, Adam inched over to the craggy wall, held out his pointer finger, and lightly tapped its surface.

"Boop. Thus ends the hike."

"This hike shall henceforth be known as the most glorious in the whole of Death Valley!"

"And lo, on the first day of this desert park, it shall be decreed that the hike was good. And that I doth love you."

We practically skipped our way out of the canyon the way we came, speaking in fake British accents and cracking Moses-era jokes about the day's exploits. I was dizzy with sun and ready for more. Hopping back into Gizmo, we plotted a course for Artists Palette.

Earth's nearest star began to sink toward the horizon as I rounded a bend onto Artists Drive, a one-way semicircular road that whisks travelers across crumbling umber cliffs to a hillside blotched with rainbow-colored minerals, as though Jackson Pollock grew three sizes and had a pastel field day with the landscape. Smudgy lumps of robin's-egg blue and blush pink erupted across the mountains, and as the sunset intensified, Adam and I threw on our gloves and hats to tramp around in the wild expanse. I stilled myself in the chilly desert air by closing my eyes and taking deep breaths, inhaling and exhaling slowly as a light breeze tickled my cheeks. For the first time that day, I forgot my arduous schedule and my stuffy nose and began to feel something like peace.

Camp was a well-known boondocking site just outside the park called the Pads. Boondocking, for anyone who hasn't hoofed it in an RV long term, is what van dwellers call sleeping in free, undeveloped campsites off the beaten path. What a boondock site lacks in toilets and amenities it makes up for in undisturbed beauty and the fact that it's, well, free. No one's quite sure what the Pads used to be, but rumor has it that an old mining firm went bust a few decades ago and packed up all its mobile housing, leaving behind only a series of level concrete slabs perfect for camping. I rolled Gizmo onto one just as the Milky Way began showing off in the deep black sky, its creamy wave of star-dust and nebulas suspended midair like a web of magic, hovering just out of reach.

⁓⁂⁓

I woke to the death rattle of my own breathing, the ragged in-out against my throat too loud for slumber. Adam seemed oblivious, thank god. He and I had agreed to start early and take in the famous sunrise view from Zabriskie Point, which meant waking before dawn and stuffing our tired faces with protein bars and bananas as we drove across the soot-black night.

After I took a fistful of over-the-counter cold medicines, the two of us parked and sauntered onto a ledge overlooking some of Death Valley's most striking badland formations, dramatic chocolate cliffs giving way to linen-hued wrinkles in the earth's crust that stretched on for miles. It was the sort of scene you could get lost in, bleary thoughts drifting off in the rose-colored glasses of sunrise, but . . . we weren't alone.

As one of the premier activities in Death Valley, watching the sunrise from Zabriskie Point has gone the way of many internet-famous natural wonders. Bundled in a puffy gray jacket, thick gloves, and my wool mohawk beanie, I tiptoed to the cliffside overlook, expecting to see a few other wild-eyed beauty seekers. Instead, what I found was a thick row of families and tourists, each one sporting a flashier and more expensive camera than the last. I tiptoed up with my prized mirrorless camera looking tiny and sad by comparison. As the world around me turned from lilac to peach, I began to feel sick to my stomach that such a stunning marvel had become an attraction rather than an escape—an excuse to walk up, click a button, and walk away as proof that *I was there*.

Sure, hopscotching from one picturesque pinpoint to another is one way of experiencing a national park, but every time I've outlined my travel itineraries with Instagrammable moments, I've found that I was looking at the parks without really *seeing* them. Like I was stroking my ego in some kind of completionist epic, hoarding visual moments like they were only real if I had a photo for social media to prove my presence in a place. Despite all the picture-taking I've indulged in, the silent, unphotographed experience of each park is far more real than any snapshot I've posed for. Without a camera, my senses have room to expand into the periphery, taking in the smell of fresh rainfall or the soft velvet of young leaves.

Eager to dodge the crowds and chart our own course that afternoon, Adam and I noticed a faint trail leading up a jagged ridgeline from the nearby parking area. We donned our packs—loaded up with nut butters, cashews, and dried mango—and dug our boots into the dirt. We had no idea what path we were on, but there was a sign marking something called Red Cathedral, and it sure as hell beat hanging out on the crowded ledge with the muggles.

The trail narrowed until it was a thin strip no more than eight inches wide in places, undulating steeply up and down a series of badlands as red as dried blood. We were in sidewalk-in-the-sky territory now, traversing a strip that felt suspended in midair, hovering above a treacherous sixty-degree slope of loose scree that threatened to shred whatever skin we gave it, should either of us fall. *No wonder the other hikers had turned back after the second high point.*

"Babe, can you toss me one of your trekking poles?" Adam shouted. "I forgot mine."

Great, now he has no way to balance his weight on this increasingly questionable route. If we take one wrong step, we're toast, we're maggot food, we're sliding five hundred feet off the edge of this fucking mountain.

"Sure thing, lover."

I tossed him one of my poles, which meant I was now hunching in a remotely upright position, leaning firmly into the slope and using my one remaining trekking pole like a cane, more doddering grandma than full-fledged mountain maven. At the top of the highest point on the ridge, the trail evaporated, and we spotted a trio of hikers heading cross-country down a saffron-tinged gully.

"Hey! You there!"

They paused and spun around for a moment.

"Are you trying to get to Golden Canyon?"

The group nodded, indicating that they were, then turned around and kept hiking. I took out my phone, grateful to have GPS and a few maps downloaded, and consulted with Adam.

"I think they're going the wrong way. See this slope here?"

Adam nodded his head.

"If we follow this gulch, right in front of us, all the way down, we'll run straight into Badwater Road. Worst case, we can road-walk about a mile, then hit the trail and cruise back up to the car, right?"

Adam, wide eyed and eager at the thought of an off-trail excursion, agreed, and soon the two of us were butt-scooting our way down a high-angle gutter of sharp gravel and crumbling sedimentary rock. I slithered along at the pace of a hungover sloth, my hands raw and reddened by the time the scree petered out. Stumbling to my feet, I dusted off my ass and stared at what lay ahead of us. Baking in the breezeless noontime sun, a maze of badlands shot downhill for several miles. Without the godlike vantage point from above, I wasn't so sure of our whereabouts. Any direction could be the right one. I pulled out my phone, tapped my GPS app, and hit "Record."

We began our rugged jaunt and passed the time by singing for an audience of absolutely no one. The rocks shored up, and the edgy shuffle of our hiking boots became more of an awkward trip down an odd-angled staircase. We were making great time. I checked my phone, excited to see how many more miles we had until hitting the bottom.

"Hey, look! If my map is correct, we should be seeing the road any minute now."

I was thrilled. With a little extra gumption, the two of us had managed to avoid the tourist hordes, plot out an off-trail adventure, and still make it over to Golden Canyon around lunchtime. *Take that, muggles.* I skidded down another hundred feet of scree, the familiar whooshing of cars making themselves known in the distance. Moving toward the sound, I carried my body across the beige hillside, eyes hungry for the end.

Sure enough, the road stretched out like a ribbon of tar, flat and impervious to the sweltering Badwater Basin below. Only Adam and I were now perched on a ledge about six hundred feet above it, with crumbling ocher cliffs to our left and harsh vertical drainages to our right. I hung my head in my hands, wishing I could disappear.

"Shit."

"Yeah, that about sums it up."

"We have to go back up," I said firmly.

Adam tried to debate with me for a minute, darting around on various nearby ledges to see if there was a way we could possibly lower ourselves down.

"It's useless," I told him. "To descend something that steep, we'd basically have to free solo. It's not worth the risk." Adam just stared back, disappointed.

We worked our way back up a thousand vertical feet of shattered badlands formations. My chest heaved. My legs burned as they tried to stabilize themselves on one trekking pole and the less-than-stellar trail we had made, following a faint lime-green stripe on my phone that marked the direction from which we came. We took two wrong turns, adrift in a crumbling sea of sameness, then had to backtrack to the thin little line on the app again. Without GPS, we would have been utterly lost. I felt the familiar sting of salt crystals forming from the sweat on my brow as we ascended. The going was rough and repetitive. In order to crest the final gutter of loose rock and debris at the top, Adam and I splayed out like starfish, crawling slowly on hands and knees until we finally reached the summit.

I wanted to cry. Whatever fears and anxieties had been rumbling around inside my body on the climb back up came pouring out of me, flooding my senses in an incomprehensible blur. *What a boneheaded move I had just allowed us to make.* As the more experienced outdoor-sperson of the group, I felt responsible for Adam. For his safety. For his enjoyment of the trips I planned. Now, instead of spending a casual day romping around on well-maintained trails and drinking iced coffee out of the van, we were both mentally and physically wiped out from what was supposed to be a fun little side trek.

Adam handed me a protein bar as I stared, catatonic, at the rippling expanse of sharply eroded cliffs below. For a long while, I just sat and gazed off, both an attempt to steady my nerves and to not vomit the meager food I had just eaten. He spoke first.

"Welp. I'm not stoked about this sketchy ridge we have to do again, but we'd better hop to it."

He was right. A mile and a half later, I had never been so happy to see the concrete and throngs of tourists in tank tops and denim. I could've kissed every one of their sunscreen-smeared faces. We jumped into Gizmo, practically melting in the unrelenting heat, and sped off to find a safe perch for sunset. Preferably without scree.

In the fading mauve light, Adam and I meandered a mile out into the wide-open expanse of crystallized salt shapes. It had rained only a few days prior, a rarity in Death Valley, and I could just make out the reflection of the Panamint Mountains in a series of small pools that hadn't yet evaporated. As if etched by giant cookie cutters, an immense field of polygonal salt formations sat at my feet and stretched on for hundreds of square miles. Badwater Basin. At 282 feet below sea level, it's the lowest point in North America and the eighth lowest in the world. Once the site of large, ancient inland Lake Manly, the water has since all but dried up, leaving only a small, spring-fed pool dubbed "bad water" by an early surveyor due to its high salinity. Needless to say, his mule would not drink.

Between the hexagonal gridlines splayed out at our feet, an occa-sional mirror-clear puddle of water had formed, glassy and iridescent, like the edge of a bubble. With the immense, black face of Telescope

Peak gazing down at us, I felt caught out of time, suspended somewhere between ordinary reality and liminal space. I was struck by a quote from Edna Brush Perkins that I had seen in the visitor center: "How can rocks and sand and silence make us so afraid and yet be so wonderful?"

Maybe Death Valley had made me long for the forest and the land of the living, but as the smooth blanket of night turned the surrounding salt flats a dazzling lavender, I took a deep breath in, lungs like happy balloons in the crisp mountain air, and knew some small part of me would miss it. My body, however, was a wreck. After three fitful nights with no sleep in the small metal cavity of Gizmo's rib cage, I could feel my serotonin levels dipping perilously low. I was a ghost with a hole in its heart. A thousand-pound slug. A withering stump of mucus where a woman might have been. My nasal passages had plugged up as I slept, until breathing became a laborious effort. It was time for real medicine. It was time to go home.

Adam, hero that he was, offered to drive the entire way back to Los Angeles so that I could at least try to nap in the passenger seat. Once home, I immediately made a doctor's appointment and got set up with a drug cocktail of hefty pink-and-blue horse pills of amoxicillin, tiny gel caps of a cough suppressant that worked by numbing my throat and lungs, and the highest recommended dose of pseudoephedrine. In three days' time, I was supposed to be back on the road, heading east. The rigid taskmaster inside my head insisted on it, and propped up by so many pharmaceuticals, she was likely to get her way. No rest for the wicked. No stopping until the parks were done. I bundled myself up in a proper bed and willed myself to recover.

Alone and on my way to Saguaro National Park, I pulled Gizmo into a truck stop outside of Tucson, taking a parking spot surrounded by other vans and RVs of all sizes and states of disrepair. Floodlights lit the paved lot, and a gentle ripple of anxiety sent needles down my spine. *This is it. No more California. I'm sifting into the underbelly of where the nomads go.*

Driving days feel like being stuck in limbo. Time washes over me like a benevolent forcefield that melts the hazy hours spent barreling across America until I am nothing but a jumble of song lyrics and the odd podcast fact. The perfect tangerine swirl of a cloud dancing mid-air might call me into focus, then I zoom back out, and six hours of deserted highway mirages pass in minutes.

The truck-stop store felt like a cartoon grocery, peppered with little bits of washed-up Americana. Stuffed animals and T-shirts bearing phallic cacti lined the shelves. Hot showers were available for purchase. A soda fountain machine the size of a monster truck made me salivate. I surreptitiously filled my water bottle for free.

"Hey there, sweetie, can I help you with anything?" Peg, a midfifties clerk with wild gray hair and wilder pink nail polish was all smiles. "We got two-for-one hot dog specials goin' right now."

"Nothing for me, thanks." Sheepishly, I backed away, grinning. Her sudden jolt of kindness felt dizzying after my eight-hour drive.

"Well, you just let me know if you change your mind, honey. We'll have hot coffee and cinnamon rolls out in the morning. Bye-bye now."

When I had set out on this journey, I had steeled my nerves in preparation for what I thought would be an occasionally grisly romp through some of America's less-savory netherworlds. I was ready for lewd remarks and slashed tires. Greasy stares and comments about roughing it solo as a woman. Perhaps too many of my ideas about truck-stop culture had come from the film *Pee-wee's Big Adventure* and essays about sex trafficking. I thought that I'd be the only woman in sight sleeping under the fluorescent lights and twenty-four-hour neon of these enormous gas stations, that I'd be outed for being a poser vanlifer, or for not being on the clock. But there, parked off a highway in eastern Tucson, my unfounded fears began to drift away. There was a smattering of other vans spread throughout the parking lot, and the truckers mostly kept to themselves, passing out soon after they parked. Apart from the incessant hissing of air brakes from nearby 18-wheelers, I felt safe at the truck stop and, surprisingly, at home on the road.

I woke in the middle of the night, as usual, suddenly needing to pee. Only this time, rather than shuffling over to the blindingly bright gas station bathrooms in my too-big T-shirt and underwear, I decided to try out my new contraption: the pee funnel. Carefully opening its bright turquoise box, I pulled out what looked like a U-shaped siphon and a tube the length of my palm. I connected them like I had practiced at home and aimed the tube into a container designated specifically for this purpose. Kneeling at the foot of my bed, I pressed the cold plastic against my crotch, praying for a seal, and . . . it worked. With not a drop spilled, I stayed warm and cozy inside the van, and I successfully peed like a man into an empty water bottle for the first time in my life. It felt strangely empowering. The next morning, I gave a special gift to a nearby tree, hoping no one would notice the school bus–yellow liquid.

Gizmo's wheels spun across the southern Arizona highway, the early morning light covering Gates Pass in gilt and honey as I backtracked a few miles west toward Saguaro National Park. Thick, rust-colored boulders sprang up from beneath the earth as thousands of the iconic, narrow-bodied, many-armed saguaro cacti came into view. Their resemblance to stick-figure people was remarkable, and I found it impossible to hike the park's trails without imagining these massive green succulents jonesing for a bout of fisticuffs or extending a spiny hand to painfully high-five the bravest hikers. I watched as tiny sparrows and finches flitted about, finding home in the most unusual of circumstances—twenty feet up in a series of pecked-out holes that looked more like a cramped Manhattan high-rise than a comfortable resting place.

I had a lot of driving to do and three days to do it, if I was going to make it to Texas on schedule for a canoe trip that I had booked. I sailed across the southern edge of New Mexico and felt my heart skip a beat in White Sands as the sunset turned an immense field of pearlescent dunes into a bubblegum Rothko painting. I hiked out with my little backpacking tent and spent the evening curled into a ball, trying and failing to stay warm amid the freezing dunefield. I tossed and turned all night in the fluffy red cocoon of my down sleeping bag, catching a mere three hours of rest. When I rose, frost had crept across the thin nylon ceiling of my tent, and it was twenty-seven degrees outside. I was exhausted and cold.

Back in the van, I slingshot my clumsy body and heavy heart across the barren, bleak expanse of West Texas. The only restaurants I saw were fast food joints, the only civilization gas pumps and grimy oil towns. My period walked into the fray full force and pummeled my insides with boxing gloves. Hunched over Gizmo's dust-caked steering wheel, I only wanted to hear the discordant vocals of an old Modest Mouse album on repeat. As I blared it at high volume for several hours, my mind fell into a trance. *The Lonesome Crowded West* kept me company past ripped-open trailer homes and soot-covered railway trains. *Well, aren't you feeling real dirty sitting in your car with nothing? Waiting to bleed onto the big streets that bleed out onto the highways . . .*

By the time I got to the trendy little village of Marfa, I was ready to collapse onto a real bed. I had little desire to peruse a series of self-important works by Donald Judd, the artist who put the town on the map, but I willed myself into enduring one more hour of activity. I meandered through a grassy field and stared at his series of hollow, eight-foot-tall concrete boxes that were supposed to be the apex of desert minimalism. I found myself bored and reminded of how obtrusive something as simple as a right angle can be when placed into the belly of nature.

Cool. A bunch of large rectangles in the desert. I didn't get it.

There's a wonderful Eckhart Tolle quote about how, when you bring your attention to anything natural, like a forest or a rock or a flower, or anything that has come into existence without human intervention, you step out of the prison of "conceptualized thinking," out of the prison of man-made ideas. He says that, to some extent, communing with nature causes us to participate in the state of connectedness and simple being in which everything natural still exists. Nature isn't split in two. It isn't anxious about the past or the future. It doesn't carry the weight of ideas or judgments about itself. A rabbit is only itself. A cactus is only itself.

To me, these sculptures seemed in direct opposition to that line of thinking. As though they were consciously adding artifice to a once unblemished landscape. Ego in the meadows. Dissertations in the dust.

❧

The next morning, after paying ten dollars for avocado toast at a third-wave coffee shop near the center of town, my wilderness-addicted brain was craving a real adventure. Tarbush and lechuguilla began to blur into frame. Creosote and coyotes. The mystical pull of the vast Chihuahuan Desert.

Greeted by a small, dun-colored shack, I pulled my van into the parking lot of Big Bend River Tours and was immediately met by a cantankerous Texan named Jason. With wraparound sunglasses, a permanently sunburned neck, and a thick southern drawl, I knew this guy was either going to be immensely awesome or a hardcore asshole. He outfitted me with a life jacket and a dry bag, then stuffed me into a van with two couples so that he could drive us forty-five minutes to the mouth of the canyon we'd be paddling.

"You know we got them invasive Barbary sheep down here near the Rio Grande, so me and my buddies like to go out and shoot 'em up on the weekends." Jason steered the van casually down a washboard road that made my teeth chatter. "They mess with the endemic bighorns."

Once plopped into the water in a carnelian-red canoe, I could see why the area's river canyons were such a big draw. Floating along a mellow stripe of tea-tinged water, the six of us inched closer to the day's objective, Dark Canyon, a menacing ravine marked by eight-hundred-foot-high cliffs of black volcanic basalt and pinkish rhyolite.

"You know what you say if you see a mountain lion?" Jason's eyes twinkled with the knowing stare of someone about to tell an epic dad joke.

"No, what?"

"Go on, git!" He belly laughed with the intensity of a strip-mall Santa. "'Cause then you sound like a redneck, and everything's afraid of rednecks."

A furry little piglet suddenly darted away from the water and into a stand of tall river cane.

"Did you smell that?!" Jason's head whipped around on his neck. "That was a javelina, man. Smells kinda like a skunk. They're more closely related to hippos than to pigs."

The light shifted in the deep shadow of the canyon, turning the water a gunmetal gray. Clouds danced and contracted above our group, an unlikely crew of two retired big-city couples and me, the lonesome writer. Despite our differences, we couldn't help but chatter away when our guide pulled over for a snack break on the gravel riverbank. Huge gusts of wind threatened to toss our hats and gear into the water, yet we couldn't stop laughing, snapping selfies against the carob-brown cliffs.

By the time we exited the canoes and helped load them back onto the trailer, I was in love with the place. We said our goodbyes, and I strapped myself into Gizmo once more, motoring across the great West Texas expanse like a tiny white spaceship. The camp that I had reserved was a secluded backcountry site down a rugged dirt road, and as I neared the turnoff, the serrated bodies of the Chisos Mountains gripped the sunset as if by force, shifting the world around me to a sea of rose and copper.

For dinner, I had planned a fancy macaroni-and-cheese casserole, complete with frozen peas and a can of tuna I'd snagged at the tiny grocery store in town. But not one moment after I finished a haphazard scrub of my dishes, the sky opened up and began pelting my outdoor kitchen with fat droplets of rain. I grabbed a tallboy of Modelo from the cooler and sprinted for the van, tendrils of red hair clinging to my face and neck, soaked to the skin. Once I was out of my wet clothes, this seemed a fine opportunity to test out the little satellite texting gadget that Adam had gifted me.

> ESCAPING SOME INSANE RAIN IN BIG BEND RIGHT NOW. WISH YOU WERE HERE TO SNUGGLE UP NEXT TO ME AND WARM MY SOAKED LITTLE BOD.

> HA! THAT'S CRAZY. IN THE DESERT? HOW WAS THE RIVER TRIP? I MISS U.

> CANOEING WAS CHILL. OUR GUIDE WAS KIND OF TYPICAL AND HILARIOUS. GOD, I MISS YOU. I FEEL SO FAR AWAY FROM HOME. I LOVE YOU SO MUCH.

Adam didn't respond to that last one. I wasn't sure if it was the impending lightning storm blocking the signal or some misguided attempt on his part to save my precious roaming text messages, but as I lay on my back in my sports bra and underwear, staring up at Gizmo's embroidered peacock-green ceiling, I realized that, ten days in, this was the longest I had ever been away from our home, and I missed him terribly.

❦

My small van rattled and shook all night as sixty-mile-an-hour winds pummeled her walls. The weather was a freight train passing right through my humble campsite, and when I finally crawled from bed, I was shocked and relieved that my kitchen table and water jug hadn't blown off into the desert.

I had a twelve-and-a-half-mile hiking day ahead of me. Big Bend's South Rim Trail is famous for being everything that Texas characteristically is not. Full of rust-colored pinnacles of rock, high Arizona pines and Douglas fir, as well as dramatic, big-mountain views that seem to stretch all the way into outer space, the loop trail begins at the Chisos Basin Visitor Center and pulls its visitors through several vastly different biospheres before dropping them back off where they began.

As a girl who had spent her childhood in East Texas, surrounded by a landscape of flat swamps, flat forests, and flat lakes, I was overtaken with awe as I began my ascent. In a few short miles, I was catapulted out of the Chihuahuan Desert and into a remarkable fairyland of chirruping titmice and bashful mule deer. Rocky monoliths stood like ancient sentries guarding the woods and their many creatures as I hiked along this rare high-altitude outcropping—a forty-square-mile Eocene eruption that stood like a lone green island in an incomprehensible sea of arid desert five thousand feet below.

Wind battered my face as I neared the South Rim itself. Edging my boots right up to the brim, I wobbled my trekking poles from side to side for balance and gazed over the cliff into the monotonous desert of Mexico. It was unbelievable to me that the rolling bronze hills I stared down at presumed to be another country. As far as I could tell, they were very much a part of the mass I now stood on. There were no discernible lines or fat stripes of paint marking "what's yours" from "what's ours," and the entire concept of king and country itself seemed utterly laughable. These mountains had overseen every Western regime put into place by bloodshed, every tribe that used the land and its resources before that, and the literal evolution of our human ancestors from apes.

I shoved a peanut butter and jelly sandwich into my face, stupefied by big thoughts and the sugar high that fluttered through my brain as I sat near the drop-off and gawked at the scenery.

"Too bad there's nothing interesting to look at." A man in his midsixties approached. He was sporting a pink plaid shirt, a wide-brimmed hat, and a tousle of long gray hair. "How d'you do?" he said, grinning and extending his hand. "I'm Kevin."

"Emily," I replied, doing my best to conceal the sticky nut butter that was momentarily gluing my tongue to the roof of my mouth.

"Would you mind a little hiking company? We seem to be going at the same pace."

Though the only child in me longed to drift off into fantasies about tramping through Mordor or befriending woodland nymphs, I nodded. It would be nice to have some company. Kevin and I descended the gradual slopes of the Laguna Meadows Trail together, and he told me how he had once been a Michigan State professor but had retired recently to spend a few years traveling to every national park he could find in his eco-friendly RV. A part of me was envious. While he could take his time on the long drives through rural America and avoid inclement weather during his park visits, I was sutured to a grueling schedule of my own (and my bank account's) making. One that only allowed for a few days in each location. One that would leave me hiking in the rain and the snow if I wasn't lucky.

We said our goodbyes quickly as we rounded a corner near the visitor center. Then I sped off into the unknown in search of a place to watch the sunset and found myself between the glowing serpentine walls of Santa Elena Canyon. Perhaps the most famous of Big Bend's time-carved ravines, Santa Elena's walls stretch skyward to a height of fifteen hundred feet above the Rio Grande. The sheer vertical relief does extraordinary things to the sunlight as its golden gleam filters down to the slow-moving, moss-hued water below, and I dodged prickly pear cacti along a short trail that tossed me right against its narrow mouth.

I strained my neck toward the heavens in ecstasy. Clouds swirled high and soft overhead. Milk poured into a blue pot of coffee.

A winter weather warning was on the forecast, and I was the only car on the Ross Maxwell Scenic Drive as I left the canyon in the fading copper light. Specks of rain began falling, catching the warm glance of the sun's embrace as they raced to the desert floor. I stopped Gizmo in the middle of the road and stood slack-jawed as the storm clouds fondled the dying sun. The sky was a neon dome on fire. I stood dumb-struck underneath the orange glow as water pelted my aching skin, my aching legs, my lonely heart.

I parked for the night down another backcountry dirt road, ate cold Campbell's soup from the can, and fell asleep. Though life inside the van was often unglamorous, it afforded me a front-row seat to so many of life's little miracles. The next morning, wrapped in my big puffy sleeping bag, I slid open the side door to find that a rare two inches of snow had carpeted the desert floor. It was the perfect excuse to check out the park's hot springs.

Kicking and jostling on an unmanicured gravelly road, Gizmo barely made it to the muddy dirt parking lot marking the trailhead. In the 1920s, there stood a thriving thermal spa resort with a post office, motel units, and a store, but the National Park Service chose to demol-ish the old Langford Hot Springs bathhouse back in the 1950s, leaving only a man-made stone pool, open to the elements, that visitors can soak in. It has since been renamed Boquillas, meaning "little mouths" in Spanish, perhaps a nod to its small pools or the slit in the earth where its trademark steaming wellspring emanates.

The sudden shock of warm water sent goosebumps scrambling across my legs as I dipped my world-worn body into the pool. I was alone, save for a few retired snowbirds escaping the midwestern win-ter. Resting my chin on my hands, I peered across the gray-green belt of the Rio Grande into Mexico and at the small men in cowboy hats hunching in the river cane on the other bank. Occasionally, one would wade across the molasses-paced current to check the money jar at his handicraft stand on the US side, then slosh back through the water just as quickly as he had come. *If I had been born thirty feet from this spring, I would be another person entirely. All the privilege of my skin color, passport, and language would disappear—poof.*

I plunged into the teal river water to cool off, floating half-naked and skyward, feeling a million miles from anywhere. How sad it seemed to make borders out of natural wonders. How trivial and arbitrary and unfair a thing to hang a life on. How hollow. How humbling.

⤖

Spit out across the snow on freezing West Texas highways, the coyotes were getting hungry. I had to swerve to avoid hitting two of the clever canines as I steered Gizmo deep into oil country on my way to Carlsbad Caverns National Park in southern New Mexico. As night fell, the towering fireballs of natural gas flares squirmed across the sky like glowing satanic orbs. It was February in the Permian Basin, the epicenter of one of America's largest oil booms. I scanned my eyes across the midnight horizon as burnoff after burnoff shot up through futuristic metal spouts, each one surrounded by an inauspicious semicircle of steel machinery. The cult of crude.

It bothered me how my own exploration depended so heavily on gasoline. Had electric minivans been available and affordable when I bought Gizmo, I happily would have lined up to deck one out with camping gear. To ease my guilt at the hypocrisy of burning thousands of gallons of fuel to write about America's parklands in locales often ravaged by climate change, I'd purchased hundreds of dollars of carbon offsets at the onset of the trip. Still, I hardly felt any better.

"That oil boom out there just made us lose our dark sky designation." A young ranger gestured in the direction of the fields as he led me and a group of twenty other park seekers down into the Carlsbad caves the following morning. "It's too bright to see most of the stars these days. Not much we can do about it. The drilling and fracking isn't technically happening on park property."

I was shocked that land so close to a federally protected site could be such a hub for carbon emissions. In the deep dark of the caverns themselves, it was easy to forget about the near-constant threats our national parks face. "Nothing dollarable is safe," John Muir once wrote when the city of San Francisco petitioned to put a dam in the middle of Yosemite National Park. He lost that battle, and Hetch Hetchy, an area once touted as being as beautiful as Yosemite Valley, became a flooded reservoir and one of the least-visited corners of the park. *If it could happen there, why not here?* I shivered as our group descended deeper, past carefully hidden sconces that illuminated the colossal towers of rock. The walls seemed to pulse like undulating jellyfish. Soon, melting chandeliers and a huge striped mound like the mouth of a baleen whale populated the underground landscape. Hiking through was like cloud gazing, only with cave formations as the object of focus. I allowed my eyes to blur and shift from shape to shape. A lingam statue. The chiffon curtain surrounding a noblewoman's four-poster bed. A horde of goblin fingertips reaching up through the earth. After the tour ended, I sat in the dark for a long while in stillness, meditating in the damp quiet instead of rushing off to self-soothe at a campground with Netflix or social media. I prayed that the caves would still be there for generations to come.

⚜

As the days ticked by, my comfort with solitude came in fits and starts, and the next parks flew past with a shock of homesickness and freezing nights spent shivering in the back of Gizmo. I hiked to the top of Texas, Guadalupe Peak, marveling at the summit's sheer prominence.

The mountain, once a thriving Permian coral reef, had since fossilized and uprooted to a height of nearly nine thousand feet above sea level.

I scanned the splotchy reds and umbers of Petrified Forest's painted desert hills and watched as my notion of a woodland was flipped on its side when I meandered through the kaleidoscopic, crystallized remains of a once tropical landscape of conifers, now lying horizontally along the trail like stone park benches. The scenery was striking, but I found myself anxious and easily distracted as I hiked, knowing that Adam was just a nine-hour drive away and would be joining me soon.

Back on Interstate 40, I drove like my wheels had wings. Arizona blurred across my rearview in a collage of brick-tinted mesas and a rotting elk corpse on the side of the road that seemed as big as a house. I hadn't pressed another person's body against mine in fourteen days. Hadn't enjoyed the sustenance of any connection other than small talk with strangers. Hadn't slept in a bed that felt like my own with a man who wanted to hold me. Unshowered and ravenous for affection, I felt more creature than girl.

As I unlocked the sky-blue door to the home I shared with Adam, my nostrils flared. It didn't smell like my house anymore. Not only that, but subtle things had been shifted around in my absence. A mess of books strewn across the coffee table. Guest room sheets thrown on the floor. Mail covering the dining room table.

Adam was on a conference call and came out of his office to give me a momentary peck on the cheek before returning to his den. It wasn't exactly the welcome I'd been hoping for. I microwaved what appeared to be leftovers from Indian takeout and mousily ate them in the breakfast nook, worried that something was amiss, suddenly self-conscious that I had been growing out my armpit and pubic hair. This was it. Los Angeles. My big comeback.

When Adam returned, he gave me a proper hug and a lingering kiss, his hands levitating for a moment before passionately grabbing my body. With sex clearly on the menu, I supposed I didn't have much to worry about after all. Still, I couldn't shake that edgy and dazed feeling. A disembodied head and boobs floating around like a phantom in a house that used to be mine.

But after a week at home, we stepped back into rhythm. I had a chance to rest and catch up with old friends, and Adam remembered what it was like to have the anarchic energy of a girl on a mission bobbing around in his house. Thrilled to once again have reliable internet, I caught up on the world outside of the parks. There was something about a virus running rampant in China. Borders were closing, and whole cities were under government lockdown. It looked awful.

Still, the whole thing seemed so very far away. Sifting through a mess of backpacking gear, Adam and I prepared for a bucket list–worthy hike we had both been dreaming about for years—a trip to the bottom of the Grand Canyon.

With Adam as my copilot, we loaded up Gizmo and flung ourselves across the enormous sandy breadth of the Mojave Desert and into Williams, Arizona, the Route-66iest town in the whole damn country. Once a crucial stop on the famous TransAmerica route from Los Angeles to Chicago, the town has been reduced to an incessant explosion of USA-inspired kitsch, begging visitors to deify Betty Boop, apple pie, and muscle cars.

It seemed funny that such a tourist nightmare could exist right outside one of the great natural wonders of the world. What I love so much about the parks is how democratic they are. How you don't have to be able to afford riverfront real estate to pitch your tent near a view of the water. When you go to a place like the Grand Canyon, it doesn't care who you are or where you came from or what you had for breakfast. Anyone can stand on the cliff's edge of the South Rim, feel a chilly updraft of wind on their face, and experience the sublime.

After a meatloaf dinner at Goldie's Diner, a quintessential example of space-age Googie architecture, the two of us hit the hay, excited to leave the mess of neon for something far more old-world and magical.

჻

As the sun began its morning slant across the sky in Kaibab National Forest, I could make out the hushed pastel tones of creamy mauves and ravishing corals beyond the tips of tall trees. I drove as Adam fidgeted in the passenger seat, scarfing down a breakfast sandwich.

"I'm so stoked we're doing this. I've always wanted to backpack down to the bottom of the Grand Canyon—"

"Or as I like to call it," Adam interrupted, "the Canned Granyon."

And so it was. Each time we read a sign or grabbed our backcountry permits or checked our map, one of us would loudly exclaim in a boastful, over-the-top voice, "Honey! I can't believe we made it to the Canned Granyon!" We found it hilarious.

When the usual housekeeping of signing permits, checking out the visitor center, loading up backpacks, and refilling water bladders was done, we parked Gizmo at the Bright Angel Trailhead, then took a park shuttle to the higher-elevation South Kaibab Trail to set up a two-night loop.

In winter, all trails that dip below the South Rim of the Grand Canyon are a bit of a mess. With the trailhead sitting at a peachy 7,260 feet, snow and ice can linger, especially in the shade. Contrast that with the warm, sunny weather typically found along the shores of the Colorado River, at just 2,200 feet, and you may find a lot of confused visitors. Underprepared travelers scurried to and fro along the steep cliff's-edge switchbacks that mark the beginning of the trail, butt-scooting when they slipped on the ice and clinging to the few small trees that lined the path. After we'd walked about a mile, the crowds thinned and the trail grew silent. We were mostly on our own.

To hike down into the Grand Canyon is to travel back in time. Given that its walls are made up of sedimentary rock, the newest stones lie on top, while the oldest layer, the exceptionally named Elves

Chasm pluton, lies way down near the bottom and is nearly two billion years old.

As Adam and I hiked down, down, down toward the churning Colorado River below, I thought a lot about what these rocks must have seen and how insignificant my time on earth will be in comparison.

"You're so beautiful . . . you could be a part-time model!" Adam was doing his favorite bit, belting out Flight of the Conchords lyrics on the trail, and given the immense beauty of our surroundings, this song seemed especially appropriate. I jumped in enthusiastically.

"You're so beautiful! You could be an air hostess in the '60s!"

Of course, the Grand fucking Canyon is in a league of its own when it comes to good looks, and the more we descended, the more I was utterly awed by the crumbling, bloodred rock and the little pinyon pines and soaptree yuccas that populated its expanse. The light shifted. The sun played funny games with our eyeballs. The shadows moved as the day warmed our flesh, and we kept hiking down. Down through layers of crunchy, iron-rich dirt. Down through cracked blue rocks like broken robin's eggs. Down past a mule train carrying supplies into the belly of the ravine.

Nearly a vertical mile into the jagged canyon, Adam and I reached the mighty Colorado River, a great swirling, rumbling brown mess of chocolate-milk water. We crossed the Black Suspension Bridge, an engineering marvel, built in 1928, which spans 440 feet across the murky current below. At the time, it was the first bridge-based river crossing for hundreds of miles, shuffling thousands of visitors across its breadth each year. Since no vehicles could make it that far into the canyon, Havasupai tribesmen and dozens of mules had to carry the necessary 122 tons of steel materials down the steep switchbacks to construct the beast.

I watched as an errant Canada goose pecked around near the shoreline. Lizards skittered across rocks in the breezy afternoon sunshine. This would be our home for two days. I was deliriously happy.

A short hike upstream brought us to Bright Angel Campground, and as soon as we pitched our tent, I could tell that our plans for the evening diverged. Adam looked exhausted.

"Do you want to meditate and nap for a little while?" he asked.

"No, thanks. I think I'll just eat a snack and read outside." No matter how hard I tried, I could never quite get my body to enjoy napping. My mind a constant engine, I always woke up feeling worse than before, envious of my friends who knew how to rest when rest was called for.

When Adam finally emerged from the tent, rejuvenated, the two of us sauntered over to check out Phantom Ranch, another 1920s heirloom of the park. Designed by Mary Jane Colter, the ranch was completed in 1922 and comprised a series of small cabins and a main lodge built out of wood and native stone to complement rather than compete with its natural surroundings. The result was an idyllic, storybook-style village sitting peacefully at the bottom of a canyon that is only reachable by foot, mule, or raft. The entire place looked teleported out of a Grimms' fairy tale. Seeing the ranch in person only made me more thrilled that we had booked a dinner reservation there the following evening.

Stars began twinkling onto the obsidian tapestry of night as we strolled along the gravel path back to our campsite and made dinner. Not yet ready for sleep, Adam suggested we lie down on a nearby picnic table and gaze skyward. I loved watching the stars blink their way into being each night. Strange orphans of far-off light emerging with evocative names like Betelgeuse, Pleiades, and Mintaka. In the crisp air, I felt as though I were inhaling and exhaling the sky itself into my lungs, one infinitesimal part of the larger whole.

"You know . . . it's good luck if you and your partner witness the same shooting star." Adam looked over at me with a devastating grin, his face mere inches from mine.

That night, we saw two.

⤙⤙⤙

The next morning we needed to get an early start if we were to hike the twelve miles to Ribbon Falls, one of the canyon's legendary hidden cascades. At 9:00 a.m. I stood at the ready on the edge of our campsite, my backpack packed and my bootlaces tightened. Adam was not a morning person. He bumbled around camp for several minutes while I waited, forgetting where he left his wallet and discarding his Crocs at the last possible moment before donning proper hiking shoes. Traveling with him sure beat being alone, but transition moments were rough. We moved at different paces, and I often gritted my teeth to ward off resentment. I wondered if the opposite were also true. *Having a type A, tomboyish, mile-crushing militant hiker girlfriend must be hard on him too.*

We set off on the North Kaibab Trail, hugging the canyon wall in the cool morning shade. Boulders in every direction appeared as though blood-forged and cut with daggers. Huge red outcroppings fell away violently into the gently burbling creek below. A seize of goosebumps crawled up my arms and across my torso, and I prayed the sun would soon inch its way above the narrow gulch.

Two hours later, Adam and I found ourselves traversing a wide, sunny gap in the canyon lined with grasses and small shrubs. Immense cathedrals of rust-colored rock dominated the landscape as the temperature rapidly warmed. The heat of the day baked into my flesh like some long-awaited radioactive kiss, and I happily stripped down to my T-shirt as we took a left-hand turn toward the falls and awkwardly made our way across Bright Angel Creek.

Ribbon Falls is a miracle hiding in plain sight: a two-tiered cascade of misty bliss that careens over the edge of the canyon wall and onto a gigantic pillar of limestone covered in a hanging garden of furry moss that glitters green in the sunshine. We ate a simple lunch of crackers, cheese, and dried fruit, then spent the afternoon taking turns sprinting under the rushing water and squealing at how unbelievably cold it was.

Back at camp, the main lodge was serving up an assortment of beer, wine, and snacks, a happy hour that ended promptly at four. Adam and I raced back along the same path we came in on, and I was desperate for a tingly sip of alcohol I didn't have to haul in myself. It seemed obvious to me that mule-delivered beer must taste better.

I asked for a can of locally brewed Bright Angel IPA, named after the very campground we were staying in. Adam grabbed a sack of potato chips and took out his wallet.

"Will that be all for you two?" The clerk, tired, barely glanced up at our sun-stained hiking bodies.

"Yep, that about does her."

"May I please see some identification?"

"I . . . uh . . ."

This was not the plan. I was supposed to stroll in, triumphant, and let my mind get hazy in the cool light of sunset as I sipped the perfect can of beer from the perfect picnic table in the perfect campsite. I didn't want to hike with a wallet or identification. I wanted to, for once, bliss out in total anonymity, if only for three days.

"I'm thirty-two years old, sir. Maybe Adam can show you his ID? He's forty-two."

"No one can buy alcohol in the Grand Canyon without some identification. It's just the rules."

"What if I showed you, like, a photo of my ID, on my phone? I have a picture of my passport too!"

"No, ma'am. I'm sorry."

I hung my head in shame and embarrassment. I barely got carded in Los Angeles. Why now at the ends of the earth?

"So just the one can of beer for you then, sir?"

Adam side-eyed me with the quixotic look of a man about to work some magic. He doesn't drink, but this guy didn't need to know.

"Uh, yeah. Yep. One can of alcoholic beer for me, please."

I couldn't believe it.

The two of us exhaled in unison as we scurried over to a wooden table, hid the unopened beer in Adam's knapsack, perused the postcards, and snuck the brew out of the lodge completely, skipping the whole way back to our tent. As the sun tilted low in the evening sky, the mile-high walls of the canyon glowed a scintillating blush pink, and my mind grew fuzzy from the beer and rhapsodically happy from the thrill of getting away with something.

"Do you want to maybe lie down for a bit before dinner?" Adam's electric hazel eyes winked as he gazed down at me intently.

We fell into a pile on our fluffy sleeping bags, clumsily trying to edge our two narrow, inflatable camping mattresses together as my tongue locked into his and my hands were soon fumbling with his zipper so that I could properly thank him for the beer. I wrapped myself in a cocoon of down, tossing my sweaty hiking clothes into a pile at the corner of the tent, feeling small and wild and animal as Adam playfully bit my nipples and pressed his body into mine again and again.

This is how it's supposed to be. No artifice. No illusions. Just pure, wanton physicality spilling out of two bodies so hungry for one another.

Dinner that night felt similarly hedonistic. Steaming vats of beef and vegetable stew adorned a table lined with cornbread and large bowls of salad. A bevy of hungry hikers descended on the feast. For dessert, the kitchen staff brought us each a monstrous hunk of chocolate cake. I waddled out of the dining room fat and happy and drunk with awe as I stared up at the night sky.

Up, up, up. In the delicate light of the next morning, Adam and I left camp to begin the long, slow ascent of 4,460 feet to the top of the Bright Angel Trail. After a mellow traverse along the roiling Colorado River, the path finally turned inward up a lush, green crack in the canyon's south wall. The two of us took our time on the never-ending climb skyward, shambling midtrail like two ants hunched with our possessions on our backs.

"Hey, this actually isn't so bad!" Adam gleefully chirped to me as the trail zigzagged along a formidable series of switchbacks, each one offering a more commanding view of the crimson-colored walls.

And he was right. At our slow but steady pace, we were making great time, and before I knew it, we were right back on top of the South Rim, crunching across an icy trail in our snow cleats while fellow travelers slipped and skidded along the frozen path. We tossed our packs into Gizmo, grabbed a bag of salt and vinegar chips, and started the long drive home.

Back on the highway, our phones were blowing up. The virus we'd heard about had made its way to the United States, and it was only a matter of time before it crept into every neighborhood. I knew I would have to make it to Utah as soon as possible.

Adam and I started trying to envision the worst. "My insane parks schedule could maybe survive a one-month shutdown, but beyond that, who knows?" My stomach turned as I said the words out loud. I wanted to throw up. The whole thing felt so Kafkaesque and unfair. I had quit my job and blown my life savings to get to this point. I couldn't afford a lengthy delay. I had planned for countless dangers and detours—how could I have foreseen an invisible virus too? *I don't want my dream project to fall apart after everything I've worked so hard for. Just five more parks, then I'll figure it out.*

☙

I sped toward Utah alone in early March, my anxiety throbbing. Though air travel had begun to shut down, most people seemed to be going about their daily lives. Cars were still on the road. Casinos were still open as I zoomed through Las Vegas and stared, dumbfounded, at a billboard for naked hand-sanitizer wrestling at a nearby strip club.

At first, the virus's main impact on ordinary life seemed to be that toilet paper and hand sanitizer were nowhere to be found on store shelves. This made relying on gas stations for water and bathrooms a nightmare. I admonished myself each time I accidentally touched a countertop or gas pump without immediately washing my hands afterward, my sleep-in-the-dirt camper soul transformed into a germophobe overnight.

I drove on. To my right stood a series of dark, wooded mountains, snowcapped and beautiful, and yet in my solitude I felt something sinister about their presence. My chest tightened. My skin felt clammy. The familiar ache of my nerves began to sink its teeth into me like a pit bull, savage and unyielding. I realized that I was guarding my fragile health like a toddler precariously balancing an egg on a spoon in some bizarre race across America.

As much as it pained me to admit it, I was only one day into this leg of my trip, and I already missed Adam. My desire to be free and feral and untamed for a year began to feel incredibly naive in the presence of a global crisis. Two people locked inside a hardship created an experience. A memory you could both look back on and laugh about. But suffering alone was just a tragedy.

By the time I reached Bryce Canyon after a nine-hour drive north, my mind was at war with itself. In the amber glow of sunset, I emerged from Gizmo and tentatively stepped toward the canyon's rim. The view spilled out for miles. Just then, as though struck by some benevolent, unknowable force, a huge grin plastered itself across my face, and my eyes welled up with tears. I stared down at the striking orange hoodoos sprouting out of the ground like a city of enormous sandstone fins, and an unexpected wave of relief washed over me. A feeling that I was part of something much larger than a virus or even a species. Somehow, in my despair, I knew that I was a small piece of this big, wild earth. An earth that didn't care if I was rich or poor, sick or healthy. An earth that would remain, beautiful and shifting and unknowable, long after my body had withered away.

When morning came, I rose early to take in the dawn at the park's famous Sunrise Point, jockeying for the optimal camera position among a dozen other bundled-up visitors as the first rays of light fanned their way across snow-dusted spires of sandstone. Standing atop a fenced-in concrete platform gave me a sinking déjà-vu feeling that conjured up the frustrations I had at Zabriskie Point. My trip was supposed to be about exploration, not adherence to a curated view and photo op, so I left the platform, hanging a right onto a narrow trail as the world was illuminated in coral. There, I sat beside a small limber pine, its scraggly roots clinging desperately to the soil for nourishment. After my last few days of excess anxiety and virus dodging, I could definitely relate. The sensation of feet on dirt was the only thing that felt sane anymore. The grounding force of wilderness was palpable.

I tramped through two-inch-deep orange muck as I set off on a day trip into the maze of rock, linking up the Queens Garden and Peek-A-Boo Trails to create a lollipop-shaped loop through the area's infamous hoodoos. "Hoodoo" comes from the Southern Paiute word for "scary" or "spirit," "oo'doo," a nod to the landscape's mysterious past. The Native people who once lived within the park's boundaries believed that the towering red pinnacles were once an entire race called the Legend People, who were turned to stone for bad deeds by the god Coyote. I was sure to tread lightly as I dipped below the rim.

Fresh snowmelt had turned every trail into a river of orange mud, and elaborate spires soon surrounded me as I carefully sloshed my boots along the path. I loved being among the hoodoos. Their time-lessness and utter indifference were oddly soothing. My mind filled with daydreams of setting up camp and sleeping in their midst for the next month to escape the wicked mess of society. No cell phone. No newspapers. I was deliriously jealous of the trees and the chipmunks, who didn't have to deal with the weight of the impending pandemic. I wanted to curl into a ball in the snow and disappear.

Once I passed the Queens Garden Trail, the crowds thinned out considerably, and I found myself mostly alone among the colossal, rust-hued altarpieces. My overwhelming sense of smallness in their presence knocked my anxiety to the ground, and I sat among the rocks for a long while, staring up at natural windows carved into ancient limestone and innumerable craggy hoodoos. *Maybe there's some great, immutable force at work here, operating at a pace I can't even fathom*, I mused as I sat awestruck beneath the hundred-foot-high pinnacles. *Maybe instead of turning away from the growing uncertainty that's staring me down, I need to somehow turn and face it. The void is the rule, not the exception.*

࿊

Morning broke with fresh snowfall in Tropic, Utah. I was supposed to meet my friend Eva later that day in Capitol Reef, but with high winds and a blizzard threatening every mountain pass within a hundred-mile radius, she had been forced to turn around, leaving me alone, white knuckling my anxiety as I carefully steered my van across the ocher-colored mesas and gorgeous ravines of Highway 12. I was in no way mentally prepared for more solitude. The few friend dates I had set along the year's course were meant to serve as big-time morale boosters. Now solo in the middle of a storm, I struggled to prop myself back up. Fat, feathery snowflakes wafted onto Gizmo's windshield as I tried to navigate the icy slush that blanketed much of the road. As a diehard Southern Californian with basically zero snow-driving experience, I was petrified.

By lunchtime I had made it to the park, dazed after what should have been a short and easy drive. I pulled over into the parking area for Grand Wash, a deep, thousand-foot-high gash cut right into the colorful sedimentary strata of Utah's Waterpocket Fold.

The most defining feature of Capitol Reef National Park, the Waterpocket Fold is a geological marvel by any standard. One hundred miles long and dozens of miles wide in some sections, it is a classic example of a monocline formation, a dramatic rift between horizontal layers of earth. Fifty to seventy million years ago, a fault line shifted, creating a vast wrinkle in the planet's crust. This section of Utah's red-rock country is now about seven thousand feet higher on the west than on the east.

Ravens sounded deep croaks from their clifftop perches as I began to stroll through the pockmarked canyon. It was a sound I had grown accustomed to in my years spent hiking in the Sierra Nevada, at once auspicious and comforting. *At least in their presence, I'm not alone,* I thought as I walked on. Thick stripes of tar-colored sediment dripped down the steep rock walls, and I craned my neck toward an overcast sky as a brisk wind whistled through the narrowing canyon. I hopped from foot to foot along the uneven gravel path, careful not to soak my boots in the shallow creek that snaked its way through the gorge.

"Finally, another solo lady hiker!" I was jolted into alertness three miles in as a bubbly thirtysomething brunette bounded up to me.

"Hey!" I fumbled my words as I tried to respond. "Yeah, nice to, umm, meet you. I was just about to turn around at the end here—"

"Ohmygosh," she gleefully interrupted me, "you *have* to hike the Cassidy Arch Trail if you haven't yet. It's steep, but it's worth it. Enjoy!"

She was gone as quickly as she came, but I couldn't ignore an endorsement like that. Besides, her beaming presence had already brightened what I thought was sure to be a dour day. I hooked a right onto a series of jagged stairs cut into the sandstone cliff and ascended a staggering seven hundred feet before traversing a gently sloping series of slabs dotted with clawlike junipers grasping at the sky. Balancing carefully as the well-worn path faded and the canyon wall fell away steeply to my left, I edged my way forward until I stood face-to-face with the arch itself.

Cassidy Arch is a massive, forty-foot-wide bridge the color of antique brick. Cut into the earth by centuries of erosion, it stands hundreds of feet above the wash below. The view from the top was phenomenal. Soul lifting. I sat on the edge of what felt like the known universe as the wind whipped a tangle of red hair around my ear and my fingers began to grow numb. In my infinite smallness, I was still a part of that vast landscape. I might be alone for the rest of my weeks spent in Utah, but I knew in this moment that it would be worth it.

⚜

Some days, it's a trifling thing to be human. As texts poured in and news of the pandemic intensified, I began to try on different shades of nihilism, as though they were outfits at a shopping mall. I needed to find one that worked. One that would keep me sane. Once again, I sped by the rust-colored hoodoos and staggering red cliffs of central Utah, only this time I resolved myself to the fact that we were all doomed. The cat was out of the bag. Free-floating particles of a potentially deadly virus called SARS-CoV-2 were on their own journey across America. My anxiety decided it was wiser to accept my fate and assume I would get sick eventually, rather than berate myself every time I forgot to wash my hands for a full twenty seconds. Still, I kept away from strangers on the trail and avoided busy visitor centers, feeling guilty that I was out in the world while my Los Angeles friends began barricading themselves indoors.

"I'll likely want dark sexual things from you when I get home," I cooed to Adam on the telephone. "I want you to hurt me. Leave marks if you can." I needed physical evidence of my penance for keeping the parks trip going as a national crisis bloomed. Even though my part-time job as a journalist was reason enough to stay out in the field, my stomach turned when I wondered how much I was putting myself and others at risk. Nauseous, I stared at the calendar and shaved two days off the Utah trip.

Arriving in Arches National Park was like being let loose in Disneyland after a week of silent meditation. Colorado had just

announced the closure of its ski resorts, and with spring break looming, every outdoor-loving, kid-toting family had descended upon the
small town of Moab. Hoping to escape the crowds, I steered Gizmo to
the very end of the park's main road and stepped onto the longest trail
I could find, an eight-mile loop around Devils Garden.

Even at 9:30 a.m., the parking lot was nearly full, and the trail was
mobbed with people. Zigzagging between clusters of other hikers, I
found the path no less crowded three miles in than it had been at the
start. The proximity to so many strangers made nature feel more like
a carnival than a temple, and after zipping around to the area's many
natural bridges at top hiking speed, I sat down in my little van and
slammed the door shut. In these conditions, it was impossible to keep
a safe distance. I wanted to scream. *Arches are such an arbitrary thing to
hike to. Who cares about a rock shaped slightly cooler than all these other
rocks?*

"While you are not safe I am not safe, and now you're really in
the total animal soup of time." The line from Allen Ginsberg's "Howl"
ticker-taped its way across my mind, and I got the hell out of Arches as
quickly as I'd come. The next day I drove south, past the wild, snowcapped peaks of the La Sal Mountains that shone like daggers in the
glare of the afternoon sun, hightailing it to Canyonlands' remote,
southeastern Needles District to go backpacking.

A wall of striped sandstone spires the color of wet clay stood watch
over the parking area for Elephant Hill. The Needles landscape is formidable: a thick maze of rounded, phallic rock formations that would be
unnavigable if it weren't for a series of developed park trails and helpful
cairns marking the way. After climbing onto Gizmo's roof to access
my enormous Thule storage box, I laid out my overnight backpacking
supplies on the mattress in the van's rear, shoved them into my pack,
and laced up my boots.

A soft breeze wafted through the huge, coral-tinted spires as I kept
my gaze fixed on the ground, careful not to miss any small stacks of

rock marking an important turnoff. Surrounded on all sides by the bright Cedar Mesa Sandstone, I felt like I was on Mars, or at least Alice falling down the rabbit hole. As far as the eye could see, colossal pillars of orange sediment stood like skyscrapers, each one topped with a dull white mushroom cap. Unlike the hoodoos of Bryce Canyon, Canyonlands' Needles were rounded at their tops, with a more eroded few looking short and squat, like a deserted Smurf village. Two miles of daydreaming later, I was at my campsite for the evening.

Away from the crowds and anxiety of Arches, I finally felt something like ease, my mind free to wander once the barrage of potential dangers was at bay. The pandemic had turned me, a fervent extrovert, into a shut-in. I pitched my tent, made dinner, and stared out as the sun set beyond the impenetrable labyrinth of candy-colored rock.

That night the wind picked up, and twice I was shocked awake as one of the trekking poles that supported my fragile tent caved in on me. Sleep came in fitful stops and starts. Dreams of something vicious lurking just out of sight plagued my tired hiker brain. *Is there an animal pacing around these thin fabric walls?* Every little sound was a cannon proving my lack of safety. I shot out of bed at dawn, my right arm numb and tingly, certain that a mountain lion had been sitting on me and licking his lips as I dozed. Alone in the wild, my logic became fuzzy.

When I arrived back in Moab and checked my phone, my heart sank. The town had just closed to all nonresidents, meaning that my plans were spinning out once again. I wouldn't be able to explore Canyonlands for an extra day; I'd have to go immediately to Zion. I understood the locals' desire for safety in the midst of so much uncertainty, but even with what little information we had been given by experts, the outdoors seemed like the safest place to be. People needed a space to feel their rage and to find the utter catharsis that only wilderness can bring. I tried not to cry as I readied myself for what was sure to be a year full of thwarted desires.

Hefty globs of rain began pelting the windshield as I drove around, trying to forge a plan B. To wait out what had become a severe thunderstorm, I parked Gizmo in a small corner of public land just outside of town. It was full of similarly stranded vanlifers. *I'll just go to Zion early,* I thought, willing myself to believe that everything was okay. My brain struggled to grasp the magnitude of the lockdown that was looming. *I'll treat myself to a cheap motel, spend half a day in the park, then land safely back in Los Angeles.* I called Adam to let him know I was coming home.

⚜

The governor of California shut down the entire state the next day, a first-of-its-kind stay-at-home order that would soon spark dozens of others. After five hours spent driving through snowflakes and across breathtaking canyons, I watched, mouth agape, as the leader of the most populous state in the union told everyone to shelter in place. Home had never felt farther away.

There's a famous Zen story about a man who was out walking through a forest when suddenly a tiger gave chase. Sprinting to save his life, with the tiger gaining on him, he came to the edge of a steep cliff, noticed a sturdy vine, grabbed it, and launched himself into the void below. The hungry tiger paced above him, and as he gazed down beneath his feet, he was dismayed to notice yet *another* tiger stalking in the ravine below. Just then, a tiny mouse crawled out from a small crevice in the cliff face and began gnawing at the vine as he held it. The man looked to his left and, at that precise moment, noticed a patch of strawberries growing out of a clump of soil beside where he dangled. He reached out, picked one, and popped it into his mouth. It was plump, delicious, and perfectly ripe.

With tigers above and tigers below, sometimes the exact right thing to do is pause and savor the beauty we can glean from the present moment, no matter how small.

It was pouring as I steered into Zion National Park and donned my crinkly rain jacket. In the frigid damp of the morning, I marveled at sky-high cliffs along Riverside Walk and watched as thin spiderwebs of clouds enveloped the famously crimson walls of the main canyon. Back in the van, I drove along a serpentine highway to the East Rim Trail as a gentle snow began to fall. The path was still and silent, without a soul on it. I listened to the few birds who were brave enough to withstand the cold as my boots made a crisp, crunching sound in the inch-thick powder. I spun around, unsure of if or when I'd be out in the parks again, grateful to be somewhere so miraculous at the dawning of the apocalypse.

I craned my neck to take in the crumbling canyon walls all around me. They were perfect. Frosted. The color of ripe strawberries.

My adventuremobile, Gizmo, at the Court of the Patriarchs in Zion National Park, Utah

Chapter 3

URBAN CONTRACTION

Going for a hike or a neighborhood walk during the lockdown felt remarkably like a bank heist. While obsessively scanning the news and waiting for the parks to reopen, Adam and I decided we'd foster two service dogs in training: a goofball standard poodle named Jetson and an enormous, mellow shepherd mix named Chinook. We hoped this would ease the languishing feeling of being trapped indoors in Los Angeles. Each time we left the house, a precise and specific series of events needed to occur, since the city had shut down its parks, beaches, and hiking trails. I researched lesser-known treks that we could easily sneak onto, though that was technically illegal and worthy of a fine. We planned multiple exit strategies and made contingencies for bystanders and witnesses.

We suited up the dogs in their purple service vests and black leashes, donned our hiking shoes, checked the route on Google Maps, double-checked the parking in Street View, and checked online maps to ensure that there was a second route nearby in case the first was blocked off or we got yelled at by a cantankerous millionaire in the Malibu Hills. We felt like criminals in our own backyard, rogue wanderers on the out-skirts of massive ocean-view estates. I frequently felt like a kid without a hall pass, wandering to the bathroom long after the bell had rung. Sure, it's no great crime to walk alone in a park, but if push came to shove, some looming authority figure could get us into very real trouble.

It was a hell of a way to hike after speeding across America for months on a self-directed walkabout. The more time I spent at home, the less like a home it felt. What makes a thing a home is the ability to leave and return. No longer a reliable and safe cradle to spring from, the house felt like a luxurious cage. My mental health wavered like a seismograph. My mind twitched. I began biting the inside of my cheek and picking at my skin. I felt locked into a waiting game to pursue my dreams again. I didn't belong there. I didn't belong anywhere.

I slept in. I lolled. I watched live-streaming burlesque shows and made Zoom dates with my closest friends. An unfamiliar darkness began to well up inside me, staring back in the mirror each day as I reflexively checked the news and made notes in my journal. A girl with a grudge against anyone who stood in her way. A shadow self I had shoved somewhere down deep and forgotten about for years.

With death in the headlines and the entirety of the world's wings clipped, I felt the virus was forcing the whole planet to stare down mortality in a very real and intimate way. I could no longer ignore the sticky gunk of having a body. Of being human. Of the palpable rage at having several months ripped away from me. I wanted to scream at the heavens until my lungs dropped out. To jettison myself into outer space until my limbs broke apart.

I suppose decay was always inevitable. The pandemic just made it more visible.

My mind became a parade of the cruelest thoughts I had to offer. Rather than swimming around in the deepest, darkest fissures of my brain, they came bubbling to the surface to bask in the chaos. I knew I had an intense personality, but even in a friend group populated by ex-goths and Burning Man devotees, my emotions felt extreme.

I hate being called on to save a generation that tanked the economy in 2008, just as I was getting out of college.

Why do I have to ruin my life for a bunch of old people with weak immune systems whom I've never met?

A hundred years ago, people with preexisting conditions wouldn't have even survived childhood.

How do we calculate the economic toll of millions of deaths versus hundreds of millions of young people being snared in a net of financial limbo?

I hope I get the virus. I hope we all get it. Let's burn this motherfucker down.

It was distressing to gaze into the pit of my own violence this way. To recognize that, no matter how many meditation apps I downloaded, I was not immune to judgment and spite. In a year that was supposed to be about expansiveness and freedom and physical exploration, I felt forced to sit still and turn inward. I fancied myself the triumphant heroine who would revel in independence and bound from park to park, asserting once and for all that she could create a life on her own terms and be happier for it. Instead, I began breaking apart to expand my definition of self. To explore the spider-filled caverns lurking inside my own chest. To say hello to the person I was most afraid to be. Nonconsensual ego obliteration at its finest.

I wondered if I could choose to see the lockdown as an opportunity. *What is the quarantine doing* for *me, rather than* to *me?*

The thought alone made me wince. Maybe if I could manage that, I'd find out that my worst fears were actually manageable. Like screaming toddlers in need of a hug.

☙

On quarantined Saturday mornings, Adam and I put the dogs in our backyard, moved all the living room furniture, and danced. In the year prior, he had gotten me absolutely obsessed with a branch of ecstatic dance called 5Rhythms. Established by Gabrielle Roth in the late 1970s, the practice is a conscious moving meditation, designed to transition between a wave of five radically different states of being—flowing, staccato, chaos, lyrical, and stillness. Ordinarily, we practiced an offshoot of this classic style in a huge dance studio with sprung wooden floors and a community of more than a hundred other writhing, sweaty bodies, but in the face of the shutdown, the entire operation had been forced onto Zoom. No matter—Kate was still its beating heart.

Kate was easily the most magical person I had ever met, a trained shaman with a sweet British accent, a wild gray mohawk, and a smile that could make anyone believe in faeries. Her no-nonsense wit was sharp as a blade, and she would just as soon kiss your face and tell you that your soul's word was "fecund" as she would call you out for not stretching to the limits of your fullest potential during dance. "Let the head go!" she would chant like a mantra, emboldening us city folk to toss our necks around maniacally and exit the river of conscious thought. "Let the bum go! Are you clenching your anus? Open your whole heart!"

I felt my feral beast scratching at my rib cage as I shimmied and shook around the living room with Adam, our fragile, flailing bodies projected onto the television from my laptop. "Once the joy is gone, then we're really in trouble!" Kate shouted through her microphone as a heart-thumping electronic beat wafted around the space. I pressed my hands to the sky and breathed deeply, grasping at whatever wisdom this muddied-up ether would grant me.

You've got to fearlessly insist on innocence, it whispered, purring the truth into my small frame as I continued to rock my hips from side to side, my mind a frayed and hazy master. *It's not ignorance to look for the light; it's intelligence.* I exhaled, bobbing my head from side to side as the music blared. I wanted to wrap my sullen arms around whatever crumbs of unadulterated joy that I could muster. If the ship was stalled, I wanted to be the one on deck still smiling.

Months earlier, in a long shamanic session with Kate, I'd faltered a bit, feeling like my upcoming project to visit every national park was somehow selfish or trite. I didn't know if I would be wasting a year of my life by jumping into the unknown, checking boxes off an arbitrary list of sites, and I definitely wasn't sure if I was throwing a hand grenade into my relationship by leaving for so long.

"But you're doing the most ancient thing in the world," Kate insisted. "The deep, hermetic work of wandering and seeking and bringing back knowledge. Roaming the wilderness—it's what humans have been doing for centuries—and it's exactly what so many women in their early thirties need to go through when they realize that they won't be twenty-five forever."

It was time to excavate a new way forward. One swirling with truth and hope and blood. A bright tunnel into my own future, carved inch by inch with my own fingernails.

❧

Adam and I watched the headlines for two months, waiting for some news of the parks reopening. In the weeks since our Grand Canyon tryst, he'd quit his job, electing to hop onto the adventure train with me for a few months before seeking new employment. I was thrilled to invite my love along for the ride in an increasingly chaotic world. We would stare down our mounting fears together.

Like heated kernels of popcorn exploding into being in a scattered and haphazard fashion, several parks in Utah, Nevada, and Colorado announced reopening dates. Adam and I looked at the map of my planned itinerary and realized that Redwood National Park had technically never closed.

"We could chart a course to the top of California," I murmured to him excitedly. "Cut over to Great Basin, then start knocking out the

Colorado parks as they reopen." Adam nodded in agreement, his eyes wide and childlike.

Though Los Angeles was still under a stay-at-home order, our cabin fever had reached a manic level. My project would crumble if I took any more time off. The money would run out, and my column would likely be canceled. Plus, the science was on our side. Experts were saying that the outdoors was the safest place to be, and with Gizmo on our team, we were essentially a self-contained unit. A mobile pod.

Still, the anticipation of social shaming stuck in my side like a splinter I just couldn't shake. Though some journalists were considered essential workers in California, I doubted that my mission to visit and document every national park counted as necessary business. There was also the issue of my heightened anxiety. I perceived every stranger as a floating haze of malicious germs first and a potential friend second. Somehow, I had to take it on faith that venturing out of the safe bubble of home and into the wild would do more good than harm.

I paid for an oil change and readied our gear. Adam took out a bright orange duffel bag and shoved it full of hiking clothes, jackets, boxers, gloves, and wool socks. He readied his Dopp kit with the barest essentials—a toothbrush, floss, razor, vitamins, condoms, and deodorant. We called my trainer friend and confirmed that we'd be dropping off the foster dogs, right on schedule. If a simple neighborhood walk felt like a bank heist, we were about to raid Fort Knox.

Swimming in the brilliantly blue void, in Crater Lake, Oregon

Chapter 4

The Great Wide Open

The dark green leaves of live oaks shimmered in the hot mid-May sun, and dense fields of golden grass twinkled and undulated as Adam and I drove north through central California. After dropping the pups off with their owner, we continued onward through tan hills freckled with jet-black cows, past Silicon Valley, and over the majestic vermilion spiderweb of the Golden Gate Bridge. We stopped for the night in Ukiah, asking a stranger in line at the gas station if they knew anywhere good to pull over and sleep.

While Adam chatted up the kind-eyed stranger, I passed a large, one-armed man with eyes bulging out of their sockets like fat, vacant marbles as I traversed the hall leading to the bathroom. He was coughing up phlegm into a ratty wad of toilet paper. Once inside, I locked the door and looked at the overflowing dumpster to my left. Blood-soaked tissues dotted the top layer. *The guy I just passed . . . We have to get the hell out of here.*

Adam finished jotting down instructions on how to find a rural pullout where cops wouldn't evict us in the night, and the two of us made a beeline for Gizmo in the dark parking lot.

"Did you just fucking say something about Kathy's son?!" The man from the bathroom was on our tail and clearly hallucinating. Neither Adam nor I had spoken a word since exiting the small, fluorescently lit store. "You did, you fucking cunt! Fucking Kathy . . . I'll kill you!"

He lunged toward the van. Adam instinctively clicked the automatic locks and started up the engine. Tires screeched as we swerved out of the gas station, hearts pumping. For miles, our eyes kept darting back and forth between the road and the side-view mirrors to be certain that no one was following us as we veered onto a dirt road for several miles, passing the ghostly apparitions of fog-laden trees and finally pulling over into a flat turnout with just enough room to rest.

Was this a harbinger of things to come? Some terrible ferryman between one world and the next? Sleep didn't come easily for either of us.

⚜

I rose to a gentle morning rain tapping on the metal roof of the van, Adam's arms wrapped firmly around me, the little spoon. Pulling away, I arched my back and pointed and flexed my toes to stir myself awake. In the fuzzy light of day, I could see plainly how simple and magical our surroundings were. Wind rustled leaves in a dense canopy overhead. Frogs croaked in the neighboring creek. The small dramas of insects were unfolding.

Our drive north continued. We passed large billboards for cannabis dispensaries and kooky roadside attractions that seemed at once antiquated and barbaric in their pandemic shutdown state. A Native American's face carved into the enormous trunk of a still-living redwood. The One Log House, an ancient hollowed-out tree that now serves as an espresso and gift shop for tourists. The Mystery Spot, a supposed gravitational anomaly that seemed more like an excuse to con money from road trippers than an enchanted natural marvel.

In a few short hours, we rolled into the tiny town of Orick, population 346. With a deserted main street featuring a hoarder-worthy antique shop, a run-down motel, a wood-carving workshop, and a gas station, the place felt less like the gateway to a national park and more like a soon-to-be-forgotten ghost town. Our plan was to backpack illegally into the park, sans permit, but we had no idea where to leave Gizmo for the night. Redwood was *technically* open but had restricted access to most of its parking areas. I pulled up to Edebee's, a bright-red one-room shack surrounded by picnic tables. Adam ordered for us.

"Two elk burgers, some ketchup, a side of fries, and, uh . . . Do you happen to know anywhere safe that we could park our van for a night or two?" Adam was clever. Killing two birds with one stone.

"Well, sure, man." The woman behind the counter didn't skip a beat. "I guess you could park 'er right here in my lot, or you could take a right-hand turn up there, unchain the fence, and leave it in the abandoned rodeo grounds for five dollars." She gestured in the direction of the trail we intended to take.

A toothy smile broke across my face as I heard the news. "Perfect!" Adam replied enthusiastically. "We'll just pay and drive there for the night, then."

This wasn't at all what I'd expected after the paranoia we had endured in Los Angeles. Small towns, it seemed, were faring much better. Fewer cases had led to less anxiety, and rather than becoming more insular and terrified of outsiders as the pandemic raged on, they seemed to embody more of a "keep calm and carry on" energy. In much of LA, it was easy to board up inside your house or apartment, ordering Postmates and Instacart and controlling every ounce of your environment, but in a place like Orick, there was physical work to be done—horses to feed, gardens to tend to. Of course, there was also a growing political divide that determined how seriously some folks took the virus, but in rural America, the temporary agoraphobia plaguing every asphalt jungle seemed steeped in class and circumstance.

Adam steered the van through lush green hills speckled with dozens of different wildflowers. The human world may have been on hold, but nature sure hadn't gotten the memo. Everything was bursting into color. I jumped out to open and close the rodeo gate behind us, and after half an hour of packing up our things behind a small amphitheater of weathered wooden bleachers, we hit the trail.

One of the signature backpacking trips of Redwood National Park is a flat, miles-long stroll along Redwood Creek that travels through some of the tallest trees on the planet, ending at Elam Camp, but with its parking lot closed off and the creek's water level high due to recent rains, Adam and I mapped out a different way of hiking into the park. According to an old map of fire roads and horse trails that I dug up online, there was a grassy berm behind the old rodeo grounds that sprouted a trail leading over a giant hill and into the dense greenery of the redwood biome, with thimbleberry and Sitka spruce jutting out under a lofty canopy of red-barked giants.

My anxiety rose as the two of us clomped across the grassy path. This happened often—just when I was about to set off on some grand adventure, I'd sense an urgent tug-of-war between my moxie and my inner child, who was always deeply afraid of getting into trouble.

"I need to learn how to turn my nerves on and off if I'm ever going to survive this pandemic," I called to Adam, who was lingering just behind me on the trail. "On when we're in a grocery store or public restroom, off when we're eating outside or backpacking."

"Hmm. That's an advanced-level skill, babe." He didn't sound so confident in my abilities. "Meditation's the only thing I've found that comes even close to helping with it."

The trail was muddy, though well maintained, and as we began our ascent up the mountain, the world transformed into a verdant tapestry of different textures of green. Big old-growth redwoods the width of two arm spans stood like furry-barked watchmen over the venerable space. Rhododendron blossoms hovered above us like glowing pink crowns, each surrounded by a circular harem of leaves. Moss-cloaked saplings dotted the forest floor here and there, a carpet of redwood sorrel and head-high sword ferns surrounding their small bodies. The place was dripping with life.

Beloved spiritual teacher Ram Dass once said, "When you hug a tree, you're hugging yourself." Eyebrows aloft, my eyes widened as I tilted my head and heavy pack backward to try to glimpse the tops of these giants. My eyes welled up with tears, the noise of mortal theatrics quickly fading into the background. I extended my sweaty arms out as far as I could reach and wrapped them tightly around an enormous wildfire-scarred trunk. They barely spanned a small portion of its staggering circumference. In that place of feeling breathless and small, I could sense my heartbeat against the pulse of the wood. The pulse of the forest. The pulse of the earth. It was the same energy that drove everything that would ever live on this planet forward, some great, unknowable spark that was as akin to real magic as we may ever find.

Panting in the ever-present humidity, Adam and I crested the top of the mountain and found the trail overgrown with thorns and vines. Within the first few minutes of our descent toward camp, we lost the path twice and clumsily maneuvered over several fallen trees. "We can turn around if you want!" I yelled back to Adam, now crashing through the underbrush. "No judgment."

"No way. Let's just try to think of it as a fun adventure and keep going. Try to focus on how cool it is that we're probably the only people in this forest right now."

I sighed and kept walking. Adam was often right about this sort of thing, and before I knew it, the trail widened and spilled onto a wooden footbridge surrounded by bright green ferns. Beyond it, tall maples covered in cat-tail moss that hung like swaying jellyfish tendrils beckoned us forward. Stepping onto the bridge, I noticed a small patch of yellow clinging to the damp boards on my right. A banana slug.

Among the more whimsical creatures of the redwood forest, banana slugs have quite a reputation in the Pacific Northwest as quirky, colorful additions to any hike. The University of California, Santa Cruz, has gone so far as to name the small gastropods as their school mascot, complete with a costumed canary-yellow slug named Sammy who makes appearances at parties and sporting events.

A pair of sensory tentacles twitched back and forth as Adam and I quickly snapped far too many selfies with the little critter. Our spirits brightened, we quickened the pace as we neared our stopping point for the night: Elam Camp.

Three picnic tables and a few hiker-established firepits marked the site. Farther down, two bear boxes for food storage crawled with more flamboyant banana slugs. The camp was set amid a grove of old-growth redwood trees. Up the hill was a damp wooden outhouse shaded by more of these enormous sempervirens. It looked like no one had been there for weeks. We pitched our tent beside a rocky wall teeming with ferns that protruded toward us like furry green arms. After dinner, I fell asleep to the sounds of a small, burbling creek that paralleled our campsite, nuzzling Adam in the cocoon of my sleeping bag.

Birdsong woke me to dappled light flitting across the sky-blue fabric of our tent. The scene was so lovely that I decided to stay in bed and read for a long while, listening to the unfamiliar sounds. The birds up north seemed so happy and triumphant, like tinkling elven bells strung up high in the treetops.

We spent our morning lounging in the tent, eating oatmeal and drinking coffee, before ambling over to Redwood Creek Trail. Considering that this track served as one of the park's main arteries, we were expecting to glide smoothly through its lush foliage, but because the park was barely open, the trail hadn't been maintained. We used our arms as machetes to knock thorny salmonberry vines out of the way, inching forward through the dense jungle of leaves. In the end, we got what we were looking for—a panoramic view of massive Redwood

Creek and its many wide gravel bars. From where we stood, the trees seemed to go up for miles.

Back at camp, I packed up the tent while Adam shoved our down sleeping bags into their stuff sacks, cinching them shut so they would cram into our backpacks more easily. There, in the heart of the woods, yesterday's anxiety felt like a skin I had shed.

In the Buddhist tradition at Plum Village, the principal monastic center of Zen Master Thich Nhat Hanh, there is a practice called "touching the Earth." Practitioners kneel on the ground three times, each time pressing their hands and forehead to the earth as if it were their best friend. This practice is encouraged to combat restlessness and lack of confidence. "The earth has been there for a long time. She is mother to all of us," Hanh wrote in *A Pebble for Your Pocket*. "Whenever you feel unhappy, come to the earth and ask for her help. Touch her deeply, the way the Buddha did. Suddenly, you too will see the earth with all her flowers and fruit, trees and birds, animals, and all the living beings that she has produced. All these things she offers to you."

Before leaving camp, I crouched down in my mud-caked boots and softly pressed my forehead and palms into the dirt three times. The trip was like a soothing balm, the earth itself my steady companion when everything else felt messy and tenuous. I tossed my pack over my shoulders and clipped my waistbelt tight, ready to hike.

Adam and I backtracked the way we had come, awed by the colossal trees and their woolly red bark as we passed a slow-moving salamander and ascended the overgrown trail. We switchbacked down through the thick woodland, saying goodbye to the lush foliage as we once again found ourselves in the cow pasture near town. Rounding the final corner, we closed in on my van and were met with a huge herd of elk, each member weighing between five hundred and one thousand pounds, casually lounging in the sun a few feet from Gizmo's grille.

It is remarkable to me that deer and elk, two animals in the same genetic family, behave in such vastly different ways. While a deer might swivel its large ears around before darting away from an intruder, an elk will calmly hold its ground, as if to say, "You looking at me, punk?"

"Uh . . . I guess we just ignore them and make dinner?" Adam was just as perplexed as I was that we were being stared down by a group of huge, uninvited guests.

Lucky for us, the elk had no interest in our burritos or guacamole, and as the fading sun lit up the abandoned rodeo in an electric amber glow, I felt the subtle hum of my confidence returning. Perhaps our illicit leap into the unknown wouldn't be so bad after all.

⚜

Adam and I sped through the Shasta-Trinity National Forest the next day, hugging a blue-green river on our right as we passed mile after mile of thick woods. After a night in western Nevada, we continued onto US Route 50, the loneliest road in America. Once thriving with gold rush and Pony Express towns, the cross-state highway is now a desolate upheaval of dust, rock, and failed dreams. Until we reached the national park, that is.

Great Basin is a high-altitude expanse of rugged mountains, feature-rich caves, and some seriously incredible trees—bristlecone pines. These conifers are the oldest nonclonal living things on the planet. They frequently live to be between two thousand and three thousand years old, with many surviving much longer than that. One such tree in California, named Methuselah after the biblical patriarch, is nearly five thousand years old, and its location is kept secret to prevent potential harm from human visitors. The park's visual centerpiece is Wheeler Peak, a craggy, 13,065-foot behemoth that towers over the barren valley below.

After a night at a free campground nearby, Adam and I woke early and readied our things. Though the trail to the bristlecone pine forest was ordinarily an under-three-mile affair, the park had elected to keep its upper road closed another week due to heavy snow, which meant that the usually mellow excursion would instead be an eleven-mile, all-day slog along Upper Lehman Creek.

We climbed quickly at first, the babbling sounds of the stream adding a friendly energy to the fragrant Engelmann spruce and ponderosa pines we passed. Then, wham! Our first view of Wheeler Peak across a meadow of sagebrush hit like some long-forgotten slumbering beast, a visual jolt of crumbling cliffs and avalanche scars. When we reached its namesake campground, three and a half miles in, my mind was dizzy with altitude. In the thin air just below ten thousand feet, Adam and I fumbled around, looking for the Bristlecone Trail. We finally located it under a blanket of fast-melting snow. Stopping to strap snow cleats to our feet, we tramped through it with quixotic glee.

Not fifteen minutes later, I was up to my ass in frigid wet snow. Postholing thigh high at times, I muscled my way forward across a steep, icy slope and struggled to break trail through the deep drifts. We were clearly the first people out to see the trees that season. Adam mostly laughed at me as he followed behind, taking videos of my clumsiness on his phone. When I rounded the next corner, I was relieved to see a sunny, mostly snow-free path heading north. Soon we were surrounded by huge gnarled trees.

Pressing my hand against the wood of a three-thousand-year-old pine without another soul around felt akin to time travel. These trees had been around during the rise and fall of Julius Caesar, the life of William Shakespeare, and the creation of the very country I now inhabited. Standing among them was an instant gateway to perspective. Proof that humans are much more fragile than our egos would have us believe.

One long, snowy descent later, we were back at the van. We slumbered again at a nearby campground, staring out at panoramic views of windswept Mount Moriah as the sun set. By morning, we were bound for Colorado, driving straight into the heart of the state's Western Slope. Nevada's arid grasslands gave way to the high mesas and wine-red tablelands of central Utah before we sped through Grand Junction, Colorado, an old railroad town now known for its fertile, fruit-filled hillsides and dozens of wineries. After winding through crumbling De Beque Canyon, Colorado River rapids to our left, we made it to Carbondale, where the snowy twin peaks of Mount Sopris stand watch.

Feeling exceedingly lucky that Adam had a half brother in town, we spent the drive listening to *This American Life* podcasts and daydreaming about what his family might have cooked for dinner. Gizmo was more luxurious than a tent, that's for sure, but when it came to mealtime, we often ate boil-in-a-bag Indian food or quesadillas. Fresh vegetables were hard to keep in stock.

We were delighted to arrive to a house beaming with family, barking dogs, salad, and hot pizza. It was a circus of love. Adam's niece and nephew, likely bored from at-home pandemic schooling, pounced on us like a couple of wildcats and demanded that we jump on the trampoline with them and then meet their new miniature pony.

Home was never something I got to hold in high regard growing up. For the entirety of my youth, we moved every two or three years within the same city, and I often found myself envious of people who'd lived in the same house their whole lives. The notion of a childhood home was foreign to me; my parents had separated before I was born, my mother's family lived in Sweden, and most of my dad's relatives stopped speaking to me after I graduated from college. Stability was a far-flung moon I found myself bellowing at as I grew older, hungry for the gift I wasn't given.

Nestled into Adam's shoulder, with the kids curled up on the floor at our feet, I fell asleep halfway through watching *The Princess Bride* in the living room, sipping every last drop of sweetness from our short time together.

"This place has the most metal, *Lord of the Rings* name of any national park," Adam exclaimed as we drove past the sign marking Black Canyon of the Gunnison, park number eighteen, two days later.

"Ha! You're right. Every other park is so prim and proper, like . . . Great Smoky Mountains or Grand Canyon, but here they cut to the chase and let you know that your inner angst is more than welcome."

Black Canyon, so named for its craggy walls of charcoal-colored gneiss, is one of the narrowest ravines in the world. The Gunnison River below furiously carves away at its striated metamorphic rock, and the park is home to the tallest vertical cliff face in Colorado—Painted Wall. Unlike other national parks, where hiking trails might navigate along a ridgeline or summit some far-off peak, Black Canyon is home to car-accessible vista points and steep climbing routes that descend roughly two thousand feet to the riverbank. That's two Chrysler Buildings stacked on top of each other. I steered toward the visitor center and nabbed us two permits to climb down into the jagged maw of the park's namesake, my excitement level rising.

Boots crunching along the dusty gravel of Oak Flat Trail, we reached a sign that pointed straight down. Not long after, we passed another sign: **WILDERNESS PERMITS REQUIRED**. The day was afoot. Soon it got steep. Really steep.

I grabbed on to a series of tree roots lining the path for balance, shifting my body weight onto the loose rock and scree below, sometimes electing to just say fuck it and butt-scoot my way down. Adam followed suit. We came to a clunky metal chain secured to a large pine that was meant to help us descend an almost vertical eighty-foot section. I took a deep breath in, hoisted myself over the rock face, and staggered down the slope, clinging as hard as I could to the chain.

"That was so badass!" I called up to Adam, who was just beginning his climb down. This park didn't treat visitors with kid gloves. We were allowed to climb at will.

As we continued down, I couldn't help but notice the flirtatious pops of wildflowers sprouting out of every sun-filled patch. Spring was fully underway in Montrose County, and viewed against the backdrop of one of the darkest canyons on the planet, it reminded me of the tale of Persephone, a flower maiden and daughter of Zeus who was captured by Hades and tricked into being his bride, the queen of the underworld. Because she had tasted some of his food—a handful of pomegranate seeds—she was forced to spend half of her year on earth and half of her year below, hence the cyclical turning of the seasons. Black Canyon of the Gunnison was a park of coexisting extremes—both fertile spring-time folly and menacing underground cleft of gneiss and schist.

The two of us skidded down the final talus slope, kicking fist-sized rocks out of our way as we neared the river. On arrival, we dropped our packs, stripped off our shoes, socks, and pants, and hopped in. The water was icy cold—fresh snowmelt from the Rockies—and I could only stand its numbing tingles for a few seconds before squealing and giggling and running onto a rocky bank at the current's edge. I propped myself up against a tree in the shade and took out my Kindle, reciting a series of Mary Oliver poems out loud to Adam.

"Did you know that the ant has a tongue
with which to gather in all that it can
of sweetness?
Did you know that?"

A breeze blew through the snaggletoothed canyon walls, mussing my bangs and giving the ravens overhead a lift into the bright blue beyond. I popped a piece of dried mango into my mouth, perfect and chewy and sweet.

Back in Carbondale, I had an appointment to get to. Adam's brother had a friend who, adhering to local guidelines, had reopened his tattoo shop, complete with mask wearing and temperature checks for safety. I had become transfixed by a passage in the Aldous Huxley novel *Island*. The particular lines that interested me were: "It's dark because you're trying too hard . . . Lightly, child, lightly. You've got to learn to do everything lightly. Think lightly, act lightly, feel lightly. Yes, feel lightly, even though you're feeling deeply. Just lightly let things happen and lightly cope with them."

It seemed the perfect mindset for a year of virus woes, political strife, and a road trip across America that would push me to the brink of my own sanity. If I could learn to tell the anxious, type A creature living inside my chest to step aside in favor of an easier, softer way, I might just make it out alive.

I had the word scrawled across the delicate inside of my right wrist in black ink, etched in my own cursive handwriting: *lightly*. Whenever I shake hands with a new friend or type into my phone or open a door, it reminds me of how I wish to behave and perceive.

༄

Rocky Mountain National Park blew by in an uncommonly happy blur of alpine cirques and sapphire lakes. Tired after weeks on the road at breakneck speed, Adam was becoming exhausted and chose to nap in the van while I mostly hiked alone. We'd discussed trying to schedule more alone time to avoid one of the primary pitfalls of road tripping with a significant other—resentment.

The scenery was impeccable. I clambered over rocky walls to avoid lingering June snow, tentatively jumped into bone-chilling bodies of water, and narrowly avoided elk on the trail. I read for hours on the shore of shimmering, sun-hungry Mills Lake and gazed awestruck at the rocky shark fins of Keyboard of the Winds. I drove with Adam to the snow closure at the top of Trail Ridge Road—Rainbow Curve—and strolled leisurely along the paved highway, passing tenacious little tundra plants as we marveled at the high peaks of the Mummy Range.

"How're you doing, babe? Better after your nap?"

"Yeah, yeah. It's just a fast-paced trip, you know?" Adam replied as honestly as he could, knowing that the disparity in our daily energy levels was one of the few things we didn't love about each other. I tried to broach the elephant in the room as delicately as I could.

"Do you think your depression is acting up again? You seem kind of down these last few days."

"No, it's not that . . . It's just . . . I think when you're on a quest, you get a direct line of energy from Source, you know? And that's why you're always raring to go, and I'm always trying my best just to catch up. This has always been *your* trip."

I couldn't argue with that. It *was* my trip. A thing I had nurtured from infancy, when it was only the seed of an idea, long before I met Adam. I had been as transparent about that as I could when we first met. About the fact that I would, at some point, leave. No matter how well we got along, 2020 was always going to be the year I struck out. I had to keep going.

﹏﹏

The chillingly dark mass of the Sangre de Cristo Range and its wreath of fourteen-thousand-foot peaks loomed high above us as we drove toward Great Sand Dunes, national park number twenty, each dune sitting beneath the enormous summits like a honey-covered hillside that glistened in the afternoon sun. Adam and I hopped across shallow Medano Creek and scaled the highest dune we could find as the sun sank low behind a white blossom of clouds. It was hardly the highest dune in North America (that harder-to-reach summit was just beyond us), but the off-trail climb gave us a sense of accomplishment as we continued to speed across Colorado. From there, we traveled east, forming a clockwise loop around the state in the exact opposite direction than I had originally intended, watching and waiting as the parks began to reopen, one by one, from their pandemic shutdowns and changing our plans accordingly.

An audio tour narrated by TJ Atsye, a member of the Laguna Pueblo tribe, guided us on a half-day driving track around the pit houses and impressive masonry of the ancient cliff dwellings at Mesa Verde, our final park in the state. Though I had traveled to the area as a young girl, my mother enthralled with the idea of visiting the Native ruins, my memories were of scanning the highway for foreign license plates and panning for gold at a nearby tourist stop. Seeing the nine-hundred-year-old structures as an adult lent them a new importance. I couldn't believe how complex the villages were, each one built brick by brick along a steep sandstone escarpment.

We drove on, out of the pinyon pines and scrubby junipers of the Four Corners, past the turquoise blue water of Priest Lake, and through the countless tall peaks that surround high-alpine Lizard Head Pass. Skirts of dense green pine spilled out for miles.

Carbondale and its creature comforts once again in our rearview, I steered Gizmo through a lichen-speckled river gorge and up and over a snowy mountain pass near Vail. I was hell-bent on getting to South Dakota with enough time to explore before circling back to visit Glacier National Park when it finally reopened. The pandemic had turned the trip into an exercise in accepting impermanence, regrouping, and then formulating new plans. Past Denver, Adam and I cruised through wide open grasslands that shimmied and shook like the waves of a great green ocean. Rolling, moving hills that rose and fell as if the earth were breathing. Blue sky as far as the eye could see.

⸎

The first thing we encountered upon driving into Wind Cave National Park was a bison as big as a Bronco. He flopped over onto a pile of dusty earth, rolled around for a moment, and stood up, shaking the dirt from his matted brown body. He seemed confident. Cocky, even. I couldn't believe the size of the furry beast. It was my first encounter with a bison, the largest land mammal in North America, and he was standing just thirty yards from my van. My heart thumped in my chest as I steered onward.

The tiny bodies of prairie dogs began protruding and receding into a lumpy expanse of grassland to our right as we pulled Gizmo over to watch. Grinning, I stepped out of the vehicle as hundreds of yipping rodents scattered. A few arched their backs and lifted their stubby arms skyward with an alarming screech, as though shouting, "Hallelujah!" to their prairie dog god. Frenetically darting between different holes in the soil, the tiny ground squirrels never seemed to sit still. After many minutes of wide-eyed watching, I turned us back toward the visitor center and parked my van in the fast-fading sunlight.

A dirt path led us to the cave's natural entrance. Repairs on the park's vintage elevator meant that underground tours were canceled, so all we could see of the cave was a small, volleyball-sized opening in an otherwise solid wall of rock. We had the place to ourselves. I held my outstretched hand over the gaping hole and, like some otherworldly sorcery, a gentle breeze blew up and swirled around my fingers. This was it: the famous wind of Wind Cave. The place the Lakota people believe all life came from. The mysterious source of all things.

⚜

In an effort to add more cleanliness and romance to our road trip, Adam and I had agreed to book two nights of cheap motels per week instead of one, maxing out my already thin budget. We rolled into the Dollar Inn Hot Springs, just outside the park, and immediately showered and changed into fresh underwear. Propping myself up on the bed with two pillows, I answered several emails while Adam shaved. As I typed, I could feel him leering at me, a target for his unsettled desire. I shuddered. It wasn't that I wasn't still attracted to Adam—I was, intimately. Only, the longer I spent on the road, the more I found my body separating into two very different kinds of animals: one that could hike over prairies and mountains and sweat and wallow and come out stronger for it, and one that harbored a more coy femininity, an object of intellect and the male gaze. The latter often had to be shoved into a box to make room for the headstrong Viking who'd planned this unyielding trip.

When I looked down at my genitals, I saw a tangled mess of pink skin, all puckered and bunched up like old chewing gum. Unshaven for months. Swollen and slit. My body was once a pleasure box, but it had become a machine primed for quick movement over vast landscapes. No time for affection, just burn, burn, burn.

I knew the moment I closed my laptop that Adam would stop whatever he was doing, and we would have sex. You'd think that I would be excited. To be clean and sprawled out on a bed with my lover. But my mind was still out in the fields, drifting. I was consumed with far more pressing matters, like what color the grass is at night and if the moon ever feels lonely.

⚜

Well rested after a night in a real bed and emboldened by on-the-road prowess, I flipped into feeling garishly pixieish the next morning, flirting like a madwoman. The longevity of my current relationship had been on my mind. Though we had been dating for nearly two years and had discussed the possibility of marriage several times, we hadn't broached the topic in a while. Prenoon coquettish Emily was going to change that.

I summoned up my most fay voice and asked, "Adam, do you think we'll ever get married?" The last of the words dangled out of my mouth like song lyrics I was sure we'd hum along together.

Adam paused. For a long while.

"Well, uh . . . I think that's something I'm trying to figure out right now."

I had been hoping for a "Yes, of course!" or a "This is a tricky year, but I love you, and I'm committed to making this work." Something encouraging. Not a verbal pratfall that would drive the air out of the room.

His response sucker punched me in the worst way. I was looking for a sign that, even though 2020 was difficult, we were a team pushing toward a more beautiful future together. At the onset of the year, my answer would have been a resounding, earsplitting, "Yes!" But lately, I had been feeling frustrated with Adam's lack of initiative and enthusiasm on the trip. I felt like I had been carrying around dead weight or guiding an ill-prepared client for free. I needed him to acknowledge that it wasn't all for nothing. Adam was one of the most intelligent and privileged people I had ever been close to, but watching his gloominess worsen as he quit his job and followed me around the country broke my heart. It kept him from fully enjoying the magic of our freewheeling months together. It kept him from embracing his own passions and embarking on his own life-affirming projects.

My stomach leaped into my throat as he spoke; I had no idea that he was having doubts too. *I* was the one who should have been unsure. *I* was supposed to be the one who got to choose whether or not we were in it for the long haul.

The conversation devolved into affirmations about what was and wasn't right in the relationship and manifestos about how van life wasn't for Adam.

"I always thought of myself as someone who could 'rough it,'" he explained, "but this trip has me feeling like maybe I'm just not."

"It isn't fair to view our entire relationship through the lens of a year full of a pandemic and what is probably the longest trip I'll ever take in my life," I butted in, interrupting his speech with righteous anger. "Nothing is normal right now. *Nothing.* It's like we're being forced to play a video game at two or three times the usual speed. Bullets and rocks are flying at our faces, and it's impossible for us to jump out of the way fast enough."

There was no escape, no offices, no ordinary steam vents. Some years were just fucking hard, and boy was this going to be one of them.

"Yeah, but I think you may be overlooking some of our core incompatibilities . . ." Adam drifted off.

"Listen, I get that it's hard. I get that I'm being a little Napoleon. But this is one of the biggest things I'll do in my entire life, and I can't have anyone standing in my way while I do it." I wanted to be honest. Kind. To give Adam a little leeway. I tried to be fair, but I had a habit of distancing myself the moment I felt like someone else was in my way. My temper raged.

For as long as I could remember, I had wanted to get married. I was never the type of girl who made wedding scrapbooks and dreamed of wearing a white chiffon ball gown, but I had a keen sense that partnership would help me finally feel valued and validated after an unsteady childhood. Since my parents had separated before I was born and my father had his own issues, I'd never had a reliable relationship with him. Instead of organizing an every-other-weekend arrangement like most divorced families I knew, my father drifted in and out of holiday dinners, showing up with sporadic gifts of stuffed animals and concert tickets, then mostly disappeared after I graduated from college. My experience was textbook, really. The girl who never knows her dad and then spends a lifetime trying to find him in other people. There was a pit at the bottom of my heart that craved the mundanity of family life. The pure physical immediacy of having another body in my domestic space. A body that would accept and acknowledge my presence on a day-to-day basis, good or bad. At the very least, it would be proof of existence. With a single mom who worked overtime to provide for us, I'd often been alone. Men came and went from our lives as they pleased for reasons I did not understand. As I grew older, the desire to pin down what I resented never having grew claws. I wanted to ensnare someone in a web of great sex and witty banter. Roses and repartee. I wanted to become a honeytrap that no sane man would ever leave. To kill the deep sting of loneliness once and for all.

I stepped outside the motel room to call my friend Alice and vent. She didn't mince words. "If you agree to come along on someone else's trip, you've got to be a good guest."

My thoughts *exactly*.

Even on our best days, Adam had become a real drag. I had been begging him to go back to therapy for months, and he wasn't interested. He moped a lot, especially in the mornings, relying on me to drive, play music, get directions, plan meals, and know where we were hiking. After over a month on the road, he hadn't suggested a single trail.

Stuffing my heartache back into my rib cage, I drove the two of us to the park so we could hike and, hopefully, heal. If there was one thing Adam and I were good at, it was taking deep breaths and remaining friendly, even after a potentially earth-shattering discussion. Clusters of two or three enormous male bison grazed atop each emerald-green hill, looking like thuggish mafia dons, and after rounding a curve populated with hundreds of yammering prairie dogs, I parked Gizmo and stuffed my backpack full of water and snacks for the day.

We stepped onto the Lookout Point Trail, narrowly avoiding a patch of waxy poison ivy, and planned to walk a five-mile loop that would take us into the belly of the park's grasslands, through a crumbling canyon, and onto the Centennial Trail to finish.

"Watch out for a huge bison patty when you get to the first bridge!" A family of hikers clomped around us on the path, the dad razzing his teenage boy. "My son's footprint is in it!"

The fresh, soupy pile of dung was splat in the middle of the trail not five minutes after we started hiking. Tiptoeing around it, Adam and I were soon surrounded by the rolling, grassy hills emblematic of the park. Two bison stood stone faced about a hundred yards away, one of them right in the center of the trail.

"So . . . I guess we just walk around him?" I was clueless about what to do in the event of a car-sized mammal blocking my path. "Does thirty feet seem like a wide enough berth?"

Adam nodded and laughed, sending me out first to timidly wander off-trail around the ice-age creature. Chum in an ocean of prairie.

I could feel my heart rate rise as I held my breath and meandered through thigh-high grasses. The bison turned his furry head and looked straight at me, the hulk of his body unmoving. Clearly, I was not enough of a threat to warrant any extra effort. Adam followed behind.

"Yip yip yip yip!"

We moved in a serpentine motion along the trail to avoid tiny potholes as it passed through a prairie-dog town.

"Sorry for stepping on your homes! We promise we'll be gone soon!" I yelled.

As we neared a mellow creek bordered by speckled, pinkish pegmatite and powdery limestone canyon walls, our conversation took a turn toward finding solutions rather than merely complaining about our current relationship woes. Clearly, the breakneck pace of the van trip was not Adam's cup of tea, and nothing I said or did could change that. Together, we sought a compromise as we walked the trail. He would find a therapist, even if it meant stopping in more cities to find enough Wi-Fi to video chat. He would continue in the van for one more month, help me drive back to Los Angeles, and meet me in Juneau, rather than drive up to Seattle together. Then, after we spent five weeks traveling through Alaska, Adam would stay home for the remainder of the expedition. I would miss him like hell, but I knew we'd come out stronger for it.

⁓⚜⁓

I woke up with one of the worst emotional hangovers of my life. For two years, I had assumed that my partner and I were in sync every step of the way, moving into the same house and planning an epic future together. But now I felt like a trickle of black ink had been flicked into the fishbowl of our relationship, and it would soon start fanning out in every direction until our entire reality was gloomy and gray. Sailing around to the national parks in a minivan was a dream trip. *How had I allowed it to corrode my relationship? Had I been blind to* that *much of Adam's discomfort?* I was so upset that I could puke.

Adam drove us north to Mount Rushmore as I sulked in the passenger seat and gazed out the window at huge stands of pine trees and the occasional pronghorn antelope. By the time we reached the national monument, I was nauseous with grief. I stared flatly at the blank faces of old white men carved into a once beautiful mountain.

When we pulled over to grab sandwiches in Rapid City, eating them while sweating in the front seats of the van, Adam tried to calm my anguish. "Don't feel bad," he said sweetly. "I never get attached to anyone."

I felt like my brain might sneeze out of my nostrils from the shock.

"Are you including *me* in that statement? Do you not feel attached to me?!"

"Yes."

I started sobbing into my panini. My stomach fell through the car floor. *Why do I feel like I'm talking to a sociopath?*

I propped up my bare legs on Gizmo's dashboard and stared, expressionless, at the green trees fluttering just beyond my grubby toes. I wanted to scream and run. To kick Adam out of the van. To say "fuck you" for ruining something I spent years of my life working hard and sacrificing for. Sometimes it felt like people dated a manic pixie dream girl to try to escape into her energy, only to find themselves caught up in the swell, tugged out by a riptide, and drowning in their loss of self.

"You're being awfully quiet . . ." Adam mumbled as he shoved the last bit of sandwich into his crumb-covered mouth.

"It just hurts to consistently be told you're extraordinary only to have everyone leave you in the end."

⤎⋅⤏

I grew up in a house where I was not allowed to get anything less than straight As in every subject, including the ones I was bad at. I skipped second grade and was still expected to earn the same high marks; it didn't matter that I was a year and a half younger than the other kids in my class. Obsessed with maintaining my perfect attendance record, I often went to school with nosebleeds or strep throat, worried about what would happen to my report card if I missed so much as a single quiz. When I told my mom that I wanted to be an artist, she didn't resist entirely but instead doubled down on my rigorous schooling, insisting that I maintain my scholastic achievements while also jetting around to dance lessons or guitar practice or drama rehearsals—events that could linger past 9:00 p.m. each night.

"Raising you was a lot like raising a boy child," my mother once told me years later. "You were always so physical and assertive. I was worried that you'd get way too rebellious once you hit your teen years, so I had to keep the rules pretty strict."

Separated from my mom at a young age and without custody, my father was generally an agent of chaos. My mother, an immigrant from Sweden without any family close by, often worked long hours crunching numbers to put food on the table. A single mom who was just doing her best to ensure our survival.

I remember dragging her out of the office early one day to attend a parents' night at school when I was eleven, so excited to hear my teachers boast about how clever and well behaved I had been in class. "Emily really is remarkable," they would tell her. "She's constantly raising her hand because she always knows the answers."

"Yeah, yeah," my mother would respond, as if swatting away flies. She had heard it all before. For me, excellence was the rule, not a cause for celebration.

After marrying and later divorcing my stepfather when I was twelve, my mom started dating, and a string of strange men came in and out of the house and tried to charm the awkward kid with the wide eyes and freakish booksmarts. They never lasted long.

I moved across the country alone to attend college at age seventeen, settling in Los Angeles and embarking on a series of long-term relationships throughout my twenties with men who were either far older, far smarter, or far wilder than I was. I yearned to impress them. I dared them to love me through my veil of quirks and intellect. I dangled my body over various flames while riding a unicycle across a tightrope and reciting handwritten poetry out loud. Anything to keep them from leaving. Anything to be the one with her hands on the wheel.

～

My hand was on the wheel as we pulled into Badlands National Park the next morning, surrounded on all sides by striped sedimentary rock formations that looked like crude, beige cardboard cutouts. Adam and I were back on speaking terms, but in the sweltering ninety-five-degree heat, not much was being said. We set out on a ten-mile loop around some of the park's infamous crumbling cliffs but had to cut it short in the unforgiving midday sun, opting instead to retreat to our campsite and read. It was too hot to be angry. Changing into a two-piece bathing suit, I sprayed myself down with cool water and sprawled out like a piece of roadkill on a shaded picnic table. Night couldn't come soon enough.

Spinning our tires across the state of Wyoming, we came to Yellowstone, the country's first national park and the birthplace of what has since been called "America's best idea." It was one of the few parks on the trip that Adam had already been to and I had not, meaning that he could play tour guide for once. I was ecstatic.

We hit an impasse on arrival, as two large bison trotted down the middle of the road. An orange-bellied pine marten scurried across the pavement. Clearly, this park was a wildlife lover's dream.

The ferocious swell of Old Faithful in the thin morning light started our day with a bang, and Adam and I were soon filled with childlike wonder as we strolled across a maze of raised wooden boardwalks to take in the extraordinary display of geothermal features at Upper Geyser Basin. A series of roiling rainbow springs bubbled up on my left and right, some a deep blue gradient that must have stretched all the way into the bowels of the earth. When Rudyard Kipling visited the park in 1889, he wrote of goblins splashing about in their boiling bathtubs. If I squinted my eyes just so, I could see them too.

Our obligatory tourist activities complete, we could explore the park more freely. After parking Gizmo near a river where sizzling, mustard-hued sulfuric vents bubbled straight into the rapids, the two of us climbed to a viewpoint overlooking Grand Prismatic Spring, a massive cyclopic eye with psychedelic coloration that unfolded from azure to tangerine to bloodred, waving its steaming, watery tendrils across the earth for hundreds of feet.

I stomped my boots across the forest floor, trying to lose the throngs of tourists that seemed to crowd around every hot spring and geyser the park had to offer. But in a matter of minutes, the world went silent. Adam and I trod lightly along a forested dirt path, occasionally whacking mosquitoes from our arms as we neared the welcome white noise of two-hundred-foot-tall Fairy Falls. Water cascaded gently down a magnificent rocky cliff, breaking into a thin lace of white as it fanned out along the rock face and neared the ground. We hiked onward, through dark hallways of trail cut into the timber, rock-hopping across a small brook and occasionally spotting puffs of steam high above the treetops. I turned right at a fork in the path and felt like I had wandered through a mystical portal.

To my left was a bubbling mudpot, where thick dollops of muck like rank eggnog glooped and glopped out of the earth. To my right was a huge cerulean pool, steaming and hissing as Imperial Geyser shot at least fifteen feet into the air, violently hurtling droplets of water onto the ground below. There were no guardrails. No rangers. No selfie-taking social media fiends. Just me, Adam, and an assortment of leisurely hiker hippies spread out across the neighboring grassy meadow, enjoying the show.

Our days in Yellowstone flew by in a blur of grizzlies and elk and waterfalls and cascading hot springs atop layer-cake rock formations that almost looked man-made, like something you'd find in a manicured botanical garden. The earth was alive with heaving, volatile forces, and yet my relationship woes had cooled to a simmer. Travel had thrown Adam and me back into each other. We were friends and confidants who needed to get along to survive in the woods, rather than bicker about what the future might hold.

⌘

Wilderness does the same thing that great art does: it reveals something jarring and unequivocally true about being human. At its best, it's uncomfortable and gut-wrenchingly beautiful.

The Teton Range is the platonic ideal for what a crest of mountains should look like. If you asked a child to draw a peak from memory, they would unquestionably scribble down something resembling the Grand Teton—a huge, serrated rock face, perfectly pointed like an upside-down *V*, with snow gracefully lining the very top.

That June, one of my closest friends from Los Angeles happened to be visiting his parents in Salt Lake City, a mere five hours from Grand Teton National Park. When I suggested that he take a respite from pandemic-induced constant family time to go backpacking in the woods with us, he jumped at the suggestion. Dylan is a sweet-natured intellectual with a master's in poetry from Cornell and an undergraduate degree in computer science. He's one of those rare modern Renaissance men that you seldom meet but feel instantly entranced by. As at home cycling up the side of a huge mountain as he is dropping acid at Burning Man and dancing all night, he's also an excellent and loving father to two boys. Having him around was sure to cut the tension that Adam and I had been feeling.

The three of us met up at a hipster coffee shop in Jackson Hole and walked around town for an hour, catching up and waiting for the rain to clear. Taxidermy squirrels wearing life vests and paddling miniature canoes decorated the window display at a shop where we tried, fruitlessly, to find Dylan a suitable cowboy hat. We drove our separate cars to the String Lake Trailhead, bullet-sized hail and rain pelting the windshields as we did our best to stay dry and finish stuffing our enormous backpacks full of gear. Then, like magic, the clouds lifted, and our trek could begin.

I led the group up toward Paintbrush Canyon, cutting a line across the north shore of String Lake, bear spray knocking against my hip like I was packing heat. I mostly listened while Adam and Dylan talked about mental health and uncomfortable family dynamics. It felt nice to hang back and be silent for a change. To watch my partner brighten up in the presence of another. To admire his cleverness and sincere listening skills. Adam and I were remarkably drained by being stuck together for months as a twosome with few other outlets for conversation. I loved seeing Adam in the context of another person. *Even if we were stuck in LA*, I thought, *the rotten bits of this year might still corrode that sweetness.*

Travel isn't the only thing that's grating. Most people have been utterly alone.
Our group ambled upward through a lush, cloudy forest.

We pitched our tents on a high plateau overlooking the sapphire
curve of Leigh Lake and her many wooded islets. A pink haze clung to
the clouds as the sun began to dip behind the thousand-foot cliffs that
flanked us. We made dinner, the three of us balancing on a sloping ledge
of metamorphic rock, and talked for hours about the many disturbing
police brutality cases that had been all over the news.

Despite the sobering topic of conversation, the entire evening felt
blissfully normal. I hadn't had a proper three-way chat in months. I
melted into my sleeping bag that night feeling like I was floating off on
a peaceful little island, both the pandemic and my relationship worries
so distant.

All morning we tramped through steep, late-season snow, dodging
surly marmots who showed no fear. We teetered on couch-sized boulders as we climbed toward Holly Lake. The patches of fast-melting slush
were blushing, it seemed, blooming bright pink with algae splotches as
the sun intensified. Breathless in the thin mountain air, Adam suggested
we stop for a lunch break at an iced-over pond, after which the canyon we were following quickly became impassable. The pond glowed
an electric glacial blue in the light, as though Excalibur itself might
suddenly rise up from its chilly depths. Our view east of Leigh Lake
and enormous Jackson Lake beyond it was breathtaking, puffy clouds
reflected in the glassy teal water.

Descending was not so graceful. While Dylan clomped down the
steep slope in all of his Eagle Scout prowess, Adam and I elected to glis-
sade as far as we could on our butts in the mushy mashed-potato snow.
Speeding toward the tree line, my body was abruptly flung sideways as
my right shin caught on an iced-over boulder. I clutched the scrape in
pain, gasping for breath as I limped my way across a small waterfall and
back onto the trail with the boys.

"You okay?" Adam asked, concerned.

"Yeah, fine," I said. "I'm gonna try to walk it off."

We packed up our little backpacker tents and car-camped at Lizard Creek the second night, rising early for coffee and oatmeal and a leisurely hike to a hot spring a ranger had told us about the day before.

Yellow-gold monkey flowers seeped out of every light-filled crack along the warm creek—fairy gardens in full bloom. Our tired group of trail warriors plopped eagerly into the first pool we came across, where scalding water trickled down a large rock streaked with orange plant matter. After a simmering half-hour soak, Adam wanted to explore farther up the water source and take a few photos, leaving Dylan and me alone in the hot shallows.

"Is it obvious that we're struggling?" With only a few minutes of one-on-one time, I was hoping to get some choice relationship advice from one of our only mutual friends. "I've been frustrated for so long, man."

"It is apparent," Dylan replied in a carefully considered tone. "But, you know . . . a relationship is its own species. It's a slow-moving four-legged animal. It's not efficient in the least. You think it's only going to take twice as long to get ready for something, but really it takes orders of magnitude longer to get ready. Once my ex-wife and I recognized that and started using that language, things got a lot easier."

We said our goodbyes in the gravel parking lot, each of us not quite ready to leave and return to the restlessness of our own lives. I hugged Dylan tightly for a long while.

"Thanks for helping me feel normal for a couple of days," I whispered.

With that, Adam and I were on our own again in Gizmo, zooming through dense pine forests and undulating grassy hills as we drove north into Montana. With my left hand on the steering wheel, I held out my right, and he clasped it tightly, threading his fingers through mine with extra care. A limping four-legged beast set loose again to wander.

⤙⤚

We arrived at Glacier National Park just in time to catch the sun setting beyond the Technicolor pebbles that lined the bottom of Lake McDonald. Adam grabbed a flat, round stone and expertly flung it against the water, its spinning momentum skipping effortlessly across the surface for several seconds. Each time I tried to fling a rock against the glassy tarn, it would give up after three measly hops. "Skip, skip, skip, FLOP." *Ah, well . . . you can't succeed at everything,* I thought.

The last of the dying light spun the high mountains into a frenzy of peach and salmon, a translucent orange feather tickling their bits before nightfall. The sun kissing each summit good night.

We wandered up to the Sperry Chalet the next morning, a Swiss Alps–style backcountry mountain lodge built in 1913. A glance at the forecast warned that our first full day in the park would be our only dry one—a chilling rain was expected to soak everything within a two-hour radius for the rest of the week. I was dying to check out some of the park's historic mountain huts while the weather was good, so I tossed the two of us onto a long trail to see as much of Glacier as possible. We traversed a recent burn zone, and light sparkled through charred toothpick trees as the far-off roof of the chalet shone a brilliant, glistening amber in the sun.

"How many miles is today's hike?" Adam had a habit of forgetting the details of the day and then echoing the same questions ad nauseam as we walked.

"Twelve miles. Maybe more if we want to check out the pass." I tried not to let my aggravation show, but I was beginning to feel like an overworked and underappreciated mom.

"Oh. And how much elevation gain?"

I sighed. Loudly. "About thirty-five hundred feet, Adam. Didn't I tell you all this last night before bed?"

"Yeah, but sometimes I forget. It's a lot of information."

"Do you even know the name of the thing we're hiking to today?" My frustration grew claws.

"The . . . something chalet?"

"The SPERRY Chalet, Adam! Jesus." How could one man trust me so fully in the wilderness yet be so skeptical about a future together? "What would you do if I fainted or you lost me on the trail and needed to figure out where we are? Would you just wander around until someone *else* told you what trail you were on?"

Even in the dazzling sunshine, surrounded by prismatic waterfalls, we were vulnerable to the tiny threads of resentment that crept into every crack and crevice we left unguarded. A venom had been let loose, waiting patiently to dissolve everything we knew to dust.

The following four days of bitter rain weren't much better. With just one person in the minivan, it was easy enough to shed off wet clothes and muddy boots, but with two adult-sized humans inhabiting the small space, the task seemed exponentially more vexing. Twice as many raincoats. Twice as many dripping socks. Twice the foot odor.

We navigated the storm and the park's many road closures—a side effect of lingering snow—by auto touring as much of the wooded wonderland as we could manage, trekking through thick mud on the way to idyllic Avalanche Lake and driving north toward the Canadian border to chow down on freshly baked huckleberry bear claws at the historic Polebridge Mercantile, a homesteader's relic from 1914.

Adam and I squeezed every last drop of juice we could out of the half-closed, sopping-wet park, but when our time was up, we were happy to leave it and sleep in a warm motel room. I knew that booking a place would also obligate physical reconnection.

Sex had become increasingly transactional and scheduled, something that needed to happen in the safety and warmth of a cheap hotel rather than in the forty-five-degree dark of a steel box. My body was a shield I held between us to keep the peace. Once showered, I allowed him to undress me and do whatever he wanted. *At least if sex happens once a week, he can't complain too much. Especially if I make myself come too.*

We continued the journey east, through fields of wheat and lemon-yellow canola flowers, passing the odd pronghorn and road-kill porcupine. Independence Day came and went in Watford City, North Dakota. At the Maltese Cross Cabin, I pondered for a long while on Theodore Roosevelt's crusade to set aside public lands. Rust-colored bison calves suckled in the road as I drove through his namesake park. Wild horses galloped across the warm tones of shrub-topped badlands. Lighting burst across the prairie after dark like radioactive veins.

Farther east, the world broke open into a never-ending series of small lakes and tremendous pine forests that rose up out of the earth like one great green mohawk. Along the drive, Adam and I talked about how absurdly myopic our minds could be when it came to long-term relationships in crisis.

"It's like, when I'm upset, my brain can only fixate on one or two issues, like you moving slower in the mornings or not being sexually dominant enough," I explained. "When the truth of the matter is that there are about five hundred other things that are all working together to make us get along and have fun on a near-daily basis."

"Yeah," Adam chuckled. "If we both got back on dating apps right now, we'd be searching for another match who possesses about 95 percent of the same good stuff we have here."

It's strange how speaking so freely about your worst fears can serve to ground and reconnect a relationship, rather than rip it to shreds. Vulnerability can have a bizarrely soothing property. After a long drive through the timberlands of northern Minnesota, talking all the way, I pulled into the parking lot for Ebel's houseboat rentals, feeling closer to Adam than I had in weeks.

We were greeted by the owner, a man named Donny, who showed us around what would become our home for three nights as we puttered around Voyageurs National Park: a one-bedroom houseboat, complete with a full kitchen, hot shower, toilet, living room, roof deck access, and a water slide off the back. It was an epic cabin on floats.

In under an hour, we loaded in our gear and groceries, got a quick driving lesson, and set sail for Kabetogama Lake. I had never captained a boat before, and holding the wheel felt strangely powerful. Passing a bald eagle majestically perched atop an enormous fir tree, we cleared a narrow passage just outside Sullivan Bay and were free to wander. Navigating northwest, we docked at our own private island for the night, one marked by a posted sign that read YODER.

After tying down each end of the unruly houseboat to the on-shore anchor points, Adam stripped off all his clothes and splashed a pot of water onto the plastic slide.

"One . . . two . . . three . . . cannonball!" He sped down the slide and flopped into the tea-colored water like a playful river otter. Next it was my turn.

"Pour some water on the slide so you don't hurt your butt!" Adam called up to me, dog-paddling.

"I'm scared!" I yelled back. I love slides but hate the sensation of falling. After the smooth white plastic ended, there was a five-foot drop straight down into the lake.

My toes curled against the molded slide as I squinted my eyes shut, took a deep breath, and let go. With a scream and an enormous plop, I fell feetfirst into the surprisingly warm water.

"You did it! That wasn't so bad, right?" Adam was beaming, stoked that I had stared down my silly little fears.

I raised my naked heart skyward, spinning and floating, admiring the sunshine and the cool sensation of wetness against my bare flesh. Skinny-dipping in a secluded cove with my lover felt like the most ancient fun in the universe. Like there was no separation between me and the liminal space of the natural world. A rare form of transformational magic I should have learned about years ago.

After a breakfast of omelets and bacon the following morning, we took the small skiff that came with the houseboat and set off in search of Ellsworth Rock Gardens. Beginning in the 1940s, self-taught artist Jack Ellsworth and his wife summered at their cabin on Lake Kabetogama, each year adding to his collection of abstract stone sculptures forged out of local boulders. The pair kept up a garden of striking orange tiger lilies for a few decades too, with the National Park Service ultimately acquiring the property in 1978, after Jack passed away. Now the Ellsworth sculptures are the most popular day-use spot in the entire park. Visitors from all over the country boat across the enormous lake to relax on the verdant lawn and meander along the artful trails.

Adam and I arrived invigorated after speeding across the glittering indigo water in our tiny motorboat. We sauntered through the nearly eighty-year-old sculpture garden, impressed that a man was able to articulate what was then likely an absurd dream and simply go for it, year after year. (I'm a sucker for a dreamer with a big idea.) We chowed down on the big picnic lunch we had brought, famished by the day's journey, then motored back to the houseboat to lounge in the afternoon sunshine.

My eyelashes twitched as I gently crawled on top of a softly napping Adam, wearing nothing but a pair of black lace panties. He blearily opened his eyes and smiled, then nuzzled his bearded face into mine, gently kissed my neck, and pressed my hips against his. With a coy grin, I wrestled his swim trunks down to his ankles. He moaned enthusiastically and, after a few moments, flipped me over onto my back and traced his nails along the sides of my stomach until my sorry excuse for an outfit was lying in a heap on the floor. He delicately pressed his face between my thighs.

It felt . . . awkward. Unenthusiastic and ungraceful. Like the person I had just spent two years sleeping with had completely forgotten what my clitoris does and doesn't like. With a knot in the pit of my stomach, I tried to redirect him.

"Like this, you mean?" He mechanically tried to do what I asked, but it didn't feel any better. Adam was going through the choreography but not listening to my body. Plus, I was on emotional defense now, hurt and confused that an ocean of disconnect could be hiding underneath such a thin veil of joy. I thought that the houseboat would be good for us. A space to decompress and spread out after being mashed together in a tiny van soup for so long. Instead, it only amplified my loneliness.

Eventually, I gave up and asked Adam to leave the room. Alone again. I felt invisible. I was in the middle of the most amazing thing that I had ever done, and I felt invisible.

❧

Days passed in a fog of boreal forest and glimpses out of Gizmo's windshield at Lake Superior's immense blue edge, which seemed to stretch past the very boundary of the earth. Soon we left the van behind and were dropped by seaplane onto an archipelago near the border of Canada. We had reached my twenty-ninth national park: Isle Royale.

Though the place was known for its incredible population of wolves and moose, Adam and I spent the majority of our trip swatting mosquitoes away from our faces and bushwhacking through shady, overgrown paths. We made our way across the forty-two-mile Greenstone Ridge Trail that bisects the island. Spiderwebs flew into my mouth as I took the lead, ascending and descending a series of hills, sweating like a madwoman in the hot, muggy climate. I bit my tongue, trying to keep the peace as Adam continued to ask me question after question like a lost boy. It felt less like having a partner and more like having an unruly extra limb that jutted out awkwardly from my hip and made the simplest actions seem like a chore. Sometimes we abandoned conversation entirely and tethered ourselves together with a set of Bluetooth headphones, listening to podcasts and stuffing our mouths with fistfuls of wild blueberries as the trail crested a thin, rocky spine, occasionally opening up to panoramic views of the island's outstretched green tendrils and the Canadian border, far across the massive lake. One sunset, we watched as a young bull moose swam right in front of our campsite at Chickenbone Lake. We climbed over boulders flecked with multicolored lichen, listened to the mournful nighttime yodels of loons, and plopped our bodies into the chilly water of Lake Superior. Still, I couldn't get over the feeling that something was terribly, irrevocably wrong. *What if this isn't circumstantial?* I wondered. *What if Adam and I actually are completely incompatible?*

Our muscles aching from the long thru-hike, we hurtled ourselves across America on the thirty-three-hour road trip back to Los Angeles. I mostly listened to music and kept my mouth shut, beginning to realize that I was nitpicking every small issue in our relationship because the big pieces weren't adding up. I wanted a partner I could collaborate with and be inspired by. Instead, I was traveling with a shell of a man who didn't know what he wanted in life, so he'd quit his job at forty-two to follow me around the country, complaining all the while that both the trip and I were not to his liking. I had hummed my siren song and convinced a city kid to live in a van with me for three months; now he was resenting me for it.

We drove across the endlessly flat farmlands of Iowa and Nebraska, back over the breathtaking Rocky Mountains, and down through the rust-red buttes of Utah. Once we were home and unpacked, my despondency took on more weight. On the road it had been easy to envision a new life for myself, free from past irritations, but sleeping in my own bed and reading in the lush, jacaranda-shaded backyard dropkicked me with grief and made the prospect of a breakup all the more real and nauseating. I began to mourn the potential loss of my home, my lover, and my financial stability.

Many years ago, our friend Dylan had told me that he had a meditation teacher in Ann Arbor, Michigan, who gave him three life-altering mantras:

1. In this very moment, there is nothing to worry about.
2. In this very moment, nothing is lacking.
3. In this very moment, there is much to be grateful for.

As a bit of a West Coast hippie, I understood the gratitude one right away. I am no stranger to taking a deep breath and listing three things I'm grateful for every night before bed. It's a practice that has inspired joy and a sense of well-being in my life. That is, when I remember to do it. But having nothing to worry about? The thought seemed dubious and wrong. How would I ever be able to afford living in Los Angeles all alone on my shitty writer's salary? In fact, how would any of my material and immaterial problems get solved if I didn't first worry about them and then devise a plan? The concept of nothing lacking baffled me even more. Dylan and I had once talked about it for a long while on his deck overlooking the twinkling lights of the Echo Park hills.

"Yeah, that's a toughie," he said, laughing as he took a sip of his beer. "It's not about nothing ever lacking in the history of the whole universe; it's more about each passing moment being whole and complete, because there isn't any other way that it could be. Because we're in the moment, *right now*, and it's real. It's immutable because it's present. Nothing is lacking because everything is always as it should be."

⚜

I struggled to sever the cords of my worry as I caravanned north in Gizmo, my girlfriend Eva following closely behind in her silver Prius. In order to give Adam a bit of rest before five straight weeks together in Alaska, she and I had constructed a plan to travel north together for six days, stopping at three national parks along the way before she turned around and headed back to Los Angeles.

Eva and Adam had been friends for years, though she and I had become close in only the past eighteen months. Adam and I had coaxed her into a backpacking addiction that began to rival my own. She was at once tough and vulnerable. An immigrant from Eastern Europe who had seen true hardship and wasn't afraid to dive deep into modern therapies to heal, she sometimes texted me holistic psychology podcasts or thumping house mixes to listen to as we drove.

It felt wild to be driving alone again after two months of being joined at the hip to Adam. I rolled down the windows and let the wind dance between my fingers as the savage lyrics of Fiona Apple and Tori Amos washed over me.

I was a child out of time, and before I had gotten around to considering my future, the five-hour drive to Kings Canyon was through, and I found myself parking alongside Eva, packing up my things, and setting off on the trail toward Mist Falls. We were in the land of great granite—big domes and rock spires jutting up right from the roadside. The Sphinx loomed large behind us as we ascended a series of polished stone slabs, a forked tongue of slate-gray rock that presided over the entire valley. Benevolent dictator of glacially polished granite.

"I think that Adam might be addicted to his own misery," Eva remarked as we climbed toward the falls. "I mean, think about it. There's always something he's complaining about. When it's not his job, he's depressed about quitting his job or the pandemic or throwing out his back or being lonely because you're traveling or being depressed because he's traveling. There's no end in sight."

At this, I genuinely laughed.

Could I stay with a man I adored who was also a veritable grump much of the time? I gazed up at the bright umber bark of a ponderosa pine and twirled for a moment, lost in thought as the thick canopy of trees swirled across my vision.

I was gobsmacked by the beauty of roaring, forty-five-foot Mist Falls. The rushing torrent of water cascaded violently across steep granite slabs, and I snapped a few photos before we scrambled down to the creek below, kicking off our dusty boots to cool our feet in the brisk water.

"This is exactly what my anxiety needed!" Eva exclaimed. "I've been stuck in boring pandemic Los Angeles for way too long."

As the light began to fade, we hiked back down the trail and parked at a picnic area near a massive rocky outcropping as the neon-pink medallion of the sun started making the canyon walls blush. Just as we were finishing up our cooking, a white sedan cruised over and parked beside us. A man ran out, clearly startled.

"You guys! You guys! I just saw a bear about a couple hundred feet that way, and he's heading straight for you." The man pointed frantically into a stand of pines. I squinted my eyes for a moment, not sure what I was supposed to be looking at, but then I saw it. It was undeniable. A huge black bear was ambling directly toward us, nauseatingly cool in its composure.

Eva let out a shriek and grabbed her food items, sprinting for her Prius like her life depended on it. The bear was now sixty feet away, still walking.

"Sir, can you please honk your horn to see if that'll scare it off?!"

I didn't know what to do, but I knew I shouldn't run. I stood up on top of the wooden table and raised my arms high above my head, shouting and waving at the massive lumbering beast as the shrill percussion of a car horn echoed in the canyon. As if utterly bored with our efforts, the brute took one final look at me waving like a lunatic, turned left, and casually crossed the road. A top predator simply out for a walk in his own home.

Adrenaline peaking after the terrifying experience, we thanked the man profusely, then opted to boondock in a crowded parking lot near Road's End rather than car-camp out in the wilderness with that hunk of meat roaming around. I slept fitfully, dreaming that a tall stranger with a flashlight and a beard would tap on my window and wake me in the night, pointing the barrel of a shotgun directly between my eyes.

⌘

It's strange how someone can drive you absolutely bananas, and then you spend one night apart and realize how much you miss sleeping next to them. Time away from Adam felt like sorcery. Big, obvious-to-every-one-but-me sorcery.

After two days in Kings Canyon, Eva and I continued our northerly route toward Lassen Volcanic National Park, traversing heavily rural Highway 99 through Merced, Modesto, and ultimately Sacramento. I called Adam as a wave of parched almond trees passed through my periphery.

"I miss you." The words spilling out of my mouth were bewildering but true. "I think that maybe the van was too tight a space and too much pressure to put on ourselves, but . . . after only two days apart, I feel the truth pouring out of my guts so clearly. I miss you."

"I miss you too," Adam offered sweetly.

I told him about the hike and the bear and the spotty nights of rest, and he told me all about sleeping in and making backyard dinner plans with friends he hadn't seen in months.

"Let's talk more in Alaska, but I think we're going to be okay," he said.

"Gosh, I hope so," I replied longingly.

"I love you."

"I love you too."

He hung up the phone, and I was once again on a highway with only my thoughts, spun out into a lunar journey across my own mind.

Amid a forest of tall, fragrant pines, Eva and I selected a camp-site near Butte Lake, a jewel-toned body of water at the foot of an immense black lava bed that could have swallowed dozens of football fields. Razor-sharp volcanic rocks gave way to fantastical dunes pigmented in fire and garnet. The focal point of the area was Cinder Cone, a now dormant volcano, littered with metamorphic rubble, that had a circular vent at its center and a trail spiraling up and around its carob-brown core.

The hike was too good to resist. We heaved and panted along the steep, scree-covered path as the sun hung low in the sky, topping out to a panoramic view of Lassen Peak, inky black lava fields, and miles of evergreen forest just beyond them. We nestled into bed that night sated and eager to explore the rest of the park's wonders.

Eva and I spent the next morning climbing into the heavens, ascending two thousand feet up the southern slope of Lassen Peak on a trail dotted with windblown whitebark pines and burgundy patches of beardtongue blooms. My head spun in the high altitude, the unyielding sun beating down on us as we neared the 10,457-foot summit. It felt like visiting an old friend. A friend named Mountaineering who often left me bloodied and bruised and begging for mercy. A friend who, after having his way with me, would leave me feeling more alive than I had in my entire life. The bruises were love notes etched in flesh. From atop its rocky crown, we could make out yesterday's cinder cone, the brilliant blue freckles of numerous small lakes, and something called the Devastated Area—an arid landscape of volcanic rock and ash where destructive forces once reigned. I pressed my hand to my heart, willing my own devastated areas to heal.

We drove off toward the Bumpass Hell Trail, first dipping our bodies into the cool, purgatorial water of Lake Helen. The day was possessed with celestial overtones. Patchy cumulonimbus clouds wafted overhead as I swam out and back for ten strokes, the sensation of my wet red braids against my breasts sending shivers across my entire body.

Rain was imminent; we knew that much. Hiking at as quick a pace as we could muster, with Eva taking the lead, we blazed across the dirt path leading to the park's largest hydrothermal area—Bumpass Hell.

"Holy shit!" Eva's reaction was concise and honest as we rounded a corner to take in the bubbling mudpots, boiling aquamarine pool, and hissing steam vents. It was her first time seeing the ground burst open with volcanic activity. The air held a thick stench of sulfur and something worse that I couldn't quite make out. Large yellow blotches of the foul mineral dotted the hillsides. It was like a mini Yellowstone, without the geysers.

The clouds darkened and rolled in with the haste of an angry buffalo, huge dollops of rain and hail pummeling us as we ran back to shelter in our respective vehicles. We called it a night so we could get up early to drive to Crater Lake.

⌇

The two of us stopped in the small city of Klamath Falls on the way to our next park specifically to check social media and make a few phone calls before dipping back into a self-imposed digital detox for our final two days.

Van life is funny. You think you're going to walk out into the wild and become one with nature while simultaneously finding enlightenment and shirking capitalism for the rest of your days, when in reality you're more likely to crave city comforts more than you ever have.

We sat in the parking lot of a Starbucks for over an hour, each reveling in the air-conditioning of our own cars, feet propped up on our dashboards and fingers deliriously scrolling across our touchscreens. I felt a twinge of shame crawl up my spine, like I knew I should be out enjoying my one wild and precious year in the national parks, but the pull of the developed world was strong. I often found myself fiending for my iPhone the moment I got two bars of reception on top of a summit or at night in camp. I hadn't scheduled enough city days on the long journey to keep up with my friends back home, hastily barreling across the parks with no regard for my own needs for rest or mental health. The buzzword "self-care" was a joke to me. After not showering for five days and eating prepackaged foods for 90 percent of my meals, my idea of R&R was flopping onto a motel bed and swiping my fingers across my phone's screen until it was time to sleep. I tried to view my ridiculous addiction through a more optimistic lens: *Perhaps because I'm living without creature comforts for so much of this year, I'm learning to appreciate them more?*

⌘

I was listening to the Kinks when I first saw it. The wailing guitar and piano of "The Contenders" screamed across the airwaves in my small van as I passed through an invisible portal leading from the ordinary world into the realm of Crater Lake. Belting out the lyrics from the bottom of my heart—*I don't want to be a constructor of highways, a sweeper of sidewalks, I gotta do it my way!*—I caught my first glimpse of a stunning natural marvel.

The lake hung in a high rock bowl, like an eagle's nest filled with an enormous floating sapphire. With wildfires raging nearby, the surrounding mountain crest was enveloped in an otherworldly haze, which only made the park feel more surreal. The landscape looked completely and utterly like a painting. Mottled, impressionistic color swaths of faraway cliffs reflected onto the deep blue water. As we hiked a short trail up to the Watchman Observation Station, I felt the other visitors were just as spellbound as we were.

The small crowd walking around the vintage fire lookout was eerily silent. Reverent. As if they all knew they were in the presence of something truly special. Eva and I sat for a long while on the nearby rocks, dangling our feet over the edge, watching the dying light as it turned the murky sky an alien shade of orange.

Our campsite that night was simple and quintessentially Oregonian, surrounded by charmingly green moss-covered trees and serenaded by the murmuring of Union Creek. We took our time making pour-over coffees and eating oatmeal the next morning, lingering in the lush, humid woodland before returning to the park. Afternoon temperatures began to soar past seventy-five degrees, and after stopping to snap photos at every viewpoint along the road that circumnavigates Crater Lake, we parked at the Cleetwood Cove Trailhead. This was the only legal access to the lakeshore, and we excitedly descended seven hundred vertical feet to the edge of the water along a steep, rocky trail lined with conifers. In what felt like mere seconds, I was toe-to-toe with the famous volcanic tarn, staring out at its impossibly blue expanse. A ring of glistening peacock-green water lapped the nearby shore, looking out of place and almost tropical at our elevation of six thousand feet. I hopped from boulder to boulder, carefully avoiding the other groups of visitors, until I arrived at a vacant spot where we could throw down our packs. Our very own slice of Crater Lake.

Instantly, Eva and I stripped down to our underwear and plunged into the water, swimming out as far as our nerves would take us. It felt like floating across a black hole, acquainting myself with the furious unknown. A dark, ominous void that was not of this planet. Occasionally, small crayfish scurried up from cracks in the submerged rocks, snapping at a too-close finger or big toe. We both squealed with laughter.

"We have these guys back home, where I'm from!" Eva shouted. "They're mean little dudes if they can get their claws on you!"

Too soon, it was time to return to camp and gorge ourselves on burgers and fries from a nearby café that was tucked into the dense forest. The week had flown by in a flash, and I didn't want my girls-only respite to end. When I hugged Eva goodbye the next morning, I felt recharged and reinvigorated in a way I didn't know I needed, excited for Alaska and unsure of what my future held.

Maybe, I thought to myself, *the liminal blue void of the lake was perfect practice for what comes next.* Maybe I just had to throw myself into the deep end of life, again and again, until the defiant act of swimming upstream felt effortless. My stomach was churning, but my plans had been set. The only way to go was forward.

Setting off in Gates of the Arctic National Park and Preserve, Alaska

Chapter 5

THE LAST FRONTIER

The savage wildness of Alaska felt ever present even before the wheels of my plane touched down in Juneau. For hundreds of miles, snowy, glaciated mountains rippled down into the Pacific Ocean like bare skin descending into bathwater. After eight days apart, the simple act of touching Adam felt similarly wanton.

Having arrived a day early to explore the town, he picked me up at the Juneau International Airport, pulled me close, and kissed me through our protective face masks. His hands hugged my hips tightly. My heartbeat quickened. I hadn't been allowed to touch another soul for what felt like forever. When you're this hungry for affection, you can't help but trick yourself into starvation wages.

"Mask kiss!" Adam's voice sounded playful and more confident than usual, like the time apart had helped him gain some clarity. "Wanna go explore downtown for a bit before our next flight?"

We climbed onto a shuttle bus, and I soon realized that, in Juneau, bald eagles are like crows or pigeons in any other city. They liked to camp out near the salmon hatchery and perch atop streetlights and traffic signs, jonesing for a free meal or a passing garbage truck. Raised for so long to revere these enormous predatory birds, I found it bizarre to witness them in an urban environment.

"Yeah, they just saw some orcas near the yacht club over there." Our driver, Randy, casually pointed out all the inner-city haunts where majestic wildlife hung out. "Down here, on our left, there's a field where I see black bears playing all the time."

I couldn't believe it. I was in the middle of the capital of the largest state in the union and about to have as many wildlife sightings as I'd had during the past several months. If this was city life, I couldn't wait to get out into the parks.

We hopped off the bus at the humble Driftwood Hotel and walked a few blocks to the town's main street, hoping to grab lunch. The strip was a ghost town. Most summers, multiple five-thousand-person cruise ships disembark each week, turning the entire town (whose population is a scant thirty-two thousand) into a frenzy of tourists shopping for gold nuggets and whale-themed novelty socks. In the age of COVID-19, that revenue stream had dropped to zero. Not a single ship was docked. Most stores and restaurants didn't even bother to open. They just stayed dark, haunting gold rush–era relics lining the streets of a modern industrial town.

After grabbing crepes at the one outdoor eatery that was open, we read our Kindles in the lush shade of Cope Park before returning to the airport. The tension I had felt driving home from Minnesota was a distant relic of our time living in the van. Fifteen minutes later, I was eye to eye with a monstrously huge stuffed grizzly bear in the lobby of the terminal. This was Alaska, goddammit.

⚜

Boat trips into Glacier Bay National Park—the way in for 99 percent of all visitors—had been canceled for the year, adding yet another pandemic hurdle to my sixty-two-park mission. Plus, the small town of

Gustavus that hosts the park's campground and visitor center had made it clear to me, via email, that they did not want tourists making the trek up. So like any good overachiever, I dug my nose into a pile of internet research and came up with a path less traveled—we would fly into the small, artsy town of Haines and visit the park by chartering a bush plane over its enormous rivers of ice.

Catapulted into the air on a tiny commercial airplane, I gaped as we made our way toward Haines. Electric-blue waterslides of ice flowed down to the Lynn Canal, dwarfing the vessel that carried us. The land was marked by not one mountain range but an entire universe of peaks and valleys that rippled along the earth's crust to the horizon. I couldn't believe how vast and undeveloped the land was.

We landed and called the guy with the only taxi service in Haines, a local with a dented white van who may or may not pick up the phone when you need a lift around town. He talked our ears off about his obsession with panning for gold up secret coves that no one else knew about. So far, Alaska was living up to every stereotype in the book.

Once settled into our hotel, we purchased an ambitious quantity of groceries for our four-night stay and cooked up a lavish pasta dinner. The sun set late in the great north, and at nine thirty, magic hour was humming through the town. Adam and I went for a walk around the harbor as the sky beyond the mountains lit up in lilac, like an old neon sign.

Two men in their twenties passed us carrying a bucket of fresh crabs. "Hey! Did you just catch those yourself?" Adam was often more outgoing than I was around strangers.

"Yeah, man! You got a place to cook 'em?"

"Uhhhh . . ." Adam and I looked at each other and then back at the men. "I mean, our hotel has a fridge and a small stovetop."

"Well, then, here you go. Enjoy!" And with that, they handed us two sets of enormous Dungeness crab legs.

We stood on the street corner for several minutes, half laughing, half gasping for air in disbelief. *Is this what Alaska is going to be like?* We traipsed back to the hotel as the sun sank, hearts open wide, as if we had just crossed the border into some wondrous new country. Snuggled into bed that night next to Adam, I fell asleep dreaming of what wonders the park might hold.

Late the next morning, I had a planning call with our bush pilot, Peter, to plot out the best course of action for our day trip into Glacier Bay. Rain and wind were scheduled for the rest of the week, meaning flying might be unsafe. As we spoke, a light drizzle intermittently fell against the hotel window, and there was a faint lift in the clouds. Sunlight began to stream through, as though the gods of weather were thinking about giving us a break.

"You know what?" Peter asked me with a tone of trickster energy in his voice. "It's starting to look pretty good right now. Can you meet me in an hour? This might be our time."

My eyes went wide as I relayed this information to Adam. We weren't packed. I hadn't charged my camera batteries or cleaned my lenses. I wasn't mentally ready in the slightest. But the pilot was right. Better to rush into the approaching sunshine than risk missing our shot. I only needed a few hours of good weather.

Peter picked us up out front of the hotel and, for the entire drive, talked about grizzly bears in town and how dead the tourist economy had been that year. He was at once surly and kind, like many Alaskans we'd encountered. Generous with information and quick to tell a joke, Peter was also the kind of man who could reshingle his own roof or fly out of a snowstorm unscathed at the ripe age of sixty. He parked out back of his airplane hangar, opening a floor-to-ceiling door that spanned the entire front of the building. I'm not really a gearhead, but Peter's plane was a gorgeous piece of machinery. A totally rebuilt 1956 de Havilland Beaver whose blue-and-white paint glistened in the sunlight like something out of the Jetsons. Retrofuturism at its finest.

"Do you guys want to see my pet eagle?" Peter grabbed a Tupperware full of yellow cheese cubes and began scattering them onto the tarmac. Sure enough, a female bald eagle swooped down out of a nearby tree and began gobbling them up. She was joined by a conspiracy of ravens who crept around her frenetically, trying to nab a free meal. A giant in their presence, the eagle hobbled around like a gnarled henchman with boxy, feathery shoulders and swallowed every piece she could.

As Adam and I stood befuddled, watching the madness play out, Peter got to work, readying the plane and radioing various officials who needed to know we'd soon be taking up airspace. He gave us a quick safety tutorial regarding the seat belts and emergency exits, noting where the sick bags were—just in case.

Offering me a hand, our intrepid pilot helped me into the front seat while Adam took up the rear. There was a quick buzzing of the propeller to warm the engine, and we were off. The ground dropped away, putting us face-to-face with a series of spectacular hanging glaciers suspended in the rocky green mountains that surround Haines. Glowing white saucers of ice, like milk left out for some giant's lost kitten. Two-thousand-foot-tall waterfalls cascaded off the Rainbow Glacier, iridescent in the afternoon sun as our tiny plane soared by.

"It might get a little bumpy here going over the pass," Peter said with the confidence of an NFL quarterback, "but don't worry, I'll get you kids back in one piece."

The vintage Beaver dipped and rocked as we soared above the Davidson Glacier, knocking us around. My stomach seized up. I was determined not to puke. When we reached the pass's high point, we had officially entered Glacier Bay, park number thirty-three.

I shivered as the air inside the cockpit grew colder, the surroundings outside a blinding shade of white. We had gained altitude quickly to sail over the snow-filled mountain pass, floating above a river of dirty blue ice lacerated with three-hundred-foot-deep crevasses that stretched down into the shadowy underbelly of the earth. A dark maze of icy chaos. We were in a vast no-man's-land, one that didn't much care if we lived or died. I sensed that a lot of Alaska would be this way. Being alone in that kind of landscape really forces you to take a good look inside and figure out just who the hell you are.

Then, as if by magic, the color returned to the mountains, and we were flying over the East Arm of the park, descending toward a milky blue inlet along the icy tongue of the Casement Glacier, gliding above Technicolor teal water that stretched out into many-fingered fjord lands. The Muir Glacier, which once reached the seawater below, now hung high in the adjacent peaks, while the McBride calved dramatically into the ocean, its two-hundred-foot cliffs of serrated ice simply detaching from the mainland and melting away forever.

"Have you noticed a lot of changes in the ice, since you've been up here flying for so many years?" I was anxious to hear the news of climate change from people in remote areas who were facing it head-on.

"Oh yeah," Peter said. "In just the thirty years that I've been up here, I've seen a dramatic reduction in the glaciers. A bunch of 'em used to touch the water and don't anymore. That McBride Glacier is the only one in the park's East Arm that still does."

Witnessing the receding ice up close added a new immediacy to my feelings about the changing climate. I couldn't believe how quickly the north was melting. In less time than I had been alive, miles of ice had disappeared, perhaps forever. The earth was breaking apart.

Peter brought the plane around in a loop as dark storm clouds crept across the nearby mountains. Time to go home. Up, up, up through the bitter wind as we flew back across the barren icefields of the Davidson Glacier and landed safely again in Haines.

In a celebratory gesture, Adam steamed the free crab legs we had scored the evening before, experimenting with a rich sauce made of powdered garlic, salt, and gobs of melted butter. Buoyed by our time apart, we felt a surge of newfound interest in each other. We ate Ben & Jerry's straight out of the container, watched a movie on my laptop, and cuddled for hours. Crawling into bed that night, I stripped off all my clothes, piece by piece, and felt the long-awaited sensation of Adam's warm belly against mine as we tumbled through the sheets. He ravaged my small frame until I was nothing but a puddle of bliss.

٭

With piles of work to catch up on and rain in the forecast, the next few days in Haines passed by in a bleary haze of article writing, emails, phone calls, and photo edits. I was becoming cranky, stuck inside the small studio hotel room, feeling like a cat on a leash. It seemed that every moment of my life had to be scheduled to get anything done. My creativity? Scheduled. Catch-ups with friends? Scheduled. Hanging out with Adam? Scheduled.

One evening, Adam and I took a long walk along the gunmetal water of the Chilkoot Inlet, boulder-hopping among kelp-covered stones as ravens and bald eagles swirled overhead. We found a patch of wild raspberries in the middle of town and began hungrily plucking them, ignoring the thorns in favor of sweetness. The fruit was plump and bursting with red juice that stained our fingertips like fresh blood. It trickled all the way down to my right wrist as I stuffed my mouth full of lush indulgences, and I couldn't help but notice the reminder I had scribbled in ink so many months before: *Lightly*.

٭

Anchorage was like so many other northern industrial cities we had passed through—big, flat warehouse buildings; trains passing in the night; drifters with loaded backpacks roaming the streets.

I rented a tricked-out four-wheel-drive Suburban camper so we could brave the infamous washboard McCarthy Road into Wrangell–St. Elias National Park. Since Adam had therapy that afternoon, I taxied to a nearby suburb to pick it up alone. Once we reconnected and had loaded up our groceries and luggage, there was nothing to do but drive for seven hours, due east.

The McCarthy Road has been a thing of Alaska legend for decades, namely for the flat tires it likes to gift travelers on their way into and out of the park. Once a railway that connected the highly profitable Kennecott Copper Mines to the outside world, the rails were salvaged for scrap metal when large-scale mining stopped in 1938. In 1971 the former railbed was covered in gravel, and a new bridge over the Copper River was constructed, giving today's visitors easy vehicle access to the largest national park in the country. Though the occasional railroad tie or spike may surface along the rutted sixty-mile roadway, thousands of people still make the journey each year, taking two bumpy hours to drive the short distance from Chitina to the tiny town of McCarthy.

Upset that Adam didn't have any trail recommendations or road-trip playlists or much of anything to say to me, I could feel myself nitpicking at him as we traveled deep into the Alaskan countryside. A thick veil of clouds twirled around the high mountains as we passed the bright white traffic jam of the Matanuska Glacier, spilling out like dimpled, frozen cement toward the highway. Though the landscape was growing more picturesque by the mile, Adam's face had been buried in his phone for hours, coordinating with his maid, his house renters, and his friends back home. Tears welled up in my eyes. After weeks of facing his relationship indecision and lack of planning when it came to our big road trip together, I finally snapped.

"It breaks my heart that you're so focused on Airbnb," I croaked.

Adam looked up from his phone.

"It breaks my heart because . . . because clearly you are very capable of reading, writing, researching, and organizing things during this trip. You've been telling me for weeks that you're too tired or too depressed or too overwhelmed by the whirlwind pace of the journey, and I've been trying so hard to be sympathetic, but it just isn't true. You don't want to help me. You are *choosing* not to help me. And it especially breaks my heart because . . . because I think you've been done with this relationship in one way or another for at least two months now, maybe more, and you haven't had the heart to tell me, so I've just been going mad over here wondering why I'm dating a completely different person than I was a year ago."

He didn't deny it. In fact, he barely protested.

After a long pause, Adam took a deep breath and said, "I think you're right, but . . . I've been trying not to have these sorts of conversations with you while we're out on the road. I don't think this is a good time to talk about it, unless, of course, you really want to?"

My jaw practically fell to the floor, bounced off the rubber mats, and flew out the window.

"Yeah, no, you're right. This isn't a good time to talk about it." I was indignant.

The two of us remained silent as we drove across the head-banging McCarthy Road and sunset began to pour its violent orange light across the forest surrounding us. When I crawled into bed in the back of the dusty Suburban, it was nearly midnight. I pulled the covers over my face and collapsed into a fetal position, willing myself to sleep.

⌘

I had an early wake-up call the next morning, so I rushed through breakfast and shuffled across the McCarthy footbridge to meet my shuttle for a guided alpine hike. Adam stayed behind. My guide, Brendan, and I began our day hiking down a rocky trail that paralleled the miles-long Root Glacier as it spilled out of the strikingly blue Stairway Icefall, seven thousand feet overhead. I was queasy with upset.

Brendan told me a little bit about the mining history of Kennecott and his childhood in New Hampshire as we passed through the ghost town, surrounded by a series of enormous hundred-year-old structures, each painted red to stand out against the mountainside. After a few miles on the dusty, undulating trail, he pointed to a small building high on the craggy ridgeline. "That there is Erie Mine, our objective for the day."

He made a sharp right up a steep, scree-filled gully and began slowly ascending a patch of late-season snow. I followed behind, panting as the morning gray lifted and the afternoon sun came out to greet us. Soon, the scree fell away, and the two of us were scrambling up a near-vertical rock face covered in moss and lichen.

"I'm not so sure about my footing," I managed to squeak out as I tentatively free soloed up the damp ravine.

"Yeah, this is the crux for sure," explained Brendan. "Just put your feet up there and there, then pull hard on those rocky knobs above you."

"Umm . . . I'm feeling pretty scared right now. Everything is covered in moss, and I feel like I'm gonna slip. Can I just climb down?"

"Sure thing."

And with that, we sat at the bottom of the near-vertical rock face, boiling water to make herbal tea.

"I'm sorry, I just . . ." I stutter-stopped to get my emotional bearings. "I'm having a really rough day. I think my boyfriend and I might have broken up on the drive in last night, and I'm totally freaked out and not my usual confident self today. I'm sorry. I can't finish the climb."

"You'd be surprised just how quickly us guides turn into therapists out here on the mountain." Brendan's demeanor remained cool and collected, as though this had happened a hundred times before and every client he guided was going through some type of breakup or life-shattering emotional crisis. After a quick bite, we packed up our bags and hiked back down the slope, the snowy, far-off crest of Mount Blackburn shining like razor-sharp glass in the sunshine.

⚜

Meanwhile, Adam had been on an adventure of his own all day, sleeping in and strolling around the abandoned mine buildings and the main drag of McCarthy. When I arrived back at camp, he was behaving shockingly normally, as though his world weren't falling apart. *Was his world not falling apart?* He suggested we walk into town and check out The Potato for dinner. Not wanting to spoil the peace, I splashed some water on my face, doctored my chapped lips, and came with.

One pulled pork sandwich, a beer, and a pile of hand-cut curly fries later, Adam and I strolled down the mile-long path back to our campsite, still not mentioning our relationship. There was a knot in my stomach the size of a Volkswagen. A terrible hole ripping my insides to shreds. In all likelihood, we would no longer be a twosome after Alaska. My home would be torn away from me, and Adam would become just another acquaintance. I decided to broach the elephant in the room.

"Adam, I don't want to get into a huge fight or sobbing conversation, but some pretty big stuff was said yesterday, and I need to ask you a few clarifying questions."

"Okay . . ."

"In the past, when you've mentioned 'not having your emotional needs met,' what does that mean to you?"

"Well, there's this, like, quality of deep listening and connection that I get with some friends but not often enough with you."

I bit my tongue in a valiant effort to let him finish.

"It's reciprocal with lots of slow back-and-forth questions," he continued. "Dylan's actually really good at it. The best phrase I can come up with for it is 'holding space.'"

By now, we were back at camp, sitting at the wooden picnic table next to the tricked-out Suburban. Yellowjackets swarmed our fragile bodies, landing on our hands and faces. I couldn't decide whether I wanted to scream or wallow.

"So you're telling me that I don't hold space well enough? That you don't feel emotionally safe or connected enough around me because I listen to you, but I don't listen in the exact right way that you want?"

"Yes."

Was it true? It couldn't be. Had my wildest dreams grown claws and teeth and turned Moloch under my watch, gobbling up love until there was none left to give? I hope he's fucking lying just to spite me.

The world teetered like a cheap carnival ride as I tried to steady myself against the pockmarked picnic table, Mount Blackburn staring me down with her staircase of icy teeth. The words erupted from my mouth.

"I think we should break up."

I told him just how trivial what he had said seemed in the face of an otherwise functional two-year relationship, how I had needs that weren't getting met, too, and how, at the end of the day, most of this probably stemmed back to childhood traumas that neither of us had any control over.

"You're impossible!" I screeched. "I don't think you understand how to compromise with a partner. No one could ever meet your needs." He heard me out, my seething woes about our relationship.

Adam held my hands as I began to cry, the only person who could console me in the wreckage. With all our cards on the table, it was remarkable how much the mood began to lift. Naked in the wake of our brutal truths, neither of us had anything left to hide behind. We were just two people who loved each other terribly but couldn't seem to make it work, no matter how hard we jammed the puzzle pieces into each other.

I felt deeply ashamed that a marriage-track relationship had gone to its grave. Embarrassed that I would be homeless come January, when the parks trip was finished. Oddly and unfairly aware of the fact that I would soon be in my midthirties.

⤖

Resentment is a carcinogen for the soul. I woke the next morning emotionally strung out and yearning for the ability to time travel, but I was committed to preserving my sweetness and grace in the wake of so much uncertainty. After all, I had no idea what would happen in the future. The Buddhist teacher Pema Chödrön once said, "Letting there be room for not knowing is the most important thing of all . . . When there's a big disappointment, we don't know if that's the end of the story. It may just be the beginning of a great adventure." I longed to possess that kind of cognitive dissonance. The ability to hold my sorrow and optimism in the same breath and allow them to commingle. I inhaled deeply and started making coffee.

It was with this desire for harmony that I sat next to Adam and strapped daggers to my feet as a team of guides prepared our group to go ice climbing. A brutal sport by any standard—a phenomenon called the screaming barfies is a regular occurrence—ice climbing when you're depressed is an even more surreal experience.

Once we had been outfitted with crampons (the shoe daggers), helmets, harnesses, and mountaineering boots by Brendan, my guide from the day before, we were paired with a young couple from Virginia and led on the two-and-a-half-mile hike to the foot of the Root Glacier. The sunlight reflected a brilliant bright teal off the icy expanse, my crampons producing a satisfying crunch each time I dug them into the frozen ground. My sadness lent a "fuck it" attitude to the day. After our guide had built an anchor and the time came to climb, I volunteered to go first. Donning my thick gloves and big puffy jacket, I tied the rope to my harness and took a breath.

"Remember to keep your arms high!" Brendan reminded me as he set up a belay, in case I fell. Wielding a set of freshly sharpened ice axes over my head, I slowly started up the glacier.

Stab, stab. Kick, kick, kick. There was a rhythm to ice climbing that I was familiar with, though I had attempted it only once, years earlier. I thrust each axe into the frozen cliffside, trying not to pretend that each puncture mark was a blow to Adam's stoic face. *Lightly, Emily, lightly.* Furiously, I broke through a frail, inch-thick layer of top ice that rained down on me like shards of frozen glass. The once vertical wall began to bend up and over my body, a fierce overhang that made my arms quiver and ache under the pressure of holding a constant pull-up position. Starfished and struggling in the middle of the cliff, I felt like I might slide off the wall at any moment.

"I'm not really loving this high-angle stuff," I called down to Brendan. "I think I might be done."

"Do you want to take a rest for a minute? Do you want to traverse over to the left, where it's easier?"

"Uh, yeah! I think I want to head left."

"Sure thing!" His voice was equal parts excited and encouraging. "Just keep kicking over to that side ledge, and you'll be fine."

Stab, stab. Kick, kick, kick. Stab, stab. Kick, kick, kick. Brendan was right. The moment I zoomed out and moved over to an easier part of the wall, the climbing became much more enjoyable. A few minutes later I was at the top of the colossal cliff of ice. Gazing out at the high summits of Donoho Peak and Mount Blackburn beyond it, I could feel a well of deep inner strength begin to return to my body.

⚜

We drove back to Anchorage two days later, trying to get some ground under our feet after breaking our world apart in the Wrangell Mountains. I am generally slow to anger, but for the entire conversation, I could feel myself seething over the fact that my partner had neglected to voice his needs for so long that resentment built up and he quietly tanked our relationship. The truth of the matter was becoming clearer and clearer to me: when being misunderstood is an essential part of your identity, it's impossible to be with someone who wants to understand you.

I was also mad at myself for forgetting my own agency in the process. After all, I was the one who had pounded the final nail into the coffin with the curt phrase "I think we should break up." Still, I wasn't ready to say goodbye just yet.

"Are you open to finishing up Alaska together?" Saying it out loud made me nervous. "You know, since we already have so much booked and are generally getting along right now . . . you know, as friends."

"Yeah, that makes sense. I've always wanted to come here, and part of me feels like we might even get along better moving forward, now that the pressure is off."

I laughed awkwardly.

"Yeah, totally. There's no reason to fight if there's nothing left to fight for. Also . . . can I stay in your guest room for the few days I'm still in and out of LA during the parks trip? I mean, I can't really move my stuff until I'm done. Plus, knowing I have a safe and COVID-free place to crash would mean a lot."

"For sure. Besides, maybe there's some trauma or karma we're both supposed to heal by remaining in contact for the rest of the year. Like, we're doomed to repeat our old patterns unless we reconcile them head-on."

If he was right, I was about to embark on the longest, most intense therapy session of my entire life. Maybe when I wasn't connected to any*one*, I'd find that, underneath it all, I was connected to every*thing*. I could choose to see this void I had been thrust into as a beginning rather than an end. Maybe it was best to live nowhere and be at home in all places.

Arriving back in Anchorage, we commenced with the usual house-keeping of grocery shopping, repacking our bags, and cleaning up the rented vehicle. I had arranged for us to stay in a larger Ram ProMaster van for the following eleven days and was excited to travel with a sink and running water. That meant we needed to spend a day driving around the city and swapping out cars. As soon as we were able, I set a course south toward Seward and my thirty-fifth national park—Kenai Fjords.

⌘

"It's called Kenai Fjords National Park, but it could just as well be called Harding Icefield National Park." Our trail guide, Emma, was a whiz at sharing obscure knowledge and ecological factoids as we made our way up a series of steep stairs cut into the slope of a mountain bordering the crevasse-filled Exit Glacier.

"You see how the melted ice forms a stream that runs directly into the ocean? These glaciers pull important minerals out of the earth. The minerals mix in with the water when it melts, and mineral-rich oceans mean lots of krill and plankton for larger animals like humpback whales to eat. So, in a big way, you could say that the health of glaciers directly affects the health of the whale population."

It was my first day in the park, and I was floored. As I climbed ever higher, Adam bringing up the rear, I felt rallied by the expansiveness of the landscape. Like I needed a space exactly this large to hold my grief. Moving my body through fluttering bursts of pink fireweed and along one of the largest sheets of ice in the country, I felt a lightness in my heart as our guide described the area's delicate ecosystem.

"When you hear on the news about glaciers melting, this is why it's so important. Without glaciers, the larger animals can't sustain themselves. Climate change is really wreaking havoc on the entire balance."

At the top of the trail, our trio gazed over the immense Harding Icefield, a thick white blanket of ice the size of Maui that every glacier in the park tumbled out of. I felt a reverence for the land stirring within me. Rising temperatures once felt nebulous and foreign, but now, standing so near to their immediate victims, they felt heart-bruisingly personal.

If we don't protect wild spaces in our own country, how will we ever reconcile the wild within ourselves?

⚜

I took this new knowledge with me the following day as Adam and I climbed aboard a small tour boat for a daylong kayaking excursion with six other guests. Steven, our guide, possessed more knowledge about local birds and mammals than anyone I had met that year, and as our vessel steered past islands cluttered with thousands of nesting seabirds, I felt like I was living inside an episode of *Planet Earth*, the biting wind numbing my rosy cheeks as an imaginary David Attenborough narrated the scene inside my head.

"Look over there!" Steven pointed toward a shadowy dip in the rock face where a cluster of fat seals lay resting. "Steller's sea lions. They're fast becoming a threatened species. Oh! And to our left are a couple of tufted puffins. Did you know that a group of puffins is called a circus?"

"Get real." The statement seemed dubious, at best.

"No, seriously." About this, our guide was adamant. "The grammatically correct name for a group of puffins is called a circus."

As the ride continued, a pod of Dall's porpoises surfed in the wake along the front of our ship. Steven darted to the starboard side.

"Whale!" he shouted, just as the fluke of its tail dipped underwater.

I could hardly contain my excitement. I had never seen a humpback whale before. "How big was it?" I asked him, grinning.

"Big."

The boat idled its engine and floated about a hundred yards from where we had seen the beast descend into the sea. Several minutes later, the whale came up, took a breath, flapped its massive tail, and dove.

"That right there is a humpback whale, ladies and gentlemen. One of the largest mammals on earth." Steven sounded rather pleased with himself.

By the time we got to Aialik Bay, a long, narrow inlet where we'd spend the next few hours kayaking, I already felt sated. I had seen every animal that I'd come on the tour to witness. What could top that?

Steven and the boat's captain readied the kayaks along a rocky beach, setting out oars, spray skirts, and neoprene gloves for each of us and showing us how to properly climb inside. His voice dipped low, and he spoke with an uncommon seriousness.

"We are about to enter the literal birthplace of kayaking. Aleutian Indians have been paddling and fishing in these waters for thousands of years. Even the modern word 'kayak' comes from the Native word 'qayak.' These right here are sacred waters."

Adam and I strapped into a tandem kayak and began to paddle the three miles to the Aialik Glacier. We could hear the rumblings of something huge and monstrous. It sounded like a car crashing into the sea.

"White thunder," Steven remarked. "That's what they call the sound of the enormous hunks of ice calving into the water. Don't worry, we're still a decent ways out."

I paddled until my triceps burned and my chest pounded. Until I was eye to eye with shimmering, pearlescent icebergs floating away from the giant glacier. Until the entire group was sickeningly close to a four-hundred-foot-tall cliff of vertical ice.

We linked our oars together, forming a large bobbing raft for stability as we opened our dry bags and began to eat lunch. I looked up from my turkey sandwich for an instant and felt a twinge of terror fly across my chest. A skyscraper-sized column of ice splintered loudly, breaking away from the rest of the glacier and landing with a deafening splash. Our entire crew started whooping and hollering.

"That was one of the BEST calving events I have ever seen!" Steven shouted.

The entire day was steeped in an untamed vastness that I couldn't quite comprehend. The earth around me was rocked by tremendous forces, yet all the creatures who lived on it were merely going about their lives.

On our return ride to Seward, I asked Steven what happens to the puffins in the dead of winter. "Do they hide out in their nests or fly somewhere warmer?"

"Oh no," he replied with a wry grin. "They spend their winters on the open ocean. It's much safer for them out there than close to shore, where predators lurk."

I felt like I was about to spend my winter alone on the open ocean of the American highway.

As our tour boat steered toward town, I felt a soul-stirring truth emerging in my core. I looked out at the immense hanging glaciers, crumbling rock cliffs, and incredibly robust seabirds and started to realize that if there was one thing big enough and bold enough to heal me, it was this dynamic landscape, right here, right now.

The birds could get eaten tomorrow by an eagle; the otters could starve when the snows came. The future was uncertain for all of us, and perhaps that was the most natural thing of all. I didn't need to make a thousand plans for where to live or who to marry or what car to buy when I was back in Los Angeles. I just needed to allow myself to be held by that wild vastness and trust that it would give me the perspective I needed to mend.

❧

As the reality of the breakup began to settle within me, I felt as though the rotting suitcase of my past had been placed directly into the center of my heart. I knew I was lucky to have Adam tagging along for the remainder of my time in Alaska, but my insides were heavy and gunked up. The slightest action could send me into a crying spell.

We drove north toward Denali National Park on a clear day dressed in summer sunshine. At 20,310 feet above sea level, Denali is the highest peak in North America, and from a distance, the glowing white of its glaciers resembled far-off cumulus clouds—I almost didn't recognize it as a mountain. Named after a Koyukon word meaning "the High One," Denali has been steeped in folklore and climbing legend for thousands of years. It seemed an auspicious place to visit in the wake of so much personal upheaval.

Adam and I rented a couple of mountain bikes before driving twenty-nine miles along the park's main gravel road to our campsite at Teklanika River. By the time we arrived, afternoon clouds had rolled in, and the high peak was enveloped in haze.

"I think I'm going to take a nap in the van and just hang out today," Adam said, yawning as he laid a blanket across the thin mattress.

"Oh, okay. I'm really dying to explore the park, so I guess I'll just grab my bike and my bear spray and head in without you."

At the campground's bus stop, hoping for a ride deeper into the park, I met a woman in her midfifties with salt-and-pepper hair and an off-putting smile.

"I wouldn't leave my bike alone in the woods if I were you. Bears love bikes."

"They DO?!" Instantly, I wondered if I should be heading out into the wilderness alone. I didn't even have a lock.

"Oh sure," she continued, grinning like the Cheshire cat. "They're shiny, they're interesting, they're colorful . . . and they have really fun tires that bears love to pop!"

"Thanks for the tip."

I eyed the bus schedule and saw that the shuttle I'd been hoping for had just passed by. There wouldn't be another one all afternoon. *Well,* I thought to myself in a vain attempt at a pep talk, *sometimes the weather is warm, and you simply must head out into grizzly country alone.*

The first several miles were nearly all uphill. Out of biking shape and fighting to keep my momentum, I passed the thin, braided strands of the Teklanika River, the dense black spruce near Igloo Creek, and the first of the fall colors beginning to burst into flame on the slopes of Igloo Mountain. I didn't see any wildlife, but then again, I was too apprehensive to look. I was proud of myself for just having the courage to bike out in the middle of the Alaskan wilds alone. I kept my eyes firmly on the washboard gravel road as I turned around at the seven-mile mark, sped back down the hill, and returned to camp, ready for dinner and a laptop movie night.

❦

The next morning, Adam and I hopped onto a green transit bus, intending to take it as far as the road was open that year—Eielson Visitor Center. The clouds had lifted, and a cool breeze whirred through the trees as the bus drove west into the park. Not fifteen minutes later, someone shouted, "Bear!" and all the passengers rushed to the left side of the shuttle for a better view.

Sure enough, an adolescent grizzly was scratching his rump on the same concrete bridge where I had turned the bike around. He eyed the camera-wielding humans nervously as he crouched on all fours and walked along the road, not ten feet from where I sat. Goosebumps tingled up my forearms. Had I been five minutes earlier or later, I might have had a very different day on the bike.

From then on, it was as though we were on an African safari, only the "big five" everyone was there to see were grizzly bears, Dall sheep, caribou, moose, and wolves. Scanning the horizon for hours on end with a gaggle of equally enthused visitors made me forget all about my troubles with Adam. Instead of bickering, we spent the entire day in a childlike state of glee, giddily pointing out a bull moose clumsily following a cow and several massive brown bears chomping at fields of blueberry bushes.

Once or twice, a caribou got caught on the street in front of our shuttle, and the driver would just sigh, muttering an exasperated, "Boy, these animals sure are dumb. Once they're on the road, they forget how to get off it." The bus would putter along behind them at the glacial pace of three miles an hour for several minutes until the poor caribou could remember how a right-hand turn works and get back into the bush where they belonged.

Adam and I arrived at the Eielson Visitor Center to a breathtaking view of Denali. The mountain was more than sixteen thousand feet higher than where we stood, unfolding ripple after snowy ripple like a huge tectonic layer cake. The two of us took off up a steep, rocky trail toward Thorofare Ridge, sweating and panting in the unyielding sun as we gleaned better and better views of the High One. We smiled at each other with the delirious expectation of what might lie at the top. Crimson bearberries and poisonous purple monkshood flowers swayed in the wind near the hill's summit. Once we crested the ridge, crumbling orange boulders greeted us, along with a commanding view of the park's namesake mountain. Wind battered my face as I gazed out across the vast alpine valley. Denali felt more like a spirit than something of this earth.

At dinner, I sat across from Adam at our picnic table, transfixed by his hands. Not wanting to ruin our precious day in the park, I sat quietly, biting my lip to ward off unwanted thoughts. Tears began to form, and before I could help it, I was sobbing into my stir-fry. The pandemic had put all sorts of new worries into my already frazzled mind—loneliness chief among them. We didn't yet know if a simple handshake could transfer the virus, and the thought that the only hand I was allowed to hold was leaving me was too much to bear.

"The speed of this breakup is akin to an amputation." I wasn't in the mood to mince words or pamper Adam's feelings. "In a normal long-term relationship, things would be getting bad for six months or more before the end, but this rapid two-month decline has me feeling adrift, like I'm lugging the dead body of our former partnership around Alaska with me. I don't get to go *home* after all this, Adam. You will never understand what that feels like. I get to pack up my things in a house I no longer live in. I get to move in the middle of a global pandemic."

Adam didn't know what to say or how to make things better. He stared blankly and quietly at me as I fixed my rageful eyeballs like laser beams on his soul.

⚜

With a fixed schedule to maintain, Adam and I had to leave Denali before either of us was ready, saying goodbye to its otherworldly presence as it hovered above the treetops on our drive back to Anchorage.

Soon we were slingshotted into the void in a little tin can of a plane, soaring over great hanging glaciers and waterfalls that glistened and undulated like thousand-foot-tall ribbons on the way to Lake Clark National Park, one of the least visited in the country. The bird's-eye view lifted my heart into my throat with sheer beauty—bright turquoise water edged by the towering slopes of dormant volcanoes. We set up our tent at a small campground in Port Alsworth, a tiny town skirting the edge of the park's enormous namesake lake, then hiked up through the boreal forest to the mirror-clear water of neighboring Kontrashibuna Lake. The beauty and solitude of the place felt akin to heaven, bordered on all sides by blue-green mountains, and since no one was looking, we took off our clothes and waded naked into the pure water to cool down and escape the humidity and throngs of flies.

"Hey," I said, offering Adam an olive branch. "I'm really glad you decided to stick out Alaska. I know I've been kind of all over the place emotionally, but this is hard. Let's just try to keep taking care of each other and let the rest work itself out."

"Thanks," he said, smiling as he gazed up with his deep hazel eyes. "That sounds like a good plan. I'm sorry it's been so hard for you."

✜

After an early bedtime, we rose to the sound of rain lightly tapping on the leaves of the trees all around us. Rebecca, our camp host, came by midmorning to see if we still wanted to go kayaking.

"It might be best to wait for a bit and leave in an hour. How does that sound?"

We trusted her advice, and soon the clouds began to clear as we were being water taxied across the pristine teal waters of Lake Clark. Since the lake itself is an astounding six miles across—a width that would make even the fittest among us question the strength of our triceps—Rebecca dropped us off at Priest Rock with her motorboat so that we could maneuver around the calmer waters near shore and explore a series of small desert islands.

We hopped onto the rocky beach and unloaded our boats, spray skirts, life jackets, snacks, and paddles. After giving us a quick orienteering session, Rebecca sped away at a brisk pace, leaving Adam and me alone in the wilderness, in grizzly country, without a clue. It was empowering. It was terrifying.

So much of outdoor recreation is about learning how to follow the rules and how to stay safe. But on a remote lake in rural Alaska, there are few rules, and safety is never guaranteed.

We pushed our boats into the water and paddled past the dense green foliage of the great northern forests, around small rocky islands and secluded coves the color of dark jade, past modern-day homesteads that made my imagination do backflips. *How on earth do the owners haul all their food out here? What do they do with their time?*

In the afternoon, the wind picked up, and Adam and I were forced to battle much stronger, higher waves to reach our agreed-upon pickup point. My boat rocked like a small earthquake as I paddled diagonally against the waves, getting splashed with icy water each time I lifted my blade to press forward. After two miles of intense effort, the waves rocked us right into the shoreline, and we pulled our kayaks safely onto the beach at the Joe Thompson Public Use Cabin, our stopping point for the day.

Soaked and tingly from the tremendous effort, Adam and I gathered driftwood to make a small fire while we waited an hour for our boat taxi to arrive. As the wood popped and crackled and the wind raged on, I felt the tips of my fingers coming back to life. I looked over at Adam and felt a sudden surge of gratitude. For the day. For the two years we had spent together. For the luck of finding a man who wasn't going to leave me, even though it was time to leave our relationship.

❧

I have no idea where the love goes when you choose to end something. It sure as hell doesn't slip through the cracks in the relationship that was broken. Instead, it hovers like a phantom. It lingers between your bodies for months and makes you wonder what on earth you were thinking when you made the conscious decision to be alone.

Like a pair of old friends who knew how and when to set their egos aside, Adam and I spent our remaining days in Alaska getting along. Dare I say we even had fun. We boarded yet another tiny plane and set off for Brooks Camp, a small outpost in massive Katmai National Park, where we landed on the glassy water of Naknek Lake with a splash.

This park was all about seeing grizzly bears up close while the salmon were spawning, and after a brief safety orientation with a ranger, we were cut loose to roam as we pleased. Sunlight sparkled on the needles of an evergreen forest as the two of us hiked onto a raised wooden boardwalk and up to a thick metal door. I pressed a heavy latch that held the caged door shut, presumably to keep grizzlies off the walkway, then slammed it closed behind us with a clamorous thud. We found ourselves above the Brooks River on a long elevated bridge as tens of thousands of sockeye salmon below swam furiously upstream. Zombielike in their instinctual spawning madness, the fish had turned from silvery gray to wine red with olive-green snouts. This coloring was a sign that their bodies were beginning to decay, the last of their energy spent on one riotous last hurrah as they leaped and hurtled for hundreds of miles from the ocean to the same small streams that bore them.

Adam and I wandered along the wooden planks, watching the fish propel themselves up the river, then descended to a gravel road and took an immediate right turn into the forest toward Brooks Falls. Three skittish ptarmigan clucked as they ran across the trail in front of us. I looked to my left and to my right. No bears yet.

We climbed onto another raised boardwalk, opened and closed a similarly hefty metal door, and stepped onto the famous Falls Platform. The moment we had been waiting for. A small crowd of tourists had gathered on the large square of wooden planks, fenced in by a hip-height barrier of two-by-fours, which offered a front-row view of the action—brown bears hungrily fishing just six feet below. A young sow sat straight up on top of the waterfall, excitedly snapping at the air each time a salmon got close. Everyone, it seemed, had come with their camera A-game, zoom lenses clicking and focusing each time the grizzly got close to her prize.

Farther out, a huge older male bear sat in a little whirlpool at the base of the falls, occasionally belly flopping onto the surface of the river to try to stun the lovesick salmon into stillness so he could gobble them up. This guy was *fat*. He had a paunch that would not quit, and I loved his sleepy yet ornery energy. I took photo after photo of his scarred face and saggy rump, watching him saunter back and forth across the torrent of water to consume as many calories as he possibly could before winter came.

Back up top, Bear Number One was having more luck. She nabbed three fish midair and hungrily disemboweled them on the nearby boulders before Old Tubby down below got angry and scared her away. I felt like I was watching two mob bosses face off in a turf war.

After a few hours of attentive bear watching, Adam and I cruised back to our room at the lodge. We gorged ourselves on the restaurant's Cajun pasta with reindeer sausage and, of course, fresh Alaskan salmon before nestling into our hilariously kid-sized bunk beds. Based on our room assignment, I felt like even the hotel knew that this was now a buddy trip.

⁂

Given the scope and danger of the ongoing pandemic, most group tours in Alaska had been canceled for the season. While this was a big win for public health, it meant, for me, that getting to Gates of the Arctic and Kobuk Valley—two of the most remote national parks—would be nearly impossible without a private guiding service. After spending hours on the internet researching what would fit my budget versus what would provide the best experience in each park, I ultimately decided to have a company build out a splurgy, custom five-night backpacking itinerary for us.

I flew to Fairbanks with Adam by my side and checked into a quirky, castle-shaped hotel that felt more like a Renaissance fair had arrived in someone's private home than a professional lodging establishment. Magazines and leatherbound books cluttered the side tables, and our host laughed maniacally every time we so much as uttered a word. There was pet hair everywhere. We began eyeing the exits.

Thankfully, the owner of the guiding company soon picked us up and took us to his warehouse, a mecca for wilderness diehards that housed every piece of outdoor equipment one could ever dream of. There we met our guide, Erica. About my age and from the Midwest, she seemed to have a permanent relaxed smile on her face, even as we talked about the forecast that called for rain nearly every day of our excursion.

"Well, you know, that's one of the things I like so much about guiding," Erica said blithely, trying to reframe the weather as a learning experience. "There are so many things in our lives that we can control, and in the Arctic, you can't really control anything. So sometimes we may just have to sit with it and be uncomfortable. And that can be really empowering."

Though I was upset about the impending storm, I knew she was right. Maybe the most feral thing of all was allowing room for not knowing. Releasing all control and remaining confident. Returning to that primal state of uncertainty. Swan diving into the darkest water and making myself swim. That safe feeling we have when we think we've got it all figured out? It's an illusion. The very essence of life is change.

Erica asked us to dump all of our gear onto the concrete floor so that it could be accounted for. She divvied up tents, first-aid equipment, individual snack bars, and several Ziploc bags full of dehydrated food among us. I carefully stuffed each and every item into my backpack, struggling to find enough space to fit it all. At the end of the day, I was carrying forty-seven pounds, roughly the weight of a large sack of potatoes. It would be the most I'd ever carried on my back.

❦

"Watch out—it's going to get a little bumpy as we descend through these clouds here." Our bush pilot, Jesse, had been flying above the Arctic Circle for more than a decade and was one of Erica's favorites, a fact she made clear by proclaiming that we were the luckiest tour group in the world that week to have him on our team.

The small plane jolted from side to side as we neared the Arrigetch Valley, a steep gorge of granitic rock set high in the far-north Brooks Range. Instead of clenching my muscles in pinned anxiety, I tried to relax my insides and simply let the rocking be. It actually helped. I pressed my nose against the window and gazed out at a dynamic landscape that was quickly shifting into its fall wardrobe, glorious mountainsides of garnet-tinged shrubs and flame-yellow birch trees growing ever closer until we landed on a thick strip of gravel wash on the bank of the Alatna River. This was it. Gates of the Arctic.

Tossing our packs out of the rear cargo hold, Jesse fired up the propeller and was gone in minutes. The three of us would be alone for the next four nights with only the stuff we could strap to our bodies. In the middle of fucking nowhere. The farthest I'd ever been from civilization.

"Welp, I've gotta pee before we start." Erica ran behind a stand of thin spruce trees as Adam and I just looked around, stunned by the silence.

As soon as she returned, we heaved our tremendous packs onto our shoulders, buckled our bear spray belts, and started hiking uphill and off trail with only a vague idea of where to go. We crossed two frigid streams as Erica encouraged us to keep our boots on and willingly soak them for stability.

"Everything you own is about to get wet anyway; you might as well do it intentionally."

I couldn't argue with that logic.

We zigzagged across uneven ground as we passed through a forest dotted with conifers and soapberry bushes. We laughed as our boots trampolined against an earth that was spongy with mosses and reindeer lichen. We sat in patches of tangerine-hued shrubs and ate our snacks. Then came the tussocks.

The tussocks, which are tricky to walk on and even trickier to walk *between*, seemed built to sprain or break an ankle. These solid, foot-high lumps of grass and muck soon dominated the once pleasant tundra as we ascended higher into the valley.

"Ugh. This *sucks*!" Adam wailed. We were all thinking it.

I wobbled in the high grass, catching myself on my trekking poles as I fell off an unruly clump of dirt. "And I thought I had good balance!" My patience was wearing thin.

"Oh my gosh, a trail!" Erica spotted a faint strip of dirt that had been carved into the slope by the area's infrequent visitors. "This'll be like strolling up a wilderness highway now!"

The going was certainly faster but still slow as we bushwhacked through saplings and adolescent aspen trees that occasionally whacked us in the face with their whiplike branches. The natural world was unforgiving. Two-inch-deep mud sucked at our boots. By the time we made it to camp and pitched our tents on an uneven bed of squishy moss, we were all starving. Erica fired up her little stove and boiled water for herbal tea so that we could warm our insides before feasting on pesto pasta and falling wearily into our sleeping bags.

The next day came and went in a similar manner, the far-off spires of frosted white peaks growing tantalizingly closer the more we hiked. We passed a dollop of grizzly bear scat on the side of the trail that made my nerves do somersaults. We soaked our boots again on a perilous stream crossing. My love for Erica's persistent smile began to wane. Damp and cranky inside my small tent, I wrestled into a set of dry thermals and bedded down in a meadow beneath the dark granite towers of the Arrigetch Peaks, which stood watch over our sleeping bodies like ominous daemons.

In the Inupiat language, "Arrigetch" roughly translates to "fingers of the outstretched hand," and I often felt held by some supernatural force as I moved through that valley toward the great fins of rock that seemed to claw up from the bowels of the earth itself.

Our third day in the Brooks Range was all about exploring. "I want to go out for a long time today," Erica declared over coffee. "I want to come back tired."

A night of rest had rekindled my enthusiasm, and her proposal sounded awesome. Up we went, hanging a left into the stunning Aquarius Valley in search of a series of pristine alpine lakes virtually untouched by modern humans. We passed through fields of swaying gold willows, each one shedding its leaves as we brushed past and exploding into a burst of marigold confetti. It was as though the trees were celebrating our arrival, saying, "Congratulations! You're here. We've been waiting for you."

With a rushing stream to our left, we ascended a steep incline of lichen-covered boulders interspersed with a thick carpet of tundra flora. Our trio crept slowly upward into an increasingly magical realm of autumn color. Bloodred bearberry shrubs and golden dwarf birches fell away behind us the higher we climbed into the rocky cliffs. We took short breaks to hunt for the last of the season's blueberries, each one deep purple and tart as a Meyer lemon. I felt like the rock-hopping would never end and carefully watched my feet as we leaped from boulder to boulder to be sure I didn't snap an ankle and have to hobble back to the plane in shame.

When the first of the Aquarius Lakes sprang into view, we all stopped dead in our tracks. It was the stillest lake I had ever seen, glassy water reflecting the sharp red mineral stripes and jagged edges of its neighboring peaks.

The three of us paused to eat a luxurious lunch of tortillas, smoked salmon, and brie at lake number two, and we craned our necks to take in the immense granite walls that surrounded us. Seeps of water spilled out of the escarpments here and there, creating sinister black stripes against the smoky gray of the cliffs. As we sat and chatted, Adam realized that the canyon produced a remarkable echo the moment any of us raised our voices above a normal pitch. We shouted as loud as we could into the abyss: "One . . . two . . . three . . . BANANA!"

Moments later, three distinct voices could be heard shouting the silly word back at us. Maybe it was the exertion or the mind-splitting solitude of the Arctic, but I hunched over and laughed until my sides were sore. I wolf-howled in glee and found an invisible wolf girl howling back at me from the rocks across the water.

How could we not go on? Each lake was more stunning than the last. We traversed under huge flakes of rock jutting out of a near-vertical cliff face and boulder hopped for half a mile to reach the southern edge of the next lake. Climbing up and over a soft, mossy slope, we reached the shimmering turquoise gem of lake three.

A series of smooth granite slabs bisected by a trickling waterfall brought us to the fourth lake, which was perhaps the most spectacular of all. Behind it was the most picture-perfect alpine cirque I had ever seen—thick shards of rock leaped into the sky in a way that would make Yosemite Valley cower. It was an earthbound coliseum.

Tired and cold, we decided to turn back instead of continuing on to the final two lakes. Our group scrambled back down the immense boulder field, and as we hiked, we discussed the concept of trails. Of how we generally feel entitled to them and how it's strange that someone gets to tell us where to go and what to do in wild spaces. We are so used to bending nature to our will, and yet, in the Arctic, nature was the one bending us. I hadn't thought much about it before, often taking the trails that crisscrossed the mountains beyond Los Angeles for granted.

"Who decides what connotates *the best* view or *the best* way to get from point A to point B?" Erica lit up as she spoke. "I think that trails take away an essential part of the wilderness experience—meandering."

I tried to let go of my desire for order and certainty as my knees creaked and my legs wobbled on the long descent back to camp. When we arrived at our tents, pitched in a quiet meadow, Adam and I built a fire while Erica boiled water for macaroni and steeped herbal tea to warm our tired bones. I fell asleep sated and blissed out.

⁓

When I awoke, I felt terrible. My tonsils had swollen in the night like two enraged golf balls, and it hurt like hell to swallow. My body was harboring a high fever that ibuprofen couldn't even dent. *Is this the onset of COVID?* I immediately feared for everyone's safety. At least we were out in the open air.

I spent much of the day shuffling between the kitchen tent and my sleeping bag, asking Adam and Erica to take turns bringing me tea and soup as a freezing rain pelted our base camp and low-hanging clouds rolled in. Netflix phone downloads were a salve I used to calm my mind. I didn't sleep a wink that night, tossing and turning in the sweaty, claustrophobic prison of my bed. Come morning, I could barely force down oatmeal and water. I held back tears as I shouldered my pack and quietly followed Erica and Adam back down the eight-mile-long valley, soaking my boots in the roaring creek, bushwhacking through the overgrown semblance of a trail, and stumbling through the muddy barrage of tussocks on our way to find Jesse and his plane.

Exhaustion was beginning to set in for Adam too, and as we neared the edge of the Alatna River, we were both strung out and muttering expletives each time an unruly branch whacked us in the face.

"Goddammit!"

"Oh lord, not again . . ."

When we got to the plane, I had a decision to make. Because I had no cough, we were pretty certain I hadn't contracted the coronavirus. Our original plan had been to fly west to Kobuk Valley, the most remote and the last on my list of Alaskan parks.

"I know you're feeling pretty awful, but we can get you there if you want." Erica was remarkably kind and stalwart throughout my day of tears and near panic. In early September, so late in the tourist season, it was unlikely that I would be able to book another flight out. I squinted through the growing pain in my throat as I spoke, knowing I had come too far to turn back when I was so close.

"Let's do it."

⤞⤝

Up we flew over the sharp fingernails of the Arrigetch, now coated with a fresh dusting of snow. Completely spent and ready for a bath and a real bed, I slumped in the back seat as we soared over the vast, unspoiled Alaskan tundra.

Jesse landed the small bush plane right onto the honey-colored sand of the Great Kobuk Dunes as the lingering northern sunset began its hours-long slide into darkness. I could barely move. I hunched my way over to a suitable tent site, helped Adam secure the thin nylon structure, and flopped over onto my sleeping bag. I had done it. I had visited all eight of the Alaskan national parks, and I felt like my life and my body were crumbling.

Apart from a brief photo outing at sunset, I didn't move for the rest of the evening. I was thwarted by some microscopic creatures who, no doubt, were throwing a fiesta inside my sad, broken meatsack. When dinnertime came, Adam brought me a bowl of noodle soup, and we watched half a movie on my phone while I slurped up what I could.

Sleep refused to come, and in the chilly expanse of the largest Arctic sand dunes, I listened as my bedfellow rustled his way out of the tent to pee in the middle of the night.

"Emily! Get out here quick!"

Adam sounded more excited than scared, and I wrestled my puffy jacket on at the speed of a mollusk, wondering what on earth could be so important.

A faint, ghostly arch hung high in the sky to the left of our tent, framing the northern edge of the horizon like a glowing white halo. Then, as if by magic, the haze began to flash and move, undulating like the apparition of a giant serpent. The northern lights. Adam and I embraced under a full moon as the lights danced and whirled over our heads. Though our great northern adventure was coming to an end, I believed the earth was winking at us one last time, making sure we knew that things were going to be all right.

⚜

Come morning, I felt as though I had been dragged for several miles behind a horse-drawn cart while gargling glass and battery acid. I was the sickest I'd ever been. My throat was wrecked, and every single joint from head to toe ached. When I peed, the color was a dark marigold. I was alarmingly dehydrated.

We packed and, once again, soared through the air in a metal vessel, the vast ocean of the Alaskan tundra stretching out forever below us. I passed in and out of consciousness as the pilot cranked up the heat and Johnny Cash poured into my headphones. My ears wouldn't pop when we finally landed in Fairbanks. My head was a balloon ready to burst.

Erica volunteered to drive us around in the tour company's van until we could find an urgent care center that was still open in the early evening. After searching for over an hour, I limped into the Tanana Valley Clinic. The nurse recoiled as soon as she saw my throat. The doctor did too. I was given an orange Otter Pop and a rapid strep test and was left to wait, curled up in a fetal position, on a faux leather exam chair covered in crinkly white paper.

"Well," the doctor began with kind certainty, "you've got a terrible case of strep throat that's well on its way to becoming scarlet fever. See how you have this rash all over your neck?" She gestured to a swath of bright red spots creeping down from my chin. "You're lucky you came in when you did."

After I was stabbed with a thick, painful needle in my upper left thigh and given an aggressive round of steroid pills, Erica dropped us off at our hotel. I was in no state to fly. I could barely get out of bed. Adam agreed to help take care of me for one extra day, changing our outbound flights and booking an extra night in Fairbanks to make sure I didn't collapse from exhaustion on my own. Short walks and single flights of stairs winded me. My entire body ached. Adam's imminent departure made me very aware that, after not having more than an hour or two of alone time for the last three months, I'd soon have an entire season of it. After that, maybe a few years.

Two days of rolling around in bed, eating pizza, and taking baths seemed to help, and with the doctor's blessing, I boarded the last of my Alaska flights, a plane going directly from Fairbanks to Seattle. Anxiety gripped my chest as we took off, and I clutched Adam's hand for the entirety of the trip, taking deep breaths and watching glaciers float by outside the window.

Ram Dass once said, "We're all just walking each other home." When I was younger, I took it to mean that you should be kind to everyone because life is difficult, and the most graceful way to live is by choosing to help others through the tough moments that even ordinary circumstances throw at us. Sort of the "everyone is fighting a battle you know nothing about" mentality. As I got older and more acquainted with his work and my own mortality, I learned that the phrase is generally understood to mean that "we are all fellow humans on the journey to the grave."

When the plane landed, Adam and I walked slowly toward baggage claim. He had a connection to LA, but for me, the Washington parks beckoned. We kept trying to say profound things to each other as we drifted through the busy airport, knowing that these were our final moments as a pair. Nothing seemed to stick.

When we reached a sign for his turnoff, I dropped my backpack and purse to the floor and wrapped my arms so tightly around him that I thought I might melt into his chest and we'd become one human. Tears streamed down my face as businessmen and hurried travelers whooshed by in a frenzy. For us, the world stopped. Above the white lip of his mask, I could see Adam's striking hazel eyes tearing up for the first time since we had agreed to end things. He looked just as lost and scared as I was.

"Thank you . . . for letting me walk you home for two years." My voice sputtered and cracked as I spoke. "I only wish it could have been longer."

Looking out over the vast North Cascades wilderness, Washington

Chapter 6

A Riot in the Northwest

The moment I got back to Gizmo, I smiled. She had been sitting in a friend's driveway for the past five weeks, and coming home to her was like seeing an old friend. I kissed the steering wheel, fired up the engine, and blasted a playlist of female-powered folk music to rock out to all the way to my hotel.

As a treat to myself after living out of a backpack for more than a month, I had booked a swanky Seattle lodge for two nights. But when I arrived at its luxe landscaping, mod furniture, and designer lighting, I felt as I often did coming back to the city after many nights in the wild—like a refugee from my own life. Scarlet fever had simmered my swagger down to dust. I knew I could quit the trip whenever I wanted, but where would I go? Hair full of leaves and clothing askew, I checked in at the front desk and received a room key from a chipper young receptionist.

I let the steaming shower run over my body for what felt like hours, lathering up my legs and belly and pretending that sadness was like any other muck that could be rinsed off with soap and enough time. Swaddled in the plush robe that came with the room, I danced around, imagining that I was a fancy lady and not some wandering ruffian with only a van as an address. I wanted to will myself into being okay again. The moment my skin touched down on the feather-soft sheets, I burst into tears. I didn't know if I was sad or happy, or just overwhelmed at the sensation of comfort against my bare skin after so many weeks without.

This is my new life, I thought. Alone in a king-sized bed in a nice hotel surrounded by trees. I realized that I could allow each new park to soothe me, or I could allow them to make me feel more alone than ever before. The power to choose was in my hands.

⚜

It was a slow start getting to Olympic, the forty-first national park on my list. After all, I had to eat breakfast, repack the van, and go to a grocery store. But those high-thread-count sheets were nearly impossible to crawl out of. I feared I might disintegrate. My body was still very much healing from the fever. Even after four nights of rest in air-conditioned rooms, my joints felt wobbly, at best. A short stroll exhausted me, and I found myself needing to sleep much longer than I had at the onset of the trip.

But the weather was sunny and warm, and after a four-hour drive through industrial Aberdeen and along a rough coastline littered with cedars and driftwood, I arrived at the Hoh Rain Forest. A winding road paralleled the Hoh River all the way into the park, dipping in and out of lichen-draped trees. Green fur seemed to cover everything in sight, hanging at times like a wizard's sleeve to cast a spell on anyone who drove through the forest. A little magic was just what I needed. I hopped out of the van and onto the Hall of Mosses Trail. Thick, humid air wrapped around my body like a hug as I crunched along the dirt path.

Up and around the loop I went, through immense maples blanketed in wisps of sage-green moss. Between moldering logs carpeted in orange fungus. Past a forest floor covered in innumerable sword ferns. The entire scene felt ethereal, dreamlike. Though my body could scarcely muster the strength to complete the easy one-mile trail, my mind feasted on the bevy of plants that called this area home. Any bit of new land was welcome, if only to distract myself from the lobotomized feeling of a recent breakup.

Sunset arrived, and the fading, dappled light lent a spooky feeling to the hike as I rounded the last corner on my way back to Gizmo. I drove off toward my campsite for the evening, a quiet patch of primeval forest with enough room to hold me and my sorrows. I slept in the tender hands of the rain forest all night, and for that, my heart was briefly, incandescently happy.

But I awoke feeling as though my physical and emotional sensations were trapped behind a pane of glass, joy a fleeting memory. A looming depression began to wrap its insidious arms around me, heart heavy and limbs dull, the palm of god pressing me firmly into the earth, begging me to return from whence I came.

It wasn't a great perch from which to experience the wonder of America's natural places.

After a half-assed breakfast of orange juice and an untoasted English muffin, I drove off in search of Rialto Beach, hoping that in my moodiness I could at least do my best brooding Jane Eyre and stomp along the rugged coastline, making Charlotte Brontë proud. The world seemed to slant ever so slightly sideways and to the left as I made my way toward Hole in the Rock, an impressive, doughnut-shaped sea stack that's only accessible at low tide. *Damn. I must have mucked up my equilibrium on that flight out of Kobuk. My ears never popped.*

Giant cedars and firs encroached upon the surf with an imposing wall of green that dominated the right side of my vision. Smooth driftwood the color of ivory dotted the shoreline. Tide pools were everywhere. I hopped around on rocks covered in slimy green kelp and peered into the tiny universes they contained. Hermit crabs scuttled by;

lime-green anemones waved their hungry tentacles; a lilac sea urchin hid behind a fistful of mussels. I was jealous of their small, simple world.

Once back at the van, I was spent. I grabbed my Kindle and a peanut butter and jelly sandwich and headed off to marvel at the surfers who dared to face the frigid waters of the Pacific. Twelve-foot waves breaking a hundred yards from shore dwarfed the long-haired hippies who were out that afternoon, and after dipping my feet into the cool ocean, I posted up on the rocky gray shoreline and read for hours.

I had been deeply uncomfortable every single day that week, challenging myself to sit with it and feel the sting of new loneliness rather than shove it away with alcohol, the internet, or sex, as I had in the past. Buddhist dharma would have me believe that the complete uprooting of my life was a blessing, one that carried the seed of transformation, but I wasn't so sure.

༄

As I neared my first encounter with Seattle traffic on the way to Mount Rainier, my mind was a bonfire. The edgy city energy made my neurons twitch and my stomach tighten. Still recovering from scarlet fever, I felt hopeless and livid and lost. This journey around the parks was supposed to be fun, and yet I was miserable, carrying the corpse of my former life with me to each new place I visited. This wasn't how I'd envisioned my trip.

I sped to the park's Paradise area at dawn the next morning after a night of solid sleep. I was in the middle of the worst fire season in US history—one that would see an area of four million acres, a swath larger than the state of Connecticut, ignite in California alone.

Mount Rainier, Washington's highest peak, glowed a horror-show orange on the horizon as I neared the cluster of saw-toothed glaciers that cling to its volcanic summit. My mission for the day was to prove that I could hike more than five miles if it killed me. I set off on the

Skyline Trail Loop with ragged breath and a throat made scratchy by the ever-present wildfire smoke, the familiar click-click-clicking of my trekking poles aiding my tired muscles as I ascended the slope. My legs dragged like I had ten-pound weights on each ankle, and my lungs strained as though I were sucking air through a straw. Dozens of cute, outdoorsy couples in racerback tanks and cargo shorts passed me, laughing in the late-morning sun, as I pushed onward. I hacked up phlegm every five minutes. My back was a slip-and-slide of fresh sweat and sunscreen. I felt disgusting, but I kept at it.

It's not a race, I kept telling myself. *It's an excuse to roam around a beautiful place in the name of self-discovery. Why do I keep forgetting that? This is what's real. Wilderness. Sickness. Loss. Beauty. What if the parks are showing me exactly what I need to learn? That if I don't slow the fuck down, I'll miss out on the miracles happening all around me?*

I managed to get my cramping legs up to Panorama Point, my mouth agape at the sheer magnitude of ice sprawled out across nearly every inch of the mountain. At such close range, the glaciers looked impossibly huge—jagged processions of watery teeth falling steadily toward the forest. Then it was down, down, down through fields of late-season aster and furry white pasqueflowers, past a lazy mountain goat lying out in the sun, across mossy streams that burst into tiny waterfalls along the lower flanks of the volcano.

I pulled into a turnout in the darkening woods to sleep that night, after driving nearly an hour past ramshackle trailers and mobile homes. The moon was bloodshot and unnerving in the haze of the worsening smoke. The air smelled of burned rubber. After eating a can of cold soup, I popped an allergy pill and prayed that the fires would lessen by morning, then pulled the covers up to my chin as I snuggled into Gizmo's soft bedding.

⚜

By morning, the air was a thick, dirty pudding scented with fire-swept trees and dying earth. The apocalypse, it seemed, was nigh. Smoke hung for miles like a dense fog that blotted out the sun and turned everything into a tanning-bed shade of fluorescent orange. The sky was falling. Mother Nature was enacting her revenge for decades of industrial mistreatment. I wanted to fucking die.

I played the waiting game all day, booking an unplanned three-night stay at a dingy Tacoma motel to escape the hazardous air. I broke my no-indoor-dining rule to post up at a nearby restaurant and eat breakfast in relative safety. *Pandemic be damned,* I thought, *the world is ending.* After lingering as long as I could, I waited in a parking lot and called one of my oldest friends from the van. The moment she picked up the phone, I broke. I was pushing the boundaries of everything I thought loneliness could be—no access to hangouts, to bars, to coffee shops, to the outdoors, to a pet, a lover, my family, a day job. "My home is no longer my home," I sobbed into the telephone while my friend dutifully listened. I had swiftly and promptly teleported out of my own life.

Four days of sweat and wildfire smoke dripped off my body in the motel shower. I had days of waiting ahead of me, days of refreshing my browser every few minutes to see if the air quality near the North Cascades had improved enough to drive up for a hike. This is the stuff that they never mention in adventure novels—how much downtime is actually spent in beige rooms with broken lamps and chipped paint.

⚜

Loneliness began to grow limbs and pummel me. Like a shark with its myriad rows of teeth, I was amazed at just how deep my own ability to dole out and endure emotional turmoil went. On my third day in the motel, I crumbled into a pit of despair. Times of day did not exist anymore, only varying shades of ash-brown sky. The world outside my window was an impenetrable haze of smoke.

I had a panic attack in the shower. Leaning my face against its cool white plastic, I sputtered and gasped for breath as mucus ran down my chin and hot water sprayed onto my naked body. My hands grasped at the slippery walls to hold myself up, my heart a ten-ton mass. Hopelessness engulfed me—no house, no steady job, no relationship, a floundering trip budget, and too much alone time. I needed help, fast.

I connected with friends who helped to pull me out of the black hole of my mind. One offered a place to stay in LA that wasn't Adam's guest room. One just held me with her voice and told me that she loved me. One reminded me that so much of what I was feeling was purely temporary and had a practical solution, adding, "You're generally a pretty happy person. You've always managed to find a job when you needed one. Things are overwhelming right now, but they won't always be, I promise."

Then Kate called. She wrapped me in a blanket of loving calm with her warm British accent. "Your tenacity and organization help get *amazing* things done in the world, but you need to be careful not to beat up on yourself."

I swallowed back tears, telling her that my project and everything I'd accomplished so far suddenly felt utterly trite.

"Oh, sweetheart, nature can never be trite. And you know what? I live with people, and I still feel like they can't always give me what I need, so I've had to learn how to give that to myself, especially this year. You need to learn how to swaddle yourself, love. How to lie on the bed in a fetal position and listen to music or just give yourself a little cuddle for five minutes. I think you have a radical opportunity right here to learn how to take breaks and self-soothe. There's really no other option."

There's a famous Buddhist story about a young warrior. The girl's teacher said that she would have to go into battle with Fear. Understandably, she was terrified. She didn't want to. It was all too much. But, following her teacher's instructions, she finally agreed. The warrior stood on one side of the battleground, and Fear stood on the other. The girl felt tiny compared to Fear's huge and rabid state. They faced each other, each holding a weapon. Suddenly, the young girl timidly walked toward Fear, prostrated three times, and asked, "May I have permission to go into battle with you?"

Fear replied, "Thank you for showing me such respect that you'd ask permission first."

The warrior continued, "How can I defeat you?"

Fear responded, "My weapons are that I speak quickly, and I get very hot and close to your face. Then, when you're totally unnerved, you'll do whatever I say. But if you don't do what I tell you, I have no power. You can listen to me and even respect me, but when you don't do as I say, I have no power to control you."

In that way, it is said, the young warrior learned how to defeat Fear.

⚜

I packed up the next morning, fighting the alarm bells in my body that rose as nausea and lightheadedness greeted me along with yet another panoramic view of gray haze. It was time to go, whether I liked it or not. Trying to remember that fear was just a sensation and I was in no real danger, I hopped into Gizmo and started the drive to North Cascades, my final stop before a rest and resupply in Los Angeles.

The Washington countryside was so ashen that it looked shrouded in fog. Ghastly lumps of mountains and small farms poured in and out of my vision until I reached the park proper, where I snapped a few photos of hazy Diablo Lake. The air smelled like an ashtray. I wondered what the animals were thinking.

With what appeared to be better weather in the forecast, I holed up in a quaint hotel room that night, eating groceries and trying to self-soothe in a lukewarm bath. Taking breaks was not my strong suit.

I wanted to burn the candle at both ends until a shooting star blazed out from the center.

Nestled into bed, I tried to picture this liminal space as a cocoon. A soft haven for deep shifts to occur. When caterpillars spin themselves into a small, woven chrysalis, they don't simply sprout wings and longer legs, then crawl out more beautiful, with the sudden ability to fly. The caterpillar's body digests itself from the inside out, turning first into an unrecognizable goo. Then there are a group of cells called the imaginal cells that morph into whatever is needed to create the adult form, literally imagining an entirely different being into the world. What emerges from the dark, threadbare space is not only a glorious new insect but also a radically transformed body, one that has unmade and rebuilt itself anew.

When I woke, it felt as though Mother Nature knew just what I needed. A glimmer of clear sunshine beamed through my bedroom window, and after coffee, oatmeal, and a dose of multivitamins, I sped off into the North Cascades in search of a worthy hike. I chose a high trailhead, hoping to breathe easy above the diminished wildfire smoke. Boots laced and backpack ready, I felt ecstatic to be back in the parks.

The air was humid and lush. Walking through it felt like being kissed on the forehead by Mother Nature herself. The forest often does that to me, the smell of it wafting not only through my nostrils but also through my entire being, filling me with a deep sense of peace. I hiked up a series of wooded switchbacks toward Lake Ann, still slow as my body recovered from illness. *Kindness, not force, will lead you there,* I whispered to myself as I steadily made my way up the dirt path.

Before long, the views opened up to tremendous metamorphic peaks that stood jagged and orange against the pale blue sky. The first of the flamboyant fall colors were beginning to show, splattering the countryside with flecks of red and umber. One moment I'd be gazing down at the dark teal water of Lake Ann, and the next I'd swivel my head around to find a charcoal-gray peak grasping at the heavens with a glittering hanging glacier tucked into its side. My lungs strained, and my pores sweat in the afternoon sun, but it didn't matter. I felt on top of the world, climbing higher toward the craggy alpine summits. I tried to remind myself to be kind to my body, to go slowly, drink water, and rest when needed. A list that seemed obvious to everyone but me.

From the top of Maple Pass, I stared at huge ripples of mountain range after mountain range unfurling like vast tectonic wrinkles. Immense white glaciers wrapped the highest peaks, suspended like a latticework of ice across their dark, looming summit spires. I tramped across the ridgeline until the trail began crawling downhill again, stopping every few minutes to gasp or take another photo of the truly remarkable landscape. After four days of horrific smoke, this literal and figurative breath of fresh air was exactly what I needed. A gentle reminder that, yes, light will return even after your darkest days.

⁓❦⁓

I drove south along Interstate 5 for the next two days, the world outside my windows a murky white abyss. The brutal wildfires showed no sign of letting up. Although I kept my air-conditioning whirring and my windows and vents as hermetically sealed as possible, there was still a faint smell of smoke inside the vehicle. A raw, scratchy sensation burned my throat. Nausea crept in, but I tried to smile. Like a goose who, exhausted, turns south and flaps her wings until some sense of home is regained, my gut knew. I needed to get back.

The Pixies became my house band as I drove through the opaque skies of Portland and the singed black hills of Ashland. The only music that allowed joy into the chaos. When your depression hits a low point, there's nothing left to do but revel in it. Passing through a hellscape of charred agricultural tarps and burned vineyards, I cranked up the volume on "Into the White" until my eardrums began to swell.

Mount Shasta hovered like a UFO in the sky as I passed, its base eclipsed by smoke while the sun shone brightly on its upper four thousand feet of rock and ice. Nearing Los Angeles, I bounced up and down in the driver's seat to keep the pain of so much driving from radiating up my spine. When I arrived, Adam had dinner ready.

Coming back felt huge and strange, like stepping into a memory of the past that you can visit but cannot alter. Adam greeted me at the door with a long, emotionally loaded hug. I struggled not to bring up our relationship all through our meal, even though I was having second thoughts about the breakup.

The two of us moved to the couch, and I could feel a physical neediness dripping off him as we talked. Our bodies couldn't stop colliding. All we wanted to do was cuddle and catch up on the last two weeks of life. We slept in the same bed that night, cuddling without having sex.

⌘

The following day, I found myself caught in the trap of wanting to constantly process our relationship in a messy attack of tears and blame. Ruth Bader Ginsburg died that afternoon, which only added to the year's apocalyptic feeling, and I found myself wandering around the house like a cadaver on strings.

"Do you still love me?" I asked at dinner, balancing a bowl of pasta on my legs as I clumsily ate on the sofa.

"I . . . feel differently about you than I did before." Adam could barely look me in the face.

I fell apart. I was a failure in every sense of the word—unlovable—and our democracy was going down with me. "Nobody cares if I live or die!" I shrieked back, my inner teenager throbbing with grief.

"Do you really believe that?"

"Yes."

I moved into the guest room.

The next morning, Adam offered to drive us both to a park where our friends from ecstatic dance had begun meeting to dance on blankets spaced six feet apart, silently getting down with their Bluetooth headphones on.

In the warm morning sunlight, our small group hopped and spun around as Kate threw us into a journey. While it took considerable effort for me not to cry each time a new song burst into my ears, Adam seemed to be having a fantastic time, smiling and laughing with the others, as though nothing were amiss. *Well, fuck,* I thought. *He's relieved.*

I fell to the ground bawling, head in hands and knees pulled up to my face, but I made myself get back up and start dancing. I was allowed to cry, I decided, but I had to keep moving. It was clear that I needed to draw an invisible box around myself and stop processing what was already done. The breakup happened. I didn't need to continue picking at the wound.

I told Adam that I would make a more conscious effort to start moving on when we got home. He shrugged.

"Okay. Sounds good to me."

The next night, I masturbated in the guest room while Adam went out with friends. When I finally climaxed, I broke down crying. Twice. Then the truth thunderbolted into my chest like a riot: I had been repressing a lot in the relationship too. I wasn't just feeling an upheaval of sadness because the partnership was ending; on some level, I had given up pleasure for comfort. I had sacrificed my own satisfaction for stability. There were trembling parts of myself aching to come back out into the world. I had forgotten how to be ravaged, how to ravage myself.

⌘

A week later, I drove toward Yosemite with the shattered pieces of my life, empowered by the thought that I could now build them back into whatever shape I wanted. When I reached the valley floor, I was surrounded on all sides by enormous walls of granite. El Capitan and Half Dome stood like friendly, stone-bound greeters saying hello to all who passed through, and the warm hues of autumn were ever present. After I pulled into my campsite at Upper Pines, my legs were itching for a walk, so I took off down the nearest trail to Mirror Lake. I let my feet carry me past gray squirrels and immense pines, all the way to a sandy pit where the lake should have been, had California not been in a historic drought. The vertical wall of Half Dome's western face blushed in the late sun.

Mosquitoes began their invisible, Doppler-like buzzing around my head, but rather than turn back to make dinner, I felt compelled to climb to the top of a nearby boulder and lie flat on my back to watch the light shift across the famous granite dome.

۞

David was an Eagle Scout with the body of a lumberjack and the heart of a poet. It was his fault that I had grown obsessively fond of backpacking in the five years leading up to the parks trip. I fell madly in love with his ability to quote Epictetus over penne arrabbiata and his infectious adventurous streak; years before we met, he and a group of friends had plotted a six-month course from Los Angeles to Rio de Janeiro. By bicycle. Riding past an onslaught of fish-taco stands, dodging dengue fever in the thick jungle, and surviving a police shakedown, his posse had managed to do the unthinkable—prove that ordinary people with nine-to-five day jobs can save up, set off on a professional-adventurer caliber trip, and survive relatively unscathed.

Not having come from an outdoorsy family, my first-ever backpacking trip was in Sequoia National Park at the ripe age of twenty-eight, under David's watch. I was a complete junk show. Donning a backpack left by Airbnb guests at my former apartment, I hunched, apelike, under its weight as my lungs quickly learned (and hated) what the air feels like above nine thousand feet. Among the assorted sundries inside my pack were a bohemian leather jacket, a full-sized towel, and a child-sized sleeping bag, covered in a purple paisley print with peace signs, from the sale bin at a suburban H&M.

David hadn't been aware that this was my first backpacking excursion. And I didn't know that he didn't know. So when he suggested a twelve-mile journey up to the summit of 11,207-foot Alta Peak and bedding down in the high-altitude meadow that shares its name, my youthful bravado and desire to impress him lit up, and I said yes. I did yoga three times a week—what could go wrong?

What I didn't know was that, once you reach a certain elevation, the air becomes noticeably thinner and thinner, until walking uphill requires a tremendous amount of effort and concentration. I felt like I was sucking air through a wet paper straw as we ascended in the afternoon sun. Without a chest strap, my backpack clung to my shoulders like a limp orangutan and swung frustratingly to and fro whenever I moved. By the time we made it to camp, I was a girl crumbled.

My stomach growled ferociously from the exertion, and David carefully assembled his little aluminum backpacking stove and delicately screwed its hose onto a fuel canister. *Click. Click. Click.* The lighter failed to ignite the gas inside the metal burner. This left us with two options: soak our dehydrated backpacking meal in cold water, making a crunchy and unsavory soup of bland calories, *or* use chocolate to bribe the hikers at the next campsite into letting us borrow their stove.

Not fifteen minutes later, we had arranged our makeshift rock chairs into a circle of former strangers and were passing around a Nalgene filled with scotch whisky that made my head spin beneath the dazzling brightness of the Milky Way. A woman pulled a ukulele out of her pack, Mary Poppins style, and the six of us howled at the moon as we belted out the lyrics to familiar pop songs.

The next morning, after a fitful night spent tossing and turning in our cramped one-person tent, I awoke to find the meadow and the

High Sierra beyond it awash in pink-hued light. It was my first sunrise in the Great Western Divide, and though I had spent most of my adult life up to that point in a strictly secular mindset, something about the soft glow and the stillness of the morning hushed me into reverence.

What impractical magic had I stumbled upon? A forest-laden Burning Man for athletic hobbits? A blister-bearing mountain temple for misfits?

A lot of people have a rare and poetic transformation in the woods. They find god or something like it and emerge reborn. I suppose the experience might be akin to one's first experience with psychedelics—the world appears one way your entire life and then, suddenly, it isn't.

What happened to me was somewhere between a god moment and a boot camp. I saw the light, sure, but I couldn't walk straight for three days. I was blistered and bruised. I was ravaged and raw. I was hooked.

It was oddly fitting, then, that my relationship with David collapsed inside a national park. The wild likes to wring out all unnecessary claptrap and excess baggage until you're left naked and exalted and clinging to the truth.

"It's not me, it's you," I found myself saying one Saturday evening in Yosemite, a full moon beaming auspiciously overhead like a spotlight as we assembled a small fire beneath the granite eye of Half Dome. "I've done everything I can to impress you. I took up rock climbing. I'm a competent outdoorswoman now. I organized a threesome. Hell, I'm even faster on trail than you are these days. Why won't you just call me your girlfriend?"

David stammered into speech before the thought had fully formed. "Because . . . I . . . I don't think we would make very good domestic partners."

"Oh."

I began trembling in great sobs, fearing my organs might melt out through my skin as I wept. My chest rattled as I struggled to take in air. My worst fears were coming true. My efforts went unnoticed. My best would never be good enough. My adventurousness and impulsivity were charming for about a year, until it was time to get serious—with someone else. I felt like the worst version of the manic pixie dream girl trope: the manic outdoorsy dream gremlin that everyone wanted to sleep with but no one wanted to take home to Mom.

In that moment, I needed to know that someone could love me unconditionally, absent of achievement, and maybe it was a fool's errand all along. But I'd been chasing down that elusive partner ever since. Only now was I realizing that maybe the only person that someone could be was me.

After my breakup with David, it took a long time to build myself back into something resembling the woman I wanted to be. I lolled around at my desk job for months. I slept with dozens of strangers. I stopped eating. I started force-feeding myself meal replacement drinks.

But as my heartsick intensified, so, too, did my love of the wilderness. I took a class to learn how to use an ice axe and crampons and started setting my sights on higher peaks and bigger adventures. Rather than elevate another man to godlike status in my mind, I began going out every weekend and throwing myself against the ragged canvas of the mountains. And though my new lifestyle felt raucous and healing, I needed more.

One day, on a hiking trip through Kings Canyon with a girlfriend, the thought hit me with all the ferocity of a locomotive barreling toward my chest: *What if I was less in love with David and more in love with the adventures he introduced me to? What if I struck out on my own and planned a yearlong journey across America, solo? Across the one thing that had stirred me awake, ripped me wide open, and stitched me back together again—the national parks.*

I didn't need a partner in crime to set off on a grand adventure. I had two perfectly good feet, a dirt-caked backpack, and a fire inside my heart.

In a blur, it all came back to me. I was staring up at the exact spot where David and I had ended things years before. Past melded with present, and I found myself experiencing a wallop of déjà vu, simultaneously feeling the weight of two shockingly similar realities. *What is it with me and breakups in the fucking national parks?* I wondered. Maybe it was something about how truth reigned supreme in the wilderness. It was all trees and rocks and elements of the ancient. The ultimate stress test for any relationship. The wild could be counted on to rip out anything that wasn't real or worthy from my life.

As the sunset turned fire red on its slow descent, I realized something else: that my moment of deep loss with David under those smooth stone slabs cradled this one. It was that singular night that catapulted me into exploring the parks and becoming so proficient in the outdoors that I would never again need a man to guide me. It stood to reason that this moment of sorrow might also be cradling some incredible, unforeseen future that I couldn't yet fathom. I had come so far in four years. Where would I be in four more?

To escape the heat and the wildfire haze, I spent much of the next morning driving up to the park's high-altitude Tuolumne Meadows area, making a pilgrimage to Elizabeth Lake before the afternoon crowds arrived. A perfect reflection of Unicorn Peak lay suspended in the glassy water while insects occasionally skittered across its slick surface. I wandered around the lake, the only person on the trail, and clambered onto a large boulder facing the humpbacked mountain. It was the same spot where, almost two years earlier to the day, Adam had suggested that we perform a relationship commitment ceremony, writing vows and declaring our love.

From my backpack, I removed a small Ganesha statue, a stick of palo santo, a lighter, and a list of vows I had written. I fingered the late-season grass, crisp and nearly golden, and snapped off two identical strands from the ground below. After carefully tying them into a circular shape on my left ring finger, I lit up the fragrant wood and started reading my script. If I couldn't have Adam, I would marry myself.

I promise to be gentle with myself and let whatever emotions arise come and go calmly and with great care.

I promise to love myself unconditionally. I promise to love my thoughts, even the less charming ones.

I promise to stand by myself in sickness and in health.

I choose patience, trusting that the work I am doing is true and meaningful and that I don't need to beat myself up to have amazing things happen.

With tears streaming down my face, I kissed the feet of my little bronze Ganesha, remover of obstacles, patron saint of new beginnings. A woodpecker began her percussive search for breakfast. I gazed up and laughed. The morning sun warmed my face.

⁓

On the drive back to Los Angeles, a stark reality dawned on me: American Samoa was showing no signs of opening up to mainlanders before my parks year was over. My epic plan to visit all the national parks would be dashed, no matter how hard I tried. Did that mean the entire quest was a failure? I had watched this dream slowly eat away at anything resembling normalcy in my life, and I had to laugh at the dark irony that I wouldn't even be able to finish. With no real home and little reason to stay in California, I decided to complete as much as I could of the freewheeling year and let the chips fall where they may, Samoa or not. I would head northeast in early October, chasing winter all the way to Florida before spinning my wheels west across the entire country to see my friends for Thanksgiving.

Back at Adam's house, the energy was thick and loaded. After inviting me onto the couch to cuddle, he brought up how much he'd been wanting to see other people. He planned to rejoin the dating apps as soon as I left for the East Coast, even though it meant that I would no longer have a place to stay that was free of COVID risks.

Entropy boiled in my veins. I pressed my palms into my face and took deep, seething breaths.

"Are you sure?" My voice trembled.

"Yeah. I think it's going to get pretty lonely over here."

You know nothing about the true meaning of loneliness.

"If that's really what you want, I think I'll go stay with Jack for a few months once I'm back from Florida."

"It is. And thanks for doing the emotional labor to make that happen. It means a lot."

Fuck you very much.

At lunch the next day, a friend was surprised that I hadn't come to this decision sooner. "You need to spend some time divorcing yourself from the notion that Adam's house is your home, or you aren't going to enjoy the next leg of your trip."

He wasn't wrong.

"You seem just as upset to be losing your idea of home as you are to be losing the actual relationship. Why not just try being a seed on the breeze for a little while?"

Two days later, I stood face-to-face with Adam on his front porch. Grief was a door I had to walk through alone. I wiped tears from my eyes and gave him a big hug before turning to grab the last of my things for the van.

"Hey," he called after me, "I don't ever want you to feel like you're kicked out. I hope you know that. I just don't want my life to feel like it's in a holding pattern just because you're traveling."

As much as it pained me to admit it, the world, of course, did not revolve around my national parks trip, and it made sense that Adam would want the next chapter of his story to start as soon as he turned the page on ours.

Back on the highway, I sped across the desert wilds of California and Arizona, passing thousands of Joshua trees and blaring Riot Grrrl music. I flung my emotions around the van like a '90s tween. Whipping my long red hair from side to side and shimmying my shoulders, I actually started to feel better. As though a lightning bolt had cracked through the metal roof, I suddenly remembered that I was single too. And that meant I was in charge of my own destiny. I could stop when I wanted, do what I wanted, and flirt with whoever I wanted.

I had one job and one job only: to take care of Emily while I drew a constellation across America with my wheels.

Biking the carriage roads at Acadia National Park, Maine

Chapter 7

EXCAVATIONS IN AUTUMN

Flinging myself across the country in the wake of so much heartache seemed a prime situation for drama, but I mostly spent my days listlessly flipping through Johnny Cash and Rilo Kiley playlists. I belted out the lyrics I knew as I passed high, pine-scented mountains near Flagstaff, countless Route 66 travel stops, and the painted flattop mesas of central Arizona. I pulled over to sleep at a Love's truck stop, the incessant hissing of 18-wheeler brakes and deranged railroad horns making the scene feel more like a three-ring circus than a legal place to sleep for the night. At 6:00 a.m., I finally rose when a car alarm failed to stop screeching after twenty minutes.

The road was mostly dull, with the occasional rust-hued plateau, field of cows, or gust of hot wind. I texted a friend to see if he had any recommendations near Amarillo. Just keep driving, he replied.

The sameness and repetition of the highway allowed a levity to grow inside my chest, as though the farther I got from Adam, the more I actually felt like myself again. I started thinking about my future as an uncoupled self. *What magic might I create? Will I get a dog? An abandoned cabin?* I wanted an excuse to be so riotously myself that it exhausted me—not bogged down by a desk job or a partner or the increasingly inhumane rent of a major US city. *When was the last time I set myself on fire in the best way possible?*

I stopped at a rest area in rural Oklahoma to catch up on sleep after the previous evening's truck-stop blunder. A warm wind pressed its hand against my face as I stepped out of the small van and into the night. Gazing up at a sky freckled with glittering orbs, I felt a stirring sensation that anything was possible. Two stars blinked back at me like wild animal eyes in the night.

What if I gave up feeling unworthy of love and instead accepted every brutal and beautiful emotion that graced my presence? Because that's what life is. It's a barrage of the abrasive and the sublime, the sick and the magical, the vomit and the glitter.

I reached Hot Springs National Park two days later and checked into a cheap hotel to shower. My teacher, Kate, was throwing a Zoom session of ecstatic dance that day, and I happily took the excuse for conscious catharsis, shaking and crawling around the carpeted room with newfound ferocity. My hips felt electric. I was sick of tiptoeing around another person all the time. Tired of trying to be a good girl for somebody else. If I was to flounder, let it be marvelous.

I tossed my legs over my head on the floral polyester comforter and started furiously kicking the mattress. I laughed with the mania of religious fervor. I twirled my body around and around until my vision blurred and I collapsed into a sputtering mess of tears and giggles. I barely made it to my bathhouse appointment.

Unlike the wide-open expanses of the western US parks, many of the national parks out east are smaller and more urban. Hot Springs is a prime example of this. Though the area wasn't designated as a national park until 1921, its mineral waters and surrounding city had been in use for over a century, growing into a popular spa town for wealthy elites to escape to and soothe their ailments. One of the main attractions is a stroll down Bathhouse Row, a preserved strip of turn-of-the-century bathhouses with beautiful historic architecture.

Buckstaff Bathhouse is the only spa in town that's been continuously open since its inception, still offering traditional soaks and treatments to paying park visitors. After maneuvering the van onto a side street with free parking, I sprinted down the antique block to make my afternoon appointment, scurrying past the tiled domes, intricate brickwork, and antique stained glass of the strip before reaching my destination. A kind woman manning the lobby desk checked me in and led me upstairs in a gilded cage elevator, leaving me with a clean white sheet and the key to a locker so that I could undress. Shoes, purse, camera, and phone all went inside, and after wrapping myself in the bundle of fabric, I shuffled along the tile floor to where my bath attendant, Madeline, was waiting.

The whole experience felt like time traveling into the upper crust of the Roaring Twenties, hardly fare for a girl who could barely keep her life together in a van. Still, I was determined to enjoy every last drop of the finery. Madeline drew a bath, gave me a loofah mitt, and handed me a cup full of ice chips.

"Okay now, you just tell me if it gets too hot or if you need more ice, okay?"

I smiled like a stoned little sloth. "You got it."

She turned on some cacophonous 1940s contraption that blew a thick stream of bubbles into the tub and let me be. It felt nice. A soft wave of pleasure rose through my body, and I found myself inching my bits toward the right side of the tub, where the bubbles were strongest. *Women in the 1920s must have done this,* I thought coyly.

I scrubbed my body raw with the mitt in between spurts from the effervescent whirlpool machine. Dizzy with bliss, I had to remind myself to wrap it up before Madeline returned and showed me to the next bathhouse delight. She took me through a series of old-timey spa rituals—swaddling with hot towels, a medieval-looking steam chamber, and a sitz bath for my hips and lower back. At the end of it all, a masseuse rubbed warm oil into my tired muscles until I was sure I would melt and become one with the table.

I tipped the girls and doddered out of the building in a puddle of joy. Sure, I'd be sleeping in my van at a truck stop again that night, but for one brief, shining moment, I felt whole.

⤳⤳

Angsty female bands rolled across the airwaves as I drove through the forests of northeastern Arkansas the next day, a roller coaster of emotions and edge. The farther away from Adam I drove, the more resentful of him I became. Dazed, I sped through Saint Louis and its gleaming Gateway Arch, frazzled by city traffic and the lack of true nature in this downtown park. I tried to be strong, but occasionally, grief snuck up on me like a thief in the night and left me bawling over my camp stove or curled up in a ball on top of my bed. I tried to remember what Kate had told me about taking care of myself, swaddling my body in a cashmere scarf that a friend had given me at Burning Man two years prior. I told myself that I was worthy. I caressed my face with my own hands.

I also decided to start work with a therapist on Zoom as I navigated my post-breakup life while straddling the whole of America. With two months of alone time staring me down and a pandemic still firing on all cylinders, it seemed the only kind thing to do for my psyche. We met over Wi-Fi in motel rooms and on FaceTime when my cell signal was strong enough. He asked me how I felt about losing my home and my chosen family; he helped me begin to unravel the hefty knot of emotions I had ensnared myself in, stuck between self-righteous anger and a deep fear of loneliness. He validated that I was mourning the loss of not only a relationship but also my former life, explaining that it made sense to feel so shaken. At times, I felt I was paying someone to be my best friend.

At Indiana Dunes, I waited out a tremendous thunderstorm that caused Lake Michigan to swell like a churning sea. With a sound like machine-gun fire, pellets of rain and hail hit the roof of my van, and a rough wind knocked the vehicle from side to side. Trees quivered and shook. When the storm finally abated, I dragged myself onto the frigid sand at dusk to watch the waves break against a watermelon sky, my fire-red hair dancing in the breeze.

༄

I had never seen fall colors out east before. For years, I had known about their heart-stopping magic from movies and television shows, but the all-American rite of passage of actually seeing them in person had never graced my life until I reached Cuyahoga Valley, my forty-eighth national park.

Tucked between Cleveland and Akron, the park was more urban than most, its sprawling woodlands home to various historic buildings and railroad stops. With a thin ripple of clouds blanketing the horizon, I pulled into the parking lot for one of the area's most beloved hikes— Brandywine Gorge—and began meandering along its mile-and-a-half loop. Steep rock walls lined with mosses and hanging gardens soon loomed overhead as I neared the area's main attraction—Brandywine Falls. A swift cascade of water trickled over terraced ledges of stone, looking more like a series of lace ruffles on a debutante's gown than the roaring torrents of rivers pouring over the edges of cliffs in Yosemite Valley. I walked on. A canopy of canary-yellow maple rustled above me, and I lifted my gaze skyward, trying not to trip over tree roots. *This is real autumn,* I thought as I hiked along slowly, watching the wind turn leaves of rust and marigold into tiny paper airplanes that wafted gently onto the forest floor. It was as if the trees were throwing a giant party, exploding into one final burst of elaborate color before embarking on their cycle of hibernation and rebirth.

When the sun began its nightly descent toward the horizon, I high-tailed my van over to Ledges Overlook, a series of rough sedimentary rocks that fall away steeply to a bird's-eye view of the park's glorious foliage. From the perch I could see for miles. Lit up in late evening sunlight, the warm rainbow of fall colors looked even more magical, and as the clouds turned a brilliant shade of tangerine, two dozen other hikers sauntered out of the woods and stood stock-still, taking it all in. When the last of the sun faded, we scattered and went our separate ways, the spell broken. I felt more at peace than I had in a long while.

I awoke wrapped in my sheets as a wash of pastel morning light made its way across the farmlands outside Akron. With rain in the forecast, I needed to hustle if I wanted to explore more of the park. After a breakfast of oatmeal and instant coffee, I spun my wheels toward Century Cycles, rented a bike, and started down the Towpath Trail. It instantly found a place on my list of the best urban riding paths.

The trail was intermittently paved and gravel, paralleling the Cuyahoga River and the ruins of locks that once served as a portage for ships carrying goods from Lake Erie down to the Ohio River. Now long abandoned, historic canals sprang up here and there beneath apricot-hued leaves that seemed to burst forth from every tree. I zoomed past old wooden storefronts and miles of fiery fall colors, thinking about my future as I raced the rain.

I would like a vintage, courtyard-style apartment. I would like a medium-sized dog. I would like to go skiing with my mother and find a devilishly handsome man to press my warm body against, but preferably not at the same time.

It felt healthy—excavating a way forward from the vantage point of a swiftly moving vehicle. Like carving a new path allowed me to enjoy the trip more. If I was chained to travel because there was no other option, travel would lose all novelty and wonder. There had to be hope. There had to be a future to look forward to.

Moments after I dropped the bicycle back at the rental shop, big droplets of rain started to fall. I checked into my motel early, eager to catch up on emails, phone a few friends, and take my first shower in days.

I was also equal parts excited and nervous for my first Zoom date since things with Adam had ended. In a fit of rage and hurt, I had signed up for a few dating apps before leaving Los Angeles, my competitive side roiling with a desire to prove that if Adam was ready to date other people, so was I, and I was going to be a hell of a lot better at it than he was.

But I didn't swipe through the smorgasbord of available men in the country's second-largest city until I was thousands of miles away. I needed to put a continent between myself and Adam before I was even remotely ready to entertain the idea of sleeping with someone new. Once my hands found their way to the familiar glow of strangers' profiles, I couldn't help myself. I grew ravenous in the wake of my own bodily starvation, swiping past page after page of potential suitors. A creep in a sundress and Crocs.

It was nice to add things to my calendar that felt akin to normal life. I put on makeup for the first time in six months and brushed my tangled mat of hair. I donned my favorite red floral dress and made sure the lighting was decent. I flirted like a lunatic for a full hour, coyly batting away questions about my recent breakup. I was determined not to let the scarlet A of a recent separation prevent me from having a little fun.

⤜⤛

My old friend Cameron and I had planned to meet up and travel to Maine together to visit Acadia, nearly nine months after our climbing misadventure in Pinnacles National Park. The next morning, I gathered my things and hit the road, driving for six hours across warm bursts of autumn colors in the rural hills of Pennsylvania and New York. After gawking at a roadside view of the Finger Lakes, glistening a fine azure in the afternoon sun, I rolled into his family's vineyard in the charming village of Watkins Glen, New York.

He stepped out of a century-old farmhouse, and I fell into his arms, crying. So much had happened since we had last seen each other. Cameron had lost a parent, and I, a partner. Meanwhile, the world kept on burning. We were in the middle of a brutal pandemic, an economic tailspin, and one of the most divisive elections in American history.

"Hey, man, I've still got some work to finish up, but then we can hang out tonight and catch up."

"Yeah, yeah." I wiped my nose with the back of my hand and found my voice trembling. "It's good to see a friendly face. I can't wait to chat later."

The afternoon passed in a flurry of raindrops and writing. I hunched over my laptop in the van, working furiously to complete a magazine assignment so that I could spend the next several days relaxing. When the sun hung low in the sky, Cameron came back outside and caravanned with me to his mom's house, a conga line of handcrafted white vans. We split two bottles of wine and ordered takeout, then babbled for hours about Adam and America and how completely surreal dating during a pandemic felt.

"But you knew you were settling." Cameron fought my heartbroken logic. "I mean, sure, you were ready to settle, but you're amazing, and you deserve way more than a plan B."

Did I mention that Cameron is an incredible friend?

He went on: "I noticed early in your relationship that Adam was taking on way more of your hobbies than seemed healthy. He didn't hold his own personality; he just sort of followed you around whenever you were doing something cool. Take another look, and try to see it all with unclouded eyes. I bet the past will appear a lot different."

❦

The two of us drove our vans through a sea of fall foliage to Maine's Acadia National Park, and I took what he said to heart on the two-day drive. Yes, I was losing a friend and a confidant, but Adam's mercurial nature often meant that I had to talk to him on his terms.

I couldn't help but wonder if I would ever be at ease in my own company. I had caught glimpses of that feeling from time to time as I traversed the national parks, often forced to endure more days by myself than I would have liked. But I still had a long way to go before alone felt more like a choice than a prison sentence.

Since he had visited the park a year earlier, Cameron was excited to show off the best of Acadia's sights when we arrived. We pulled up our vans near the Precipice Trail, an almost vertical wall of sloping granite with metal rungs and ladders embedded into the rock to aid hikers on their ascent. A nightmare for anyone with a fear of heights.

The trail started easily enough, offering step after step of stone-cut stairs. But soon it opened up into a glorious scramble through swiftly changing leaves of flame orange and bloodred, requiring us to crawl on all fours through a miniature cave and traverse narrow, exposed walkways with stomach-turning drops to our right. Cameron, a dedicated rock climber, practically flew up the challenging bits with the grace of a dancer, occasionally pausing in a dramatic pose for the perfect photo. I, on the other hand, was not expecting to traverse a cliff all morning. Occasionally, the hiker before me would have wet, muddy shoes, leaving the metal ladder rungs that I clung to for safety slick and unreliable. My muscles clenched, and I gritted my teeth.

"Dude!" I yelled up to Cameron. "This is a lot spicier than I thought it would be!"

"Yeah, but you got this! I've seen you climb before."

I carefully crisscrossed my footsteps on a smooth granite boulder as we neared the top of the mountain, staring down at a carpet of fall colors hundreds of feet below. A few more steps up a series of iron rungs and we were at the top of Champlain Mountain, the ragged Atlantic coastline stretching out for miles like a strip of torn paper against a deep palette of blue.

After a much easier descent along a more traditional trail, we cruised around the park's scenic drive, stopping to climb around on high ocean cliffs as the waves pummeled them repeatedly, spraying us with a fine mist. We ate dinner at Stewman's Lobster Pound so that I could try my first lobster roll. It was every bit as delicious as I had hoped—creamy mayonnaise on a toasted, buttery bun and gobs of fresh crustacean meat.

With full bellies, we were off to our campsite for the next three nights: a wolf sanctuary run by a duo of eccentric women just outside of Mount Desert Island. I was so spent when we arrived that I fell asleep before I could even hear them howl.

Cameron and I had wanted to explore as many of the park's carriage roads as we could during our visit, so the next morning we got up early and rented bicycles. These forty-five miles of historic roadways are an essential part of any visit to Acadia, a gift of philanthropist John D. Rockefeller Jr. in the early twentieth century. Each gravel lane was specifically designed for visitors to take in the park's unique beauty, curving around waterfalls or toward the edge of steep drop-offs to glean the best views. Nowadays, no cars are allowed on these quaint backroads, though hikers and cyclists are welcome.

We parked near Jordan Pond, the rounded hills of the adjacent countryside looking nothing like my beloved California peaks. Full of bright patches of honey and rust-tinted leaves, fall was in full swing, flaunting itself as the most brilliant of the four seasons. Cameron and I donned helmets and sped downhill to a junction, then bore right and began a steep climb that made my quads ache. Though I had spent the year in the outdoors, I was certainly not in biking shape, and I breathed deeply, moving at what felt like the speed of a snail.

The crushed stone road circled up and up and up, spiraling around the edge of a great mountain as it passed over storybook bridges carved from ivory-colored stones. We crunched our wheels through gradients of fallen leaves—yellow to orange to red to brown—and skidded mercilessly across the gravel when we took a corner too quickly. Once we crested the summit, we were rewarded with a phenomenal view of Acadia's freshwater ponds and acres of dense woodlands.

We zoomed down at breakneck speed, only to rise, zoom down again, and rise another time. The trail was a tough fourteen miles, and by the time we neared the end, my thighs were on fire. I hobbled to the popover counter at Jordan Pond House and ordered two pastries and a tea. We sat outside under a canopy of light gray clouds talking about our futures.

"Do you think you'll be a vanlifer forever?"

"Nah," he replied. "I just want to make sure I settle down in the right city when I do pick a spot. I really want a dog, though."

"Me too. Being on the road alone is tough."

Tea gave way to craft beers and movies inside of Cameron's huge van. It was the human connection I'd been craving for months, and we laughed and drank well into the night.

﷼

My eyes cracked open to a splitting headache and a familiar wave of nausea as I rose in the dark to ride with Cameron to Cadillac Mountain for sunrise. My tolerance for alcohol had shrunk down to nothing.

Cameron swerved his van around the paved road leading to the top of Cadillac Mountain, the first spot in the United States to receive the sun's glow each day. His headlights spilled out a faint beam of white light as we ascended higher and higher. We were not alone. Hundreds of tourists had already gathered on the cracked granite slopes to marvel at the show. We stood side by side, just in time to witness the sky break open into a dazzling display of fuchsia and pink, a frigid breeze numbing my nose and fingers. Alive with the light of a distant star, the horizon turned from periwinkle to gold. As the sun rose higher, the crowd dispersed until it was just Cameron and me gazing out at a few small specks of islands floating in the Mount Desert Narrows.

Leaving Cameron that afternoon was harder than I expected. After nearly a week together, the time had come for him to go home and for me to head south. He gave me a huge bear hug as he said his goodbyes, reminding me to stay strong as I stared down a solid month alone in the van.

"I'm going to miss your dumb face," I said, laughing.

"I'm going to miss your dumb face too."

⤞⤝

I checked into a hotel so that I could shower in peace before logging in to my weekly Zoom therapy session. I told my new therapist all about my mind's tumult and how I had no idea why my brain was having so much trouble accepting the breakup and moving on.

"I'm usually so much more resilient than this," I offered, frustrated.

"What do you do when you first wake up?" he asked curiously.

"Well, I umm . . . click through my phone for about thirty minutes and check social media before hopping out of bed to make breakfast."

"I want you to meditate or do yoga or stretching or something that's 100 percent just for you for the first fifteen minutes after you wake up. Really try to own this time apart. Think about all the great things you can only have when you're single. Then let me know how you're feeling."

It wasn't a terrible idea. I had become so engaged with my phone as a Band-Aid for loneliness that it was like I had grown an extra, electronic limb. The next morning, groggy from a night of sleeping in a foreign bed, I tried it. I queued up a short yoga video on my laptop, took deep breaths, and focused my body. If nothing else, starting my day with an iota of calm would focus my trip, if not my life. Like Kate said, I needed to invite softness in.

Pointing my van south, I drove through the evergreen forests of Maine and the unfamiliar traffic of Connecticut's toll roads, inching my small home across the tippy-top of Manhattan before veering inland to the verdant farmlands of rural Virginia. Two days later, a chilling rain soaked me to the bone as I ascended more than two thousand feet to the summit of Old Rag Mountain in Shenandoah National Park, and I was grateful for the heat and sunshine I found on my next day's hike along the Riprap Trail, crunching my boots through piles of leaves grounded by the storm. I was rounding a series of wooded switchbacks in the sticky warmth of the late afternoon, and my mind couldn't help but wander to Adam. So much alone time is a playground for an obsessive mind. I remembered a promise Adam once made: that he'd never leave me abruptly—like he had so many other things in his life. The end of our relationship had felt so dramatic and intense that I hadn't really remembered until this moment. He knew my father's absence and my mother's grueling work schedule had left me with rampant fears of abandonment, and he'd promised not to leave without trying harder than he ever had before—even going so far as to say he'd do couples therapy. But he hadn't fought for us at all.

The next morning, I was livid. Glaring at my phone, I sped through the hills of West Virginia's coal country. I decided to text Adam.

Can you talk later today? It's important.

Yeah, bu. His casual attitude made me want to scream. I'll call you in about an hour.

When he did, I launched right into it—how I felt abandoned and discarded and that he had broken his promise. Adam listened, but he didn't see it that way.

"Don't you think that both people should *want* to go to therapy for it to even work?"

I couldn't argue with that. The tension cooled, and we caught up on each other's lives . . . but then I threw out my Hail Mary.

"Listen, I still think that there's a lot of good stuff here, and if you wanted to try to salvage the relationship, I'm open to that."

Never one to be particularly decisive, Adam replied instantly. "Yeah, I'm definitely open to continuing the conversation."

My heart did a backflip inside my chest.

"One of my friends recently told me that a lot of men freak out when they first become fathers," Adam continued. "They suddenly aren't getting the quality of love and affection that they were used to and often lash out and have affairs. I felt like that a lot with your big parks project."

I tried to soothe his bruised ego, assuring him that I doubted I would ever visit every national park during a global pandemic again. I couldn't stop smiling. It felt amazing to have my best friend back.

"Before I let you go, I feel like I should check in and see what 'keeping the conversation going' looks like for you?"

Adam paused. "Oh, well . . . lately, I've been leaning more toward a no than a yes. Like, after taking some space for the past month, I think it's more a good thing than a bad thing that we separated. You know how I like Eckhart Tolle, and you think that he's boring?"

"Umm, yeah?"

"Well, it's like that. I think that my default channel is stillness, and your default channel is adventure. Our energies don't line up quite right."

I inhaled sharply. "You're breaking up with me because I don't like Eckhart Tolle?!"

All the hurt and the sorrow and the rage of the initial breakup slammed back into my system, and tears began to stream down my cheeks.

"Look, I don't need an answer today," I quavered through sobs, "but I know I can't wait for you. I'm cracking a door open inside my heart and inviting you in, but I need to know if you want to start working together to repair this, even if it's just a weekly phone call."

Adam sighed. "If I had to give you an answer today, it would be no."

That gutted me, and I fell over the steering wheel wailing, not caring if I flew into a ditch or flipped the van off a mountain.

"Try to think of it as cultivating a new friendship with me," he continued.

"Adam, I need to sign a lease on my own apartment and start living my life again," I said. "It's time for me to start individuating."

I bawled for hours beneath a canopy of darkening clouds until, under cover of night, I pulled into a rest area off a busy interstate in central Kentucky, wanting more than anything to numb myself with alcohol or drugs, like I had done in my twenties when the world was too much. But I knew that was only an attempt to escape the void rather than befriend it. As crickets chirped outside, I fell into a deep sleep, nestled into my freshly woven cocoon and feeling very much like primordial goo.

⚜

When I awoke, an electricity was pulsing ripe and hungry inside my veins. I felt ravenous for male attention. My sexuality had grown teeth and begun gnashing away at my insides, tenacious and eager to rip apart relationships and leave children fatherless, if only to have someone, anyone, lie on top of me. It was as if my organs understood that I would be back in Los Angeles in under four weeks, and a lecherous beast wanted to claw its way out of my stomach and devour any man who would have me, pandemic be damned. Agony and ecstasy commingled. A ferocious moon rising.

I took this feeling with me as I embarked on a self-guided morning tour of Mammoth Cave, national park number fifty-one. My moody, worn-out heart was grateful for a mellower hiking day, and as I walked down the staircase leading to the cave's entrance, a soft trickle of water cascaded down from above. The sound seemed to usher me into a new, calmer state of being as I hiked farther into the longest cave in the world. In the belly of the immense cavern, all light vanished, save for the occasional amber-tinted spotlight aimed at the steep limestone walls. I walked on, overhearing a ranger whisper to a group of visitors that the main hall I had just entered was large enough to park a 737 aircraft in. I tilted my head back to take in the towering domed ceiling. It reminded me of the Italian cathedrals I had seen in my youth. The fact that these structures had been built by nature made them even more impressive.

I strolled past antique saltpeter mines that dated back to the War of 1812 and the stone ruins of a tuberculosis ward that once housed dying patients. By the time I climbed back up and returned to my van, it had started to rain.

The heavens opened up, and I drove back to the previous night's rest area off the busy Kentucky interstate, where the patter of raindrops and whooshing of distant cars serenaded me. I ate a peanut butter and jelly sandwich for lunch and stared blankly at the wood-paneled doors of my van. I had nothing to do until tomorrow.

I lay on my bed, swiping through a dating app to numb my boredom, declining page after page of available men. At one point, I came across an extremely overweight gentleman named Giovanni, and I felt the world stand still. He had a kind face and an instantly endearing smile, and for some reason, I could not take my eyes off his profile. I read the entire thing from top to bottom, praying that the algorithm would somehow notice my screen time and show his info to more women. Though he wasn't my type, he seemed so deserving of love. So unabashedly deserving of joy and of being held in exactly the way that he wanted to be held in the world.

Things started to take a turn for the weird. My heart lit up and felt as though it would swell to such a size that it might balloon out of my chest. I instantly started crying. These weren't sad tears; they were expansive tears. It felt like a glowing energetic thread was dangling from the heavens and somehow locked into the top of my head, beaming light straight into the center of my being. The knowing came fast and pure: Every human on earth is a world unto themselves. A whole world of madness and joy that is totally and completely absurd and yet totally and completely worthy of love. And not just any old rinky-dink love. Worthy of the precise kind of love that they've always been looking for.

I felt like my chest would burst open from the download, all bony ribs and exposed organs, but I couldn't unknow what I then knew. Sometimes your heart breaks wide open. You can slap a Band-Aid on it and close it back up, or you can fearlessly and audaciously hold the channel clear and allow light to blossom across your whole body until you catch a tiny glimpse of what it might feel like to love the world unconditionally. If we're lucky, pain can break us open into compassion.

I knew in that moment that whatever hurt I felt from losing Adam was worth it. It was riotously opening me to a world I wouldn't have otherwise known.

❧

Waking to more rain and a gray ceiling of clouds, I drove south through narrow backcountry roads and cute Amish villages, then zoomed along the open highway until I reached Great Smoky Mountains. I had decided to splurge on a night of camping inside the park, and once I rolled into my assigned site at Cades Cove, it was time to make dinner and hit the hay. The rain did not let up.

In the morning, I curved the van around a narrow mountain road, a rocky, moss-covered cliff hugging my right side while a raging creek churned to my left. I hit the brakes as a mama black bear and her adolescent cub scampered up a hillside not ten yards from the pavement. A few minutes later, a flock of enormous wild turkeys quietly pecked their way across the road. It was clear that this was one of the last remaining outposts of wilderness on the East Coast. Great Smoky is the second-largest national park east of the Mississippi, bested only by the Everglades.

The temperature was barely above freezing when I reached Newfound Gap, a famous lookout point on the border of Tennessee and North Carolina. At its high elevation of 5,049 feet, the clouds from the recent storm lingered, and I was immersed in a world of chilling fog. I ambled through miles of dark, spooky forest along the Appalachian Trail, occasionally passing another hiker or a soggy, wooden backpacking shelter. As I wandered through the woods, small icicles clinked on tree branches, shattering into dozens of pieces whenever they fell and hit the trail. When I reached the viewpoint at Charlies Bunion, a cold wind stung my cheeks, and the ground opened up for hundreds of feet below me. Pillowy white clouds rushed past, wafting up and over the rocky hilltop where I then stood. Eventually, my toes began to tingle and my fingertips went numb; I knew it was time to turn around.

On the hike back, I shivered as I paced through the misty forest. Boots clomping along the muddy dirt trail, I made it back to Newfound Gap just as the sun began to shine through a spindly web of dispersing clouds. From my vantage point along the path, I could gaze out at row upon row of rolling green mountaintops. The view stretched on for miles, and it was spectacular.

⤛֍⤜

Every national park is an opportunity to come home to yourself. As I began to feel new legs and innards sprout beneath the tightly woven cocoon of my own grief, I took solace in the fact that I was being held by the most ancient of circumstances—the pristine air of the natural world.

I drove down to South Carolina, where I kayaked through soot-colored water among the scraggly exposed knees of thousands of bald cypresses in Congaree National Park. It was forest bathing on steroids. A swamp so dense with foliage that bootleggers and runaway slaves once formed small villages within its shady expanse. Big patches of chartreuse moss stuck to downed trees like the fur of some great alien beast. I allowed the dappled sunlight to warm my face as I floated slowly through the woods.

Back in the van, I spent nearly ten hours driving to reach Florida's infamous Everglades. When I arrived, the first thing I did was hop onto an airboat tour with a dozen other visitors, all of us transported across the endless horizon of sawgrass slough as if by magic. An enormous white egret the size of a six-year-old soared past as the sun's golden rays bounced off the brackish water. The boat grew quiet. Out of a tangle of grass, a large female alligator swam directly toward us, her back scales jutting up like rows of tiny gray shark fins. I could not take my eyes off her. There was something so peaceful and powerful in the way her muscular tail effortlessly sliced through the water. She was a master of efficient movement.

In a few seconds, she was on us, slithering back and forth along the edge of the boat, not two feet from where I sat. Her intense green eyes glared up at me with a familiar ferocity. We were definitely kindreds.

❧

I tried not to have a heart attack when I got back to the van and watched as my plans for the next two weeks crumbled. Though I had purposefully chosen to visit Florida outside of peak hurricane season, the tail end of a fierce Category 4 storm would soon rip across the southern tip of the state, canceling boat trips, flooding roads, and shifting guided tours. I was gutted. After checking into a motel near the park, I jumped onto its weak Wi-Fi, typing vigorously into my laptop to rearrange everything—flights, hotels, paddleboarding, and most importantly, a long-awaited ferry to the Dry Tortugas, my last of the eastern parks. It was one more nausea-inducing slap in the face after a year of upheaval. *Serves me right for thinking that a life outdoors could ever be predictable.*

Trapped by the tropical storm in sopping-wet Homestead, Florida, I tried to hone my new daily meditation practice from the comfort of a stained yellow couch in my motel room. Sirens sounded their shrill whooping outside while a tenacious wind howled. Other guests came and went loudly. The lobby's free breakfast was nothing more than a pair of hard-boiled eggs and a cup of cheap Dannon yogurt. I bit my teeth into the white plastic spoon, trying to stay present and mindful, antsy to keep moving.

A lull in the storm meant that my guided day trip around Biscayne National Park could proceed only three days late, so I excitedly drove to the visitor center and boarded a boat with my camera in tow. Though my captain, Jim, had been guiding in these waters for almost a decade, our small boat was no match for the high waves rolling into Biscayne Bay from the rumbling Atlantic. I held on to the railings tightly, my clothes soaked through, even in full rain gear, as he steered us across the open water to the park's more serene keys. When the rain abated, we stopped in a mangrove-lined lagoon to paddleboard through a labyrinth of leggy roots, hunting for small sharks and baby parrotfish among the trees. Clumps of coral and sea sponges clung to the submerged trunks. Jim pulled up a jellyfish with a ruched white underbelly that looked like the ruffles on a toddler's christening gown.

"Touch it," he offered, and when I did, I pulled my hand back quickly, my fingers pulsing with shock. He chuckled. "Yeah, these guys don't exactly hurt you, but you'll definitely feel uncomfortable for a few seconds."

When he plopped it back into the water, it hung suspended like a huge olive marble before contracting its entire body and drifting slowly down to the sand. I wondered how it must feel to live at the bottom of the ocean, bound to whatever nourishment happened to float by.

I moved into an Airbnb and was again held captive by the weather. The storm had circled back and pummeled nearly the entire length of Florida with biblical rain. Five-foot waves crashed into the Keys, and a scuba diving trip that I had been looking forward to for months was canceled at the last minute, leaving me picking at my cuticles and swiping through dating apps. I watched online yoga videos and hours of Netflix. I tried to get my writing work done to the constant patter of raindrops outside. I swaddled myself in my beloved cashmere scarf and meditated for fifteen minutes each morning. No matter how much time or distance I put between myself and Adam, a strange well of sadness seemed to hover just under the surface, and my lack of constant motion gave it time to gain strength.

⚜

After nearly a week of microwave dinners and unscheduled time indoors in the soggy town of Homestead, I decided to go out and practice some much-needed self-care. I called a well-reviewed massage place, and a sweet lady referred me to one of her favorite massage therapists, Jacob. I shot him a text, and he called to set up a time to meet that night.

"Do you have anywhere you have to be after?"

"Not really. I'm just waiting out this storm so I can go on to the next park."

"Good. I'm getting really into some Chinese medicine stuff, and there's a chance that if we hit something really deep, we might want to take up to three hours."

"You'll be wearing a mask, right?"

"Yeah, yeah. I live with my ninety-two-year-old mother, so I've gotta be careful with COVID, you know?"

"Oh, okay. Perfect!"

I jumped at the opportunity to loosen my muscles after months of hiking. Eager for the day to be over, I passed the time in my small room with yet another Zoom date from the apps. The rain never stopped.

Around eight o'clock, I left my Airbnb and drove into the cloudy, moonless night. Fat pellets of rain continued to fall, and the windshield wipers made a high-pitched squeaking sound each time they cleared my vision. Pulling into a sparse outdoor strip mall lit with fluorescent streetlights, I parked the van and walked upstairs to the massage studio. Jacob was the only one inside, and he quickly unlocked the door, a surgical mask taming his shaggy gray hair and sun-spotted face. He looked to be in his early sixties. He was high energy as he asked me a barrage of questions.

"When was your last menstrual cycle?"

"I think it's supposed to start in a week."

"If we do anything today that's going to start it early, will you freak out?"

"Umm . . . I don't think so."

"Do you wake up in the night to pee?"

"Yes."

"How often?"

"Usually once. Sometimes twice, I guess."

He squeezed my upper thigh so that my cellulite was showing.

"Mmm. You're retaining too much water. We'll work on that tonight."

I didn't think much of it. He seemed like an eccentric old hippie who was just really amped to be getting some extra cash. Jacob sent me into a small massage room and closed the door so that I could undress. A large beach towel with blue-and-white stripes covered the table where a crisp sheet would usually be. I took off my shoes, dress, and underwear and positioned myself face down beneath the terrycloth fabric.

"Ready when you are!" I shouted.

He slathered my naked body with too much coconut oil and got to work, moving his rough hands across my pale, dimpled flesh for over an hour. It was a decent massage, but the longer he pressed his fingers into my skin, the more I understood that a more sinister energy was flying around in the room with us. As he massaged me, Jacob began opening up about his childhood and his life in southern Florida, talking a mile a minute and interrupting whenever I tried to get a word in edgewise.

"When I was a kid, you know, my dad used to have this house in Ibiza, and we would fly out there all the time. Lemme tell ya, those parties were off the hook! People drinking and doing drugs until the sun came back out again. Women barely wearing anything. It was crazy, man."

"Oh, that's cool. I've only been to Barcelona . . ."

"Yeah, yeah. Spain is like radical, man. I used to grow weed, you know? Once I got my own house out here in Florida. That is, until they made it a felony, you know?"

"Ha ha. Yeah, sorry, I'm not much of a pot smoker."

I tried not instigating any conversation, but he couldn't read the room. The manic puppet of his gaping mouth kept vomiting out words.

"I think a lot about how being a massage therapist is pretty weird, you know? Because it's like this monetary transaction, when usually, when I'm touching a naked woman, it's more of an energetic exchange, if you know what I mean."

I knew what he meant.

The frenetic blather went on as Jacob pressed his thumbs deep into my bicep and jostled my left arm so that it grazed his cock through his pants. *Surely I must be imagining this, right?* He told me to flip over onto my back.

Emily Pennington

"I've been studying massage for over twenty years now, and I've been getting really into these Thai and Shiatsu pressure point releases. Here, watch. I'll do a pectoral release on you right now."

He jammed his thumb and index finger into the tender flesh just below my right armpit and held for several seconds. Wanting to be the kind of person who can take hard sensations without wincing, I gritted my teeth and continued to breathe deeply. He turned the back of his hand toward my right breast and began a gentler massage stroke, which prompted me to open my eyes. I felt like I was being toyed with.

"You see, this one here is a great massage technique because I'm really close to your breast, but I'm not touching your nipples or anything, because my hand is turned backward."

Jacob's fingers were millimeters away from my right nipple, and I squirmed on the table, suggesting he finish up on my legs. After slopping more coconut oil onto his palms, he ran his hands back and forth along my upper thighs and tried the same trick as before—flipping his wrist backward and announcing how close he was to my genitals without ever technically touching them. He asked me to put my hands over my pubic bone, then pressed down with the full force of his weight, as though he were engaged in some sort of womb-sucking energy voodoo.

It's not uncommon for a predator to test where the boundary is before blatantly exploiting it. They'll trace their fingers across every corner of a room, breathing their toxic air into a space to see what nooks and crannies will hold under pressure. Jacob knew I didn't have anywhere to be that night. He knew I was alone, and he knew that I was open minded enough to meet a strange man at night in a new city.

It was nearly ten thirty. Exhausted and emotionally frazzled, I knew that I wanted to leave.

"Hey, I'm getting pretty tired, and I have to write tomorrow. Think we can finish up soon?"

"Okay, okay. Just let me do this one thing—I really want to get you into some of these stretches before you go."

With a wave of his hand, he positioned my legs into a sort of "thread the needle" yoga pose. My left ankle was crossed over my right knee, but my right leg was held straight up to the ceiling. Every inch of my crotch was completely exposed.

"Don't worry, my eyes are on you . . . on you."

A meaty palm worked its way across my calf and hamstring while my eyes remained fixed on Jacob's face.

"I'm not gonna sneak a peek, you know? My eyes are on you."

Jacob's eyes glanced down at my genitals several times while he played the part of the unassuming old hippie. When he tried the same thing on my left side, I abruptly ended the massage. He left the room. Adrenaline coursing, I threw on my dress and shoes. I needed to get out.

"Hey—you wanted to be paid in cash, right? I need to go to an ATM really quick while you close up."

"I'll go with you! Yeah, just wait a few minutes while I clean this stuff up."

I felt trapped. I sat on a stiff gray sofa in the entry room, the oppressive mint-green paint and framed Sanskrit mantras laughing at me from the walls. I would have given a thousand dollars for a shower and a memory wipe.

After carrying his bags downstairs, the handsy masseuse followed me to a nearby bank and waited while I took out a stack of twenties. Behind me, he hung out of a dented white Subaru and sucked down a cigarette. In the fluorescent white of a streetlamp, I could make out the deep grooves and wrinkles in his world-weary face as I handed him the money. I took a deep breath. Finally, the experience was over.

"Listen, I gotta follow you home. I just need to make sure you get home safely."

Trying to be polite and uncertain of his motives, I deflected. "No, I'm fine, thank you!"

"No, no, no, I wouldn't feel right not following you at least part of the way home."

"Seriously, I've traveled all over the world. I think I'll be okay."

"Really, though, I'm just going to follow you to 160th Street, I promise."

Something snapped me out of my people-pleasing fear, and my voice got firm as I snapped back.

"HEY. Do NOT follow me. Do not EVER follow a woman home at night. I am in a cargo van; no one is going to mess with me, buddy. They probably think I'm a fucking dude before they pass me on the street, so just . . . BACK. OFF."

I sped out of the parking lot and immediately took a wrong turn. The traffic light glowed red, and I couldn't see the headlamps of his car in my mirrors. Body coursing with hours of pent-up energy, I called one of my girlfriends and broke down.

I sobbed because I didn't have a safe home to come back to. I sobbed because I felt so uncommonly alone. I sobbed because, more than anything in the world, I wanted to call Adam and couldn't. Laila listened. She was horrified, creeped out on my behalf as I unraveled the story for her. At the end of it all, she told me the thing I needed to hear the most—that she was proud of me. That I set boundaries and stood up for myself. I made it clear that I was not a person to be fucked with, even though I was the one in a vulnerable position.

I felt, as I often did that year, that I was caught between two worlds: grateful that I had such good friends and shitty to be reminded that, as a woman, my power and safety could be ripped away from me suddenly and without warning.

Still, I was determined to retain my optimism. I would not let a stranger cloud my life with a jaded heart. After a terrible night's sleep, I cried in the bed of my guest room for hours. I told myself that some people have been so deeply hurt by the world that they feel the need to take pleasure rather than simply asking for it. This man deserved my pity but not my time.

❦

Waking to a bruise-blue sky, I drove my van to the Miami airport. The terminal was a mess. Thousands of people were bustling around, crowding the counter at Starbucks and jostling for position to board whenever their gate monitor made an announcement. Save for the fact that nearly everyone was wearing a mask, it felt as though the pandemic had never happened. My anxiety was on red alert. Volume to eleven, burners set to high, flames shooting toward the ceiling.

I hadn't slept well in two nights, the lingering shame of my massage experience pulling my chest to the earth like a necklace wrought from a bowling ball. In three hours, I was transported across the Atlantic Ocean, passing over the verdant green humps of the Bahamas and landing in the US Virgin Islands, the site of a rare, tropical national park. I had to hustle if I wanted to make the three o'clock ferry to Saint John, so I grabbed my backpack and purse as soon as the plane landed and jogged through the airport to the taxi stand, hiking shoes squeaking across the slick tile floor.

Two taxis, a ferry ride, and a short walk later, I made it to the dock where a sunset sail that I had booked would soon depart. Palm trees bordering massive beach resorts swayed in the breeze, the fingers of their immense fronds dancing as Bing Crosby's "Dream a Little Dream of Me" played softly from the boat's speakers. My body, transported to an entirely new world in only half a day's time, started to relax. Mother Nature rocked the anxiety out of me with each passing wave, lulling my frayed nerves while illuminating the clouds overhead in glowing shades of amber and rose. Our boat bobbed gently as the tide rolled in, and I stared for a long while at the ever-shifting line of the horizon, sensing how far I'd come in such a short time.

Energy vampires are little to be feared, I thought to myself as I wrestled with what had happened during the massage, *because energy and resilience spring from an eternal source. Love springs from an eternal source. And no one can ever take that away from me.*

When the boat docked I checked into a modest hostel with a twin bed, free towels, and a shared single-stall bathroom. Warm water poured over my weary frame as I stood in the tiled shower stall and rinsed off the day. Dozens of small bites emerged on my ankles. *Ah, well. It's not officially nature until you're getting eaten by something.*

The next day was as close as I would come to a day off for weeks, so I lingered in bed until late in the morning, messaging friends in Los Angeles and editing photos before rising to a breakfast of coffee, orange juice, and granola. The ocean was calling to me, and though I had never been a beach person, the idea of finding a secluded, sandy nook in Virgin Islands National Park where I could linger and read for the entire afternoon sounded too good to pass up.

Slathering my body in reef-safe sunscreen, I high-stepped up a trail to Lind Point, passing turpentine trees and the odd cactus as my breath quickened in the worsening heat. I was in the islands now, and the tropical humidity clung to my lungs so that every small movement felt like a chore. I breathed deep and took my time ascending. At the top of the path, the dense, green jungle opened up to a clearing with a bench facing the aquamarine expanse of the ocean. I could make out dozens of small boats and ferry vessels spilling out beneath rolling green hills, which were dotted with guesthouses.

I hiked on. Through a tunnel of emerald green, a sign appeared marking the path down to Salomon Beach. I had never heard of it, but since my goal for the day was to find an uncrowded spot to lie out in the sunshine, I hooked a sharp left and quickly descended. The gnarled roots of towering trees cluttered the trail, and from time to time, a small hermit crab scurried across, surely terrified that a giant was tramping around his home.

The beach was perfect: soft white sand like powdered sugar and warm turquoise seawater. I rolled out my towel, crunched into an apple, and simply gazed out at the waves for a long while, their metronomic whooshing lulling me into a Zen-like state. It was as though the earth had a heartbeat, and I was somehow inside it, held firm by an unknowable, benevolent force.

I went for a swim. Then another. Then another. Leisurely breast-stroking across the length of the secluded cove, I hovered above colorful coral reefs and thought about the small universes that were fastened right below my feet. The swell rocked my body like a mother swaying her baby to sleep. Floating faceup in the mellow water, I felt small and powerless and knew that I needed to let Adam slip peacefully into the waves forever. It did not serve me to hold on to the weight of my former life.

I sat cross-legged on the flour-soft sand and closed my eyes. Taking deep breaths as the tide rolled in, I tried to release my need to be "right" or "good" or "desirable." I released my need to be anyone's girlfriend. I released the futile fight to prove my worth. I knew that my worth was inherent. It was time to walk forward into whatever my new life held for me.

The sun began to hang low in the sky like a great golden spider, and I knew I needed to get back. I waded out into the sea and dipped my body into the salty water one last time, hands to heart, then to my third eye. Thanking the ocean for holding me. Thanking the sunshine for healing me. Thanking the steady rhythm of the earth for keeping me present. Tears welled up in my eyes, and I bowed forward and plunged into the warm water, somersaulting in the waves as gravity released its hold on me. The ritual was complete.

༺❦༻

By the time my flight left for Miami, I had spent three full days in a tropical wonderland, and though my mind was awash in dopamine, my body dragged far behind. The glands in my throat had once again swollen to a considerable size; I wore my thickest mask and kept my head down as I shuffled through the tiny airport and boarded a plane back to the States. I prayed that this wasn't another scarlet fever situation.

High seas battered my ferry vessel as I made my way out to the last of the eastern parks, Dry Tortugas, a small sandy speck floating seventy miles off the coast of Key West. This was my fifty-seventh park, and the saltwater glowed a bright cerulean in the midday sunlight as we edged closer to shore. I strolled around the walls of the island's Civil War–era fort for hours, wondering how the men who'd once lived there had coped with the mind-numbing solitude.

My subsequent drive from Key West to Los Angeles passed through a dilated stretch of time, and I watched as each one of the forty-four hours of highway washed over my body and into my rearview as though they were happening to someone else entirely. I hovered above my dirty white van like a ghost, equal parts anxious and excited to return to the city where I had spent the entirety of my adult life. At times, I had to pull the car over and meditate in a fetal position for fifteen minutes until my mind had recentered itself enough to keep on driving. Other times, graced by a show of blush and lilac, I could feel the desert sunsets burst into my body and lull me into a state of explicit gratitude.

I arrived in Los Angeles to a waxing crescent moon and a dry breeze. Rolling down my window in bumper-to-bumper traffic, I howled at the night sky, cranking up the volume to the Decemberists' "Los Angeles, I'm Yours" and belting out every single lyric. Before I had time to press repeat, I was parking against a curb near Adam's house. I opened the dusty van door and lingered on the pavement for several minutes, looking up at the three stars I could make out under the glow of city streetlights. In the cool night air, I felt more grateful than I had in my entire life to live there. Los Angeles. The dirty, dingy whore of a city who would always accept me exactly as I was without judgment.

Adam opened his front door before I rang the doorbell, and we stood and stared at each other for a long while, our grins as big as the continent I had just crossed. He pulled me in tight for a hug. It was strange and overwhelming and comforting to feel the warmth of his body against mine after two months apart. We ate dinner together, catching up on my trip and our mutual obsession with therapy. Knowing it was too late for us as a couple, I told him I hoped that not every relationship we'd ever have was doomed.

It took me an hour to stuff a suitcase full of city clothes and extra toiletries while Adam cleaned up our plates and drifted around his office. I was still angry with him, but I didn't allow the swarming ants of my own thoughts to spill out into my former home. It wouldn't have done any good anyway.

We hugged goodbye, and I stood on the bricks of my former stoop, holding a purple suitcase, having no idea what was next.

Gizmo at Sequoia National Park, California

Chapter 8

A Bed of Moss

I settled into the tiny library guest room in my friend Jack's house and tried my best to be at ease with the fact that home was still a moving target. But only two days after arriving, I woke in the night with an alarmingly high fever. I had sweat through my sheets and my nightshirt. My muscles ached as my mind flew into a panic. *Is this COVID?* A pervasive little nasal drip licked the back of my throat, and as soon as it grew light outside, I put on a mask; dragged myself out of bed; grabbed water, tea, and a protein bar; and drove to Dodger Stadium for a free throat swab. I texted Adam to warn him that he may have been exposed.

He texted back with genuine concern and a suggestion for a pricey concierge doctor who promised to email test results in under twelve hours. After waiting in a line hundreds of cars long at the enormous stadium's parking lot, I sped over to the fancy doctor's office to get a second swab for safety. I messaged Jack that I was going to lock myself in my room as soon as I got back and make myself scarce until I had the results. He was seventy-two years old, and I couldn't imagine anything crueler than a friend being punished for their generosity.

My fever continued to rage, I was lightheaded, and a persistent headache rocked my brain. My energy waned. I rolled around in the dirty sheets with a space heater on, intermittently napping and mentally self-flagellating.

Seven in the morning is a hell of a time to wake up to a positive test result. With my roommate still sleeping, I crept into the kitchen wearing my thickest mask and quickly grabbed breakfast and a few snacks so that I wouldn't infect the air once he was up and about. Waves of shame rolled through me. *What should I do?* Was it more moral to self-quarantine in a shared living space with a friend in a high-risk age group or fork over the money to rent a secluded guesthouse for a week and hide out until I was no longer contagious? It was one of those terribly complicated adult quandaries that school never prepares you for. I chose the latter. Feeling like your every move might accidentally murder a close friend is not a way to live.

Once again, I packed up my suitcase and drove what remained of my tattered life to a furnished one-room pad in the middle of an unfamiliar backyard. I was a fugitive in my own city with nowhere to go but down. I had groceries delivered while I showered and stumbled into bed, my mind and nervous system shaken. I felt like an untouchable. Like the most terrible person in the world for lying my way into a vacation rental. Adrift in the same sea of solitude and silence that I had come to know so well that year.

Like a slow molasses baby, I traced my feet across the floor of the small room, occasionally microwaving dinners or streaming movies to pass the hours. There was a heaviness in my chest whenever I took deep breaths, and I felt my organs swelling and moving from within as I rested. Sometimes, a ragged cough pulled up thick phlegm from the depths of my being. My fingers and toes tingled, as though falling asleep. My heartbeat fluttered.

"Finally catching the virus after nearly a year of successful evasion feels like sleeping with a celebrity," I joked with a girlfriend on the phone. "There's been so much hype in the news for months, and then suddenly it's inside of you. All your friends want to know what it feels like."

After three days, I couldn't smell or taste anything. I felt like a hungry ghost. A shell of a person, ordering bland takeout, pacing inside a single room, crying out to no one. People never mention how comforting one's sense of smell is. How its subtle immediacy can pull us fully into a sense of home or discord. Food became a joyless parade of texture. I ordered delivery Thai and couldn't taste a lick of it—just a mushy experience of noodle sensations on my wet tongue. Soup was a hot, watery liquid full of vegetable shapes. My morning tea brown and lifeless. What I wanted most in the world was to self-soothe with sensory comforts, and what I got was yet another invitation to dissociate completely, to fall backward into the murky void of my own head.

For more than a week, I stayed in bed as much as possible, trying to thank my body for healing from everything I had put it through that year, to commit to taking good care of myself, as though I were an attentive parent. Vaccines wouldn't be available for my age group for another five months. Slowing down was my only recourse. So much of having COVID was about being thrown into the less-than-stellar reality of having been incarnated into a meat-covered skeleton and choosing to love it, as best I could, each time a new upset threatened my very existence. Lying down like a wounded animal on a bed of moss and breathing into the pain, I knew that my body would carry me wherever I was supposed to go. It felt at once timeless and radical to let go and lie still. To focus 100 percent on my own recovery. If I was to continue doing great things, I needed to be a lot kinder to myself.

⤛⤜

Ten days of quarantine later, I could comfortably move around without my lungs heaving, but my sense of smell and taste were still gone. The CDC maintained that I would not be contagious as long as I had no fever. Considering that I had four parks left to complete in under a month and that I'd be traveling solo in a private vehicle, I reasoned that I could safely hit the road.

It seemed only fitting that the next park on the agenda was the place where my journey began: Sequoia. After wiping down every surface in the guesthouse, after driving north through a lingering haze for four hours, and after curving my tiny van around a death-defying mountain road, I parked in a pullout with a view of the bare granite mound of Moro Rock and just stared, ravaged by the world.

Both awestruck and crestfallen, I wandered around the Tall Trees Trail, craning my neck skyward to take in the towering giant sequoias. These enormous plants could live to be three thousand years old, and I wondered how they had faced so much fire and war and uncertainty and remained steadfast through it all.

I drove to the parking area for Moro Rock, hoping to summit the backside of its glacier-polished granite just as the sun began to set, turning the entire Kaweah River Valley a profane shade of coral. My lungs could barely keep up, though the trail was little more than a few hundred yards of stone-cut stairs. A raven's throaty croak sounded as I neared the top, and as my boots hit the mountain's crest, I was rewarded with a view I hadn't seen since my first-ever trip to the park at eighteen years old, in college and so confident it hurt. The bird hopped around from rock to rock in the dying light, blue-black feathers ruffling in the breeze. I tried to remind myself that this was my homecoming, the place where I first fell in love with the national parks, the genesis of the trip, but the weary weight in my soul could barely muster the energy for short one-mile hikes, let alone self-reflection. That night, parked in an illegal campsite hidden behind a massive dirt berm, I fell asleep for nearly ten hours as the temperature dropped close to freezing.

I woke feeling rested and refreshed and like a different person entirely, my breath icy and lingering in the chilly morning air. Before I returned to Los Angeles, I intended to soak up as much ancient tree wisdom as I could, so I sped up the twisting park road once again, pull-ing off near a circular stand of sequoias that rose like Roman columns from the forest floor. Leaving the door cracked and the keys switched off in the ignition, I stepped out of Gizmo's warm embrace and edged slowly into the belly of the wooded ring. I gazed up at the trees' lower branches, eighty feet above my head and thick as a large oak trunk. My vision blurred as I kept my eyes fixed on the sky, spinning in a circle and letting the leaves transmute into a kaleidoscope of rusty bark and emerald needles. I walked between trees ravaged by centuries-old fire scars and grazed my fingertips across names that had been carved in the 1940s, feeling like the only person on earth. Their bark was furry and red like an animal, and as I pressed my palms against a trunk as wide as my van, I silently prayed for the patience and resilience that these trees seemed to carry so effortlessly.

This was my first *real* park. My first love. A relationship I'd always carry with me no matter where I went.

When it was time to go, I steered around the hairpin turns of the park's main highway, bursting into tears when I finally realized what the year had truly been about. It was never a vacation; it was an initiation. A modern-day rite of passage to strip away anything that was superficial from my life, no matter how desperately I clung to it. David had as little to do with my identity as Adam; it was my job to define myself for myself. These days, we don't get assigned vision quests; we have to create them for ourselves. And that's exactly what I did. I spent a year wandering the wilderness, and this was where it led me: to a bone-deep knowing that I was strong and capable and joyful and resilient. All pain was conspiring to bring me home.

❦

Four months of celibacy had electrified my body, as though some fiend had snuck in after nightfall and plugged me into a wall socket. The slightest human touch felt like being on drugs, a potent cocktail of skin and hormones. I found myself lingering for too long in masked embraces each time I joined a friend for an outdoor picnic or stargazing meetup, ferocious and fay. I had denied myself so much that year in service of living off the grid, and I had watched my romantic life shatter like a glass dropped onto a hardwood floor. Pandemic dating could hardly scratch the itch. Humans were not designed for extreme isolation, and the wild animal of my own desire had become frightening inside the eggshell of my chest.

I set an in-person date with Aaron, a former competitive Scrabble player with a quick wit and a taste for electronic music festivals. We had met via Zoom a month earlier while I was still gallivanting around the East Coast, but this was our first chance to properly say hello. The evening went well enough, but I could tell from the jittery barrage of words that fell from his mouth that he was not the next love of my life.

Hey! I think you're really fun and interesting and attractive, he texted the next afternoon, but I just didn't sense the chemistry needed for a long-term relationship, and I'm kind of in the phase of my life where I'm looking for my person.

His tact and honesty impressed me.

Same, I typed back. I had a great time with you, and though you're a formidable texting partner, I didn't see relationship potential either.

Oh . . . Well in that case . . . He stuttered back into my life like a hungry cannibal. I'm not usually a friends with benefits person, but since neither of us has been touched in so long, and the pandemic is nowhere near over, maybe we could grab a drink and hook up one night?

I chuckled, feeling suddenly sly and powerful. I might actually be down. Let me see how I feel tomorrow.

Two nights later, my van was parked outside the stucco walls of an apartment complex in the San Fernando Valley, cool night air humming across my bare legs. Aaron greeted me and unlocked a large black gate, leading me past a long strip of landscaped bushes and down a vacant, beige hallway to his unit. I asked for a glass of water, nervous and itching for someplace to put my hands, then circled his room like a new pet he'd brought home, eyeing his books, his family photos, his wall hangings.

"When did you hike the PCT?" I asked as I held his gaze coyly, sitting down on a freshly made bed of crisp gray sheets.

In an instant, the tone shifted, and Aaron's breath was hot against my face as he kissed me hard and pinned down my wrists. I exhaled sharply, relieved. He was a hypnotically good kisser. *Maybe this won't be so bad after all,* I thought.

My clothes were almost entirely off before his sweater even hit the floor. Dress, lace panties, leather riding boots—all tossed aside. The entire act felt like a dance. We tumbled into each other for a long while, making out like teenagers.

"I'm going to have to be honest with you, it's been a while for me, and my insecurities are definitely acting up. This first time might not last very long." Aaron grinned sheepishly.

The raw, unexpected honesty of the moment made me laugh. What else but a global pandemic would force such an endearing, unguarded confession at the onset of a sexual fling?

There was something oddly beautiful about the entire experience. The admission of abject aloneness on both sides. The vulnerable communication between strangers. The fact that the year had thrown two consummate relationship seekers into a casual tryst for the sake of sanity. It felt real and rare and exposed in all the right ways.

We collapsed into a heap on his pillows. Then, both still naked, we started chatting about life and podcasts and how I wanted to move into a new apartment soon. I found myself fluttery and heated.

"Can I touch you?" I asked as he told me about a book he was reading. "Being allowed to have skin-on-skin contact feels like rolling . . . I'm so dizzy . . ."

We didn't rush. In fact, I stayed out well past my bedtime, falling into his sheets again and again until we were both spent. After Aaron walked me to my car, he kissed me softly and said that he couldn't wait to meet up again soon.

On the drive home, I saw that I had a ninety-three-dollar parking ticket stuck beneath my windshield wiper, flapping in the breeze, but I didn't mind. It was all worth it. I wasn't an untouchable anymore; I was a real girl.

Hiking in Haleakalā's enormous crater, Hawai'i

Chapter 9

Everywhere and Nowhere

I kept feeling like I was getting away with something simply by existing in the world. That was the odd gift of having had the coronavirus and developing antibodies; a veil had been lifted. My mind felt elevated to a bizarre new level by way of having gone through unforeseen terror. Though I still wore a mask in public, my fears about seeing people subsided.

With this newfound vigor, I boarded a ferry to Channel Islands National Park in Southern California, my friend Eva in tow. She seemed woozy about being around so many strangers, even though our seats were outside. There was a growing spike of new cases around the country, one that we both knew would only grow worse until after the new year.

"Do you want to postpone our Hawai'i parks trip until mid-January?" I asked, wanting to soothe her nerves and caring less about my timeline now that American Samoa was almost certainly off the docket. "I've sort of been wanting to look for my own apartment anyway. I feel bad staying with a friend I almost infected."

"Honestly, yeah. It would be a huge relief." Eva sighed as though she had been wanting me to ask for weeks. "I'd rather go later and actually enjoy our time there than feel stressed out 24/7 by the virus."

"I totally agree."

Just then, a flash of rubbery silver crested a wave to my left, then another, then another. A massive pod of dolphins, at least a hundred strong, leaped out of the water with contagious joy. The captain's voice came over the boat's loudspeaker, compressed and crackling as he spoke.

"Ladies and gentlemen, what we have here is a group of common dolphins. We've been seeing them pretty regularly out in these waters, and the pods can have up to six hundred members. We're gonna try to lower our speed and cruise alongside them for a few minutes."

It was an encouraging beginning to a day full of sunshine and hiking on Santa Cruz Island, the largest in the park. Once the boat docked, we immediately hopped onto the Pelican Bay Trail, ascending steeply through a tangle of chaparral and live oaks. The views were tremendous, all ocean and amber-hued hillsides. Occasionally, a tiny island fox would peek its head out from the wavering grass as if to say a quick hello before continuing on in its quest for food. We ate lunch on a rocky beach surrounded by sea cliffs, basking in the bliss of being out of the city.

"This is *exactly* the escape I was waiting for!" Eva exclaimed, and as we found our way back to the boat in the yellow haze of late afternoon, I felt the kind of lightness brewing inside me that only a day in the park could provide.

꧁꧂

The next two weeks passed in a blur of apartment hunting and trips to the big-box department stores that always left me feeling vacant and childlike. I settled on a large studio in a pet-friendly 1920s building with a shady garden out front, and the task of repurchasing all the furniture I had given up to live with Adam the year prior had turned into a full-time job. There was a deep sense in my bones that the thing I most needed after a year abroad was to nest and create a safe foundation for myself. Hawai'i would have to wait.

But my body wasn't cooperating. As ecstatic as I was about having a real bed and a shower, the uncomfortable realities of city life came rioting back at me. An endless procession of traffic sputtered up and down my block with an insanity-inducing barrage of sound. It seemed as though there was no end to the motorcycles and trucks that used the street as a go-between to avoid bumper-to-bumper jams on larger boulevards. On less than four hours of rest per night, my neighbors' footsteps were like bulls fighting a matador. Less than two, and birdsong became as blistering as a car alarm. My heart raced and fluttered in the middle of the night, uncertain what was an actual threat and what was just a bad muffler.

I also struggled with a lack of things to do. In the van, I had a purpose. There were places to drive to and parks to hike through nearly every day. Nature soothed me in my most trying times. But back in Los Angeles, the constant sun and smog and **FOR RENT** signs plastered across ecru stucco buildings began to pummel my spirit into the ground. With the city's bars and restaurants shuttered, I was living in a ghost town. I spent an entire week lying comatose on the couch, staring indolently at moving pictures on my laptop screen without so much as a fleeting memory of the plotlines. Sartre was wrong when he said, "Hell is other people." If we're not careful, hell is our own minds.

During a routine checkup, a nurse practitioner asked, "How long have you had anxiety for?"

"A few years, I guess. Maybe forever."

"Would you ever consider going on daily medication for it?"

I began to tear up in the blue-gray light of the exam room. Though many of my close friends managed their anxiety and depression with medicine, I had never considered the option for myself, mainly because

I believed that it constituted a massive failure on my part. Sure, other people might take drugs to level out their brains and improve their quality of life, but I wasn't like that. I was strong. I was unique. I could arm wrestle whatever demons befell me and come out on the other side laughing.

"Umm, no thanks. I think I'm fine with just my emergency Xanax prescription."

My sleep didn't improve.

⌘

How do you admit to yourself that you can no longer trust the narrative of your own mind? The thought rolled around my head like sand in the soft belly of an oyster as I drove north to visit my mom for Christmas, passing the frozen edges of the Sierra Nevada and the bleak, alkaline expanse of Mono Lake. *If I don't feel at home inside my own skull, where am I supposed to go?*

I opened the front door to the shrill yipping of my mother's chihuahua. She and her husband sat on the sofa and sipped what appeared to be their second glass of wine, talking over the constant yammer of a local news channel. It wasn't even 5:00 p.m.

"How was the drive, sweetie?"

"Good. It was interesting, you know? Driving through the Sierras felt like coming home to my favorite place, only . . . I'm a different person now."

I dropped the news about how I had been grappling with the idea of going on anti-anxiety meds, wanting to get her support before taking the plunge. She stared at me, perplexed, and raised a solitary eyebrow, pausing for a long moment before speaking.

"You know, Emily, there are lots of other things you can do to help anxiety, like breathing exercises, or meditation, or working out, or talking to someone," she declared, taking another swig of wine. "It's like when you were a kid and you almost got diagnosed with ADHD. I decided to not put you on the drugs, because I knew you didn't really need them."

"But, Mom, I exercise more than anyone I know, and I meditate every day. This feels *different*. Something feels wrong."

"Well, I suppose if you do decide to go on the pills, it should be with a plan to go off them at some point. Like by July or in a year or something like that." No one ever asks when people plan to go off their thyroid medication.

"Sure, Mom," I snapped as I left the room to unpack.

I was gutted, trying to reach out for solace in a sea of uncertainty and finding myself instead floating endlessly over waves of shape-shifting emotions. I felt like a fucking cowboy inside my own mind, jolted up and down by the maniacally kicking beast that I was tied to.

My mother drank a bottle and a half of wine on Christmas Eve and passed out on the couch while yelling at her smart speaker to play Van Morrison. I couldn't sleep. In the morning, she came clean, admitting to me that she'd developed a drinking problem, and that she didn't know when or how to stop. I told her I would help her find a good therapist. I told her I could send her a list of online AA meetings. I told her I was around if she ever needed to vent.

I was dangling at the end of a thin rope and had been for months. For an entire year, I had yearned for a home that kept being stripped away from me. I craved a safe place to land that no one was able to provide, and I fell face-first into the dirt each time I counted on someone else to cradle my woes. I knew then that it was up to me to be the arms I wrapped myself in, the sweet song I sang myself to sleep with, the safe space I came to at the end of a long day. Maybe that's why dialing in my mental health felt more crucial than ever. In spite of the ever-shifting void, I needed a place to land within myself. Home should have been inside me all along.

⤞⤝

On the day I left my mom's house, she was rushed to the emergency room with intestinal bleeding. I dropped the phone when I heard the news and tumbled into a full-blown panic attack, hunching over my steering wheel and sobbing. I pulled over and allowed my mind to spin out for a few minutes, staring at the dizzying expanse of mountains before me. If I could have, I would have turned around immediately and rushed to her side, but in the wake of the pandemic, hospitals had stopped allowing all visitors. I couldn't see her. I didn't know what to do. The day was brisk and sunny, and the blue sky seemed to taunt me with cheeriness as I continued to drive the long six hours back to Los Angeles.

After two days of observation and a truckload of antibiotics, my mother recovered and was released, but my own health was in a tail-spin. I was done despairing, ready to pull the ripcord and take whatever medical advice I was given. I had spent too much time crawling around in the dark without a lantern or a map.

I texted Adam for the name of a psychiatrist he trusted. I think it's good that you're finally taking care of yourself, Em. Ever since getting on my new meds, I've been waking up without a constant sense of impending doom.

⤞⤝

My first session with the psychiatrist was nothing like talk therapy. Instead of inquiring about my feelings and how my week was going, he got right down to business, going through a questionnaire about my family's history with addiction, divorce, and mental illness. There was a big question mark around my dad's side of the family, since none of them had spoken to me in more than ten years, but I had heard stories as a teenager about my father's drug and alcohol use. I gave the doctor as much information as I could remember.

"Mm, addiction can mask a lot," he murmured, typing notes here and there as I tried to hold myself together and not cry or babble too much.

I walked to a grocery store three blocks from my new apartment to fill the prescription he gave me, stalking the fluorescently lit aisles and fingering tantalizing mounds of organic goat cheese and vegan ice creams while I waited. It seemed absurd to me that I could walk into a brightly decorated supermarket blaring Katy Perry's greatest hits and pick up a psychoactive substance that would soon dig its fingers into my brain and leave my personality slightly altered.

Puffs of sage smoke wafted around my apartment as I put on a song called "Samadhi" and tried to turn what felt like a pharmaceutical chore into a personal ritual. "Samadhi" means "to come together" in Sanskrit, which seemed fitting. I wanted to yoke together the chemically dysfunctional side of my mind with and the wonderful, amazing, happy part. Both halves were mine to own and love; I just needed the volume turned down.

The doctor told me to start with five milligrams of duloxetine, which meant I would need to split the dosage nightly before bed. I spilled the contents of the small, generic orange pill capsule onto my coffee table as sitars vibrated through my apartment. Dozens of tiny white balls bounced across the wood, and I gathered them up with my hands, scooping each palm gently across the flat surface to create a small pile. I imagined the little white spheres caressing the maze of my brain, melting over the lumpy pink mass that contains my thoughts and everything I understand to be me. It felt strange to know that something so small could hold such hugeness within it.

Tears slowly began to trickle down my cheeks, and I pressed my palms together in front of my heart, squeezed my eyes shut, and said a little prayer.

I am grateful for the opportunity to change.

I am grateful to have the resources to get the help I need.

I am grateful to have the time to try something new that might better my life and create more harmony and peace.

With that, I opened my eyes, licked my right index finger, dipped it into the medicine, and swallowed.

❧

The side effects came on during a therapy session the next morning, and it was all I could do to mutter for him to stop talking so that I could grip the armrest of my velvet sofa and breathe. I was embarrassed and nauseous, my chest dropping into my gut like a kettlebell. It felt like having a doctor watch me come up on a bad mushroom trip from the less-than-kind vantage point of a Zoom camera. My therapist told me to stick with it if I could bear the discomfort. "Most people go on these meds and give up after two or three days, because they freak out. The truth of the matter is that they should settle in under a week, and you'll be feeling much better."

I had entered into the ordeal cocky and certain that I would be one of the rare and lucky exceptions who faces no side effects and runs through fields of joy into her new life. But this, of course, was fantasy. I called my friend Alice.

"Expecting zero side effects is basically setting yourself up for failure." Her no-nonsense advice was exactly what I needed. I laced up my shoes and stepped out into the dappled light of my building's garden. Winding a little maze through the lush, green parks and vintage houses of my new neighborhood, I could feel my panic subsiding, as if moving my body were a way to wave a wand across any tension that befell me.

❧

When the time came to fly to Hawai'i, I hadn't slept for more than four hours at a time in over a month. Still stuck in my handmade cocoon, hoping that one day I would blossom, I boarded a plane to Maui and sat next to Eva, trembling from stress and exhaustion. The five-hour flight was turbulent from beginning to end, and by the time we found our rental camper van in the huge, sunny parking lot, my head was throbbing.

"Let's get you set up quickly so I can show you how everything works and you can be on your way." Sean from Campervan Hawai'i was friendly and no-nonsense, walking us around the twenty-foot vehicle with a special attention to detail.

"This right here is your sink nozzle that can pull out all the way and make an outdoor shower, and over here is where we hide the platform to fold out a second bed."

The van was massive compared to Gizmo, an RV complete with a toilet, dinette booth, and front swivel seats. Driving it on the remote roads into Haleakalā National Park would surely be a challenge, but Eva and I did our best to smile and feign confidence as we signed the paperwork and took off.

A pounding force radiated up from the back of my skull to my front temples. After a quick stopover at Whole Foods, I had Eva take the wheel. I hung my head in my hands and prayed that this wasn't another side effect of my new medication, that the warm, tropical air and a good night's sleep might somehow cure me.

We had arranged to stay at a hippie commune that doubled as a bee farm, where we navigated up a steep gravel driveway in the black of night. Apart from a solitary porta-potty and a vacant stand selling local honey, the place was barren. Not a single one of the tent dwellers came out to greet us, and the entire property seemed to occupy a twenty-degree tilt. There wasn't a level spot in the joint to park the van. After an hour of lurching forward and backward in the campground's loose rocks, the two of us settled on the flattest surface we could find—a patch of dirt right next to the john with a mighty view of the ocean.

After dinner, my headache worsened, so I climbed into the van's tilted but spacious rear bed, setting up a blockade with extra pillows so that I wouldn't roll off in the night. By the time the sun had blinked its dazzling yellow eye open, I had racked up another miserable night spent sparring with my thoughts.

Eva and I took our time that morning, brewing coffee, scrambling eggs, and cutting up exotic fruits so that we could bask in the sweaty embrace of the island's humid air and take in the view. One of the things I appreciated most about my year on the road was how often it forced me to slow down and breathe in the small moments, the ones in between the Yosemite Valleys and the Grand Canyons. Feeling well enough to drive, I gave Eva a break and decided to circumnavigate the island counterclockwise so that our afternoon could be spent waterfall-hopping.

The thing is that no one ever told us about "the back road to Hana," a terrifying feat to accomplish in a regular sedan, much less a massive RV with the turning radius of a hippopotamus. So as my body acclimated to the new drugs, my mind scrambled to acclimate to a rural backroad that was rocky and rutted and practically falling off the edge of a sea cliff.

"Are we even allowed to be here? How is this a road?!" I shrieked to Eva and whatever deities would listen as I spun the steering wheel around to avoid rolling into the ocean and never being found.

"It's called a highway, right?" she squealed back, just as confused as I was.

"Yes! This isn't some little backcountry campsite road. It's called the . . . Pi'ilani Highway, I think."

Gritting my teeth on the hairpin curves, I gasped and shouted expletives each time a car approached from the opposite direction or the passenger-side tires nearly edged off the cliff. On the verge of cardiac arrest, Eva and I rolled into Haleakalā with our hearts pounding, flustered but ready to shake off the morning's terror with a good hike. I filled my water bladder and stuffed my backpack full of snacks. Brow already slick with the sweat of the day, I laced up my hiking boots and hit the trail.

A thick buzz of insects hung in the air like a fever as we ascended stone steps through a salt-sprayed coastal rain forest. The bright hibiscus flowers and sky-hungry banyan trees elicited the notion that we had been strung up in a large slingshot and flung halfway across the world. The sun was relentless as we climbed, hot air steaming out of my lungs and into the lush jungle. The two of us strolled across wooden boardwalks and rugged stairs hewn from black volcanic stone, eventually finding ourselves amid the gentle creaking of a towering bamboo forest.

I stood in the shade for a long while, letting a breeze tousle my bangs as the soft clicking sounds of bamboo trees knocking against each other radiated out like two river stones tapping. It was as though the forest itself had a pulse, and we were inside of it. Jutting our chins upward and spinning around endlessly to a choir of ancient souls.

The apex of the hike—Waimoku Falls—rushed down a cliff face four hundred feet high, the torrent of fresh water bordered on all sides by imposing green vines and tropical shrubbery. Spent from the day's exertion, I dipped my hat in a nearby stream and scooped a load of cool water onto my head. It trickled down my face and shoulders, giving me goosebumps as I turned around and marched back along the trail.

❦

By the time we made it to the van, my hiker's high had turned into an intense fatigue brought on by the heat. The bottom of my skull rumbled, and I could feel a restless irritability and the beginnings of another headache start to stew.

"I miss my old brain," I muttered to Eva, slouching over the small laminate table as I tried to eat an egg sandwich and a few slices of pineapple. "This whole thing is so scary, because I don't know if or when I'll ever feel normal again."

"I get it, girl. A few years ago, my anxiety was so bad that I couldn't even commit to something as simple as volunteering on a Tuesday night, because I didn't know if I would be able to function."

"Really? What did you do?"

"I had to start working with a nutritionist. I got into therapy. The breathwork I've been doing every morning also really helps."

"I have a feeling it's going to be months or years before I'm back to where I was, if I'm ever there again."

"Listen, this stuff takes time. But investing in yourself is the one thing that's always worth the effort. There's only one you on the planet, and if you don't take care of your health, you're going to constantly feel chewed up by the world. Trust me."

My stomach churned, and my brain wanted to punch a wall. I knew Eva was just trying to help, but my month and a half of no sleep could ripple the waves of reality and make any sound that entered my airspace feel like a dental drill.

"Can you drive, please?" I knew it was time to switch myself off for the day. "I'm down to listen to any music you want as long as I don't have to drive."

But the Hāna Highway was long and winding, hugging the sharp curves of the island's largest volcano beneath a leafy jungle canopy, and twenty minutes after Eva had begun her shift, she was anxious and eager to have me take the wheel again.

We rolled through small villages and past black-sand beaches, continuing our large circle around the island and back to camp. A brief pit stop for some fresh coconuts gave us a burst of new energy, until we drove on and saw that a massive tree had recently collapsed, blocking

236

the road. Small cars and trucks were passing beneath its fat branches just fine, but when the officer on duty saw our tall van, he strolled over.

"You're going to have to turn around, miss. Your van's too big."

Eva and I looked at each other, the light in our eyes fading.

"Are you sure we couldn't just slowly drive up to the tree trunk and check if we'll fit?"

"No, ma'am. You'll have to go back the way you came."

Eva looked like she was about to cry. "But, sir, that other highway is insane! We can't drive on it!"

It made no difference. We would have to either brave the death-defying cliff's-edge road or find somewhere to camp on the opposite end of Maui. We slowly turned around.

"I wish we could just pull up to one of those little farms we passed and ask to park for, like, twenty bucks," I said, doubtful that it would ever happen. But the moment I finished the sentence, we passed a neon-orange bus with bubbles and swirls painted on its side. A large purple sign with cartoon letters soared up from its roof: COCONUT GLEN'S ICE CREAM.

Had I stumbled into an exhaustion so deep that my mind was conjuring Willy Wonka–style hallucinations? I pulled the van into a small dirt parking lot, and Eva hopped out, doing her best to play it cool.

"Hey there, listen . . . This tree fell onto the road a few miles up, and now we have nowhere to sleep for the night because that crazy backwoods highway scares the shit out of us. Is there any chance we could give you twenty dollars to stay here? We'll be gone in the morning."

A cute twentysomething brunette covered in mandala tattoos was working the booth. Her lips curled up in a serene smile as she answered: "Sure! I don't see why not."

This is why I love hippies.

She directed us to a flat, grassy parking spot that seemed specifically designed to hold their wandering van friends, and just as we were getting settled, a black-and-white spotted pit bull ran up and started begging for scratches.

"Oh, don't worry about him—that's just Snoopy Dog!" the sweet brunette shouted as she started closing up shop. "Last call. You want anything?"

"I'll take a passionfruit scoop, please."

It was like the world was throwing us a bone right when we needed it most, and from the comfortable vantage point of our new home in the rain forest, I could feel my headache begin to lift. I fell asleep early to the occasional whooshing of cars along the road, feeling like I was exactly where I was supposed to be.

⌘

The funny and sinister thing about having an anxiety disorder severe enough to warrant medication is that there comes a point when your life is so disrupted that you find yourself in a constant bargaining mindset. It's like going through those pesky five stages of grief, only your mind trips over the one that makes you feel like an esoteric stockbroker, and you get stuck there, possibly forever. When I first spoke to a psychiatrist, I had been adamant about not losing my sex drive, supremely confident that my body was strong and would weather the storm without side effects. I thought my mental health would be a one-month problem, tops, like getting your transmission rebuilt or trying to get through a James Joyce novel, then poof! Better sleep and the return of the old Emily.

But my mind's state had moved into a level of severity I didn't even know existed. I would have gladly traded a year of sex for the ability to flip the channel to my previous self. There were sharp, daily mood swings and jolts of physical discomfort. There was the fact that my heart would seize up for no reason in the middle of the night, stirring me awake for hours at 3:00 a.m. It was unsustainable. While hiking along the lush, tropical trails of Hawaiʻi, I often caught myself locked in an imaginary Faustian bargain with whatever deity would listen, desperate to barter anything or anyone I held most dear for a sliver of sanity.

⤳

My troubled, divine bargaining spilled into the next day as Eva and I threw on our hiking shoes and set off on what is perhaps the most famous hike in the national park: the Sliding Sands Trail, an eleven-mile trek into the belly of the Haleakalā Crater, a rugged no-man's-land where few things dared to grow. In Hawaiian, "Haleakalā" means "house of the sun," and the volcano that bears this name is steeped in ancient lore. Many years ago, the demigod Maui wanted to make the days longer so that his mother's tapa cloth might dry better and crops might grow faster. As one of the strongest and cleverest of the gods, he devised a plan. One morning, Maui ran to the top of the towering volcano, and as soon as the sun began to peek up beyond the horizon, he lassoed it, holding its bright rays firmly in place. The sun begged Maui to let go, and he agreed on one condition—that the sun slow its daily crawl across the sky to provide the island with more sunlight. To this day, the summit of Haleakalā has an average of fifteen more minutes of light than the coastal towns below.

As Eva and I stepped out onto a small ledge just beyond the parking lot, we nabbed our first glimpse of the steep drop into the immense belly of the volcano. With a crater the size of the island of Manhattan, Haleakalā is a mostly dormant volcano that last erupted more than 230 years ago. Seeing it up close was like gazing out at the surface of Mars: brilliant rust-hued cinder cones rising up like tremendous ant hills in a landscape of compacted ash and jagged igneous rocks.

We hiked down, passing craggy outcroppings the size of city blocks and dried lava fields made up of pockmarked gobs of black stone. There were hardly any other people on the trail. As we neared the crater's floor, dozens of small, faint-green plants began to freckle the crust of the earth.

"I think I've heard about these!" I shouted back to Eva. "Silverswords. They only grow here, on the volcano."

The plants each looked like a thistle bud ready to burst into bloom, or a succulent you might purchase for your mother at a bodega in Middle Earth. They were endangered, that much I knew, after thousands of tourists in the early days of the park tried to smuggle them out as souvenirs. Now they sit like tiny, gray-green crowns upon the crater floor, waiting up to ninety years to bloom once and then die.

The two of us brightened up at the sight of a little greenery, and after hiking twenty-eight hundred feet straight down into the volcano's mouth, we giddily took a sudden left onto a thin path marked only by a faint dimple of footprints in the rocky ground. Guarding our shins against several narrow hallways of dark, ragged lava rock, we soon found ourselves climbing between two enormous cinder cone mounds the color of burned terra-cotta. We were blissfully lost in a gorgeous wasteland. The stark scenery helped to flatline my negative thoughts for much of the afternoon, but by the time I was huffing and puffing my way up the main switchbacks en route to the van, I could feel the little monsters in my brain begin to whip out their claws again.

The next morning was worse. After another night without sleep, my waking life was suspended somewhere between dreamland and consciousness. I could feel my mind hovering above my wrecked body, watching its parade of terrors like a late-morning soap opera. I couldn't speak without snapping, my mouth a trigger-happy scorpion. Eva trod lightly. I begged her to take the wheel on our drive to Mākena Beach so that I could space out in the passenger seat with my head down and my sunglasses on, sincerely wishing that I could skip the next few months of my life.

In the sticky heat of the day, I hurled my body into cerulean waves and allowed the current to carry me wherever it wanted. Tears streamed down my face, mingling with the salty water as I stared up at the bright blue sky and felt smaller than I had in my entire life. *Please,* I pleaded with the ocean, *help heal my broken mind. I'm not sure how much longer I can take this.*

We lay on the beach all day, intermittently napping and dunking our bodies into the water. Tiny black ants crawled across my legs and belly as I tilted my head into the shade of an umbrella to read, fearing that this trip around the country had very much become a trip away from myself.

❧

The shrill, robotic sounds of our airplane's wheels lowering alerted me that we would soon be landing on the Big Island, the last stop on my yearlong journey. I tossed my headphones into my purse and grabbed my two carry-on bags, now bursting with snacks, towels, and souvenirs.

"Only one park left to go." Eva sighed. "How are you feeling?"

"Decent. I just wish I could enjoy it more, you know?"

After following a gaggle of masked tourists in floral shirts and pink terrycloth sundresses, we showed our negative COVID test documents to a woman at a makeshift kiosk outside, then waited eagerly for our new wheels. Not five minutes later, a twentysomething surfer dude who could have been straight off the set of *Dawson's Creek* rolled up in a vintage Volkswagen Eurovan, our home for the next four nights.

We shrieked like teenagers with excitement as the young man showed us how everything inside functioned. It was a bohemian dream. A propane stove, mini fridge, pantry, closet, and two beds, one in the pop-top and one on the pullout couch. I couldn't wait to get that thing on the road. Compared to the previous island's massive RV, this vintage VW would give us serious street cred. The moment he dropped the keys into my palm, we thanked him profusely, cranked up a thumping mix of house music on Eva's phone, and hightailed it to a grocery store. It felt like old times. Before my head broke, and I couldn't sleep, and the world wasn't a melted and rotting Dalí painting of my own making.

As night began to fall, we cruised across the island's saddle road, a steep highway between two slumbering volcanoes that stood on opposite ends of the landmass. We eventually neared a hand-painted wooden sign that read MOON GARDEN FARM and pulled onto a muddy dirt road lit only by the faint threads of garden lights. I climbed out of my seat and let the warm night air wash over me as a chorus of frogs croaked out a thunder of deep, mournful cries.

✼

I was beginning to realize that courage isn't something we're born with; it's forged in the fire of our own experience. Molded in the muck of our traumas and our willingness to overcome them with grace. I woke the next morning having only slept two hours, but I could feel a familiar tug inside my heart to hike anyway. To keep going. To finish what I had started.

So after a quick breakfast, Eva and I drove for twenty minutes along a jungle highway until we pulled off and parked in front of the visitor center for Hawai'i Volcanoes, my sixty-first national park. I breathed a sigh of relief as I donned my backpack and adjusted my trekking poles.

In the time since we delayed our trip, an eruption had begun on Kīlauea, the most active of the five volcanoes that make up the Big Island, and we were excited by the possibility of witnessing new earth being made. We strolled along a level path through the tropical forest, past bright yellow sulfur crystals looking like radioactive waste and hissing steam vents wafting noxious gases into the air. After crossing the park's main road, we merged onto the Crater Rim Trail and began hiking faster toward a large tendril of smoke emanating up from the mountain's collapsed summit. Leis and flower crowns hung in bunches along a fence to our left—offerings to the goddess Pele. In Hawaiian, her full name is Pelehonuamea, or "she who shapes the sacred land." As a deity, she is revered as much for her powers of creation as for her powers of destruction. They are two sides of the same coin; one cannot exist without the other.

When we reached the final viewpoint, I gazed out at the smoldering chasm of the Halema'uma'u Crater for a long time, watching the clouds and smoke dance overhead as I felt a hot breeze kiss my face. It seemed as though a volcano had erupted in the very core of my being, and there was still so much new earth to chart. I had watched my day job, my relationship, my social life, and my mental health blow up, leaving me learning how to live in an ever-shifting, groundless world. I had a new apartment and the occasional urge for companionship. Some of my life had been completely obliterated, and some, like the boiling earth below, was rugged and infant and yearning for exploration.

Eva and I returned to the van and headed off for the Kīlauea Iki Trail, parking and descending over four hundred feet to a crater that had exploded into a fiery lava lake in 1959, with a fountain of molten rock spewing nineteen hundred feet into the sky. Now the dormant volcanic site is one of the most popular hikes in the park, dotted here and there with hearty pioneer plants like the 'ōhi'a tree, which burrows its roots into the unforgiving terrain of dried lava beds and shoots up tufted red blossoms. I was surrounded by evidence of reincarnation, the stubborn insistence of the earth that all things can and must be made new again.

Together, Eva and I rambled across the immense black lava field, hopping over enormous cracks where pressure had once built up and broken apart the old ground below. We curved around fissures of jagged, lead-gray teeth and leaped across huge voids, playing hopscotch on the rough earth. It was exhilarating.

When we had again scaled the edge of the monstrous crater, I paused for a moment and looked out across the ever-changing landscape, slung halfway between heaven and earth. These mountains were the birthplace of all things, it seemed, and I felt so lucky to be a part of their story, if only for an instant.

With a crackle of oil on the stove, Eva and I fried up eggs and tortillas in our new van for a late lunch. We sat and ate and waited for the sun to go down, munching on carrot sticks and hummus in the trailhead parking lot before shifting into gear and cruising over to the park's more active crater. A small cluster of tourists was gathering on the viewing platform, and I threw on a thick jacket and hurried out of the van to stake out a space while Eva parked.

As the sun dipped slowly beyond the seemingly infinite edge of the horizon, a faint wisp of pink began to crawl up from the crater below. Though we couldn't see the eruption from where we were standing, at night the supernatural glow of lava caught a rising white specter of volcanic gas as it lifted hundreds of feet toward the stars above. Once all traces of sunlight had disappeared, the gleam intensified, illuminating the smoke in shades of bloodred and fuchsia. A pulsing, glowing chasm of molten rock shining beautifully through the dark.

The entire scene felt remarkably womblike, young earth gestating in the steaming maw of this torrid hellscape, wrapped in warmth. Churning for months until it became something of substance. Seeping with possibility. Like the caterpillar in her tightly wound chrysalis, the nascent planet was utterly unrecognizable from what we call home. It took time to sprout legs and start moving.

⌘

My mind continued to resemble primordial mush as Eva drove us to Carlsmith Beach Park the next morning. Unlike traditional white sand beaches, the frequent lava flows on the eastern border of the Big Island made for coarse, black rocks along the shoreline, surrounded by grassy lawns where people could spread out on their chairs and towels. It was like hanging out in a backyard, only to have the ground suddenly give way to brilliant aquamarine lagoons lined with pocky volcanic boulders.

Eva read on her beach towel while I rolled around in the shade, facedown, quietly begging my mind to stop screaming obscenities at me. I had essentially finished my trip, and yet I felt like I had failed in some massive, unforgivable way. I hadn't found myself; I wasn't even close. I had lost my partner, my anxiety was worse than ever, and on top of it all, I couldn't even sleep. As I flopped around on the grass, I started texting Alice that my mental health hadn't improved, that I was beginning to have minor suicidal ideations.

It's not that I want to kill myself, I tried to explain as my clumsy fingers tapped away across the slick phone screen. It's just that . . . I don't know if I want to stick around if life is always going to be like this. It's too painful.

The most opinionated of my friend group, Alice immediately jumped in with a plan. This doesn't sound normal. Are you taking the medication as prescribed?

Yes.

And your sleep hasn't gotten any better at all?

No. It might actually be worse.

That's the thing about some of these psychoactive drugs—they occasionally have really severe side effects like making people suicidal. You're going to have to call your doctor immediately.

But . . . it's Saturday.

Doesn't matter. He should have an emergency hotline or something for situations like this.

Holding back tears, I relented and called my doctor's office. I clicked through when the automated message reached the very end: "If you are experiencing a medical emergency and need to contact the doctor outside of normal business hours, please press nine to be connected to his cell." Fuck. I had never imagined myself as Medical Emergency Girl, but as I sat there, listening to the phone ring, I realized how eager I was to have someone pick up.

"Yeah, this is Dr. Blum."

"Hey . . ." I said, trying desperately not to blubber as I explained what was going on. "I don't know what's wrong with me. I'm here, in Hawai'i, and it's been a week, and I'm still not sleeping, and I feel like my brain is falling apart, and I don't know what to do. I'm depressed, and I'm anxious, and I'm terrified. Does this mean I need to go off the medication?"

"Well . . . probably not." Dr. Blum was one of those classic old-school Jewish doctors. A beacon of friendly confidence and eccentricity. "*Could* these pills make you more anxious? Not likely. More *depressed*? Yeah, that's not really how they work. My bet is that we need to get you sleeping. Do you have any Xanax with you?"

"I've only got a few left, but yeah."

"Good. Take one tonight before bed."

"And what if I wake up?"

"Take another half every time you wake up until you get eight hours of rest, and call me tomorrow if you're still not sleeping." With that, he hung up, and I felt a huge wave of relief fall over my body. Though I didn't love the idea of lining my stomach with more drugs, I had a plan. I had my doctor's approval, and I had a plan.

I plopped my body into the park's cool, salty water and bobbed up and down in the waves of a small inlet, breathing in the sea and the sun and wondering if I would ever feel like myself again. As I floated along, buoyed by the gentle rocking of the ocean, a dark shape began to move toward me. It hovered just below the water's surface for a few moments before finally coming up for air two feet away from where I swam. A sea turtle. Peaceful and round like the dimpled cheeks of a Buddhist monk. We stared at each other for a spell, her eyes wise and knowing, silently taking in the moment before she dipped below the waves again and gracefully propelled herself back into the deep.

When you ask the world for healing, you begin to see it everywhere you look.

꧁

A soft beam of golden light fell across my eyelids as I arched my back against the molded gray wall of the old Eurovan. I interlaced my fingers and stretched my arms skyward, gently pointing and flexing each toe while the choir of frogs died down. It was dawn. It was dawn, and I had slept through the night. What a simple and miraculous thing.

The sun shrugged its pink haze across the horizon, and I gazed out the rear window onto rolling fields of grass and citrus, pulling the crinkled sheets over my pale flesh as I waited in silence for Eva to wake up. No longer burdened like Atlas, holding up a spinning globe of anxiety and madness, I could feel a lift in my chest. The ability to inhale with ease. The notion that the natural world still contained some magic.

With our cell phones straining to connect to the outside world on two fleeting bars of service, Eva and I logged in to Kate's weekly dance session, popping wireless earbuds into our heads to catch the muffled bliss of ritual. The grass was moist with morning dew, and the nightly amphibious song had just about vanished. A soulful, lyrical tune blurred into my brain, followed by the bright vowels of Kate's voice.

"Good morning, my lovelies. It's been a long week, hasn't it?"

The solid mass of my sternum disbanded, at once supple and liquid, and my eyes welled up with the long-awaited tears of coming home. I traced my left foot across the wet grass and lunged deeply into my right hip, bending forward in prostration to the sun, the soil, and the sky. My arms undulated outward like the thick limbs of an octopus in a wavy procession that would have made Kali proud.

It was the end of my trip, and how fitting it seemed to spend the final few days held firmly in the grip of so much new earth. New earth that wasn't always pretty. New earth that nearly killed me. New earth that was vicious and goopy and filled with poisonous gas. Destructive and rageful and dark. Bubbling up from the inside out as though possessed. Beginnings aren't always beautiful; they are bloody and sutured and limping. Messy and terrible and heart-ripping.

Births are violent, sanguine affairs. Why should my own be any different?

Kate's voice blasted into my eardrums. "Your sweetness and your resilience are what's going to save you," she hummed, warming the space between my temples. "Your joy is what's going to save you." I fell to my knees in the muddy grass, fat gobs of soil staining the skin of my legs, my forehead rolling against the wet blades, my hands digging wildly into the ashen muck of the ground. "Because none of us has any idea what's going to happen this year or next. If you're going to be handling poison, make sure you've got a bucket of honey. You've got to bathe your soul in a bucket of honey to suffuse your sense of sweetness."

A thousand green fingers of grass brushed up against my bare shins as I began to lose myself in great, quivering sobs. I would never again be the same person I was, and the acceptance of this fact rocketed straight into my heart while my body rolled madly into the hillside, weeping and howling and giggling like a possessed child. My guts spilled out onto the earth—a bloody, yawning chrysalis breaking apart into a new self. A self that knew how to be gentle. A self that knew how to be terrible. A self that did not bend to the whims of others, that took care of its body and chased beauty with abandon. To survive, I would have to learn to enjoy the broken parts. To revel in the chaos of feeling breathlessly alone and ripped open. Bewitched by my own freedom and terror.

If I were to thrive in the new normal, the pursuit would not be to bandage whatever wounds befell me and heal them as quickly as possible but to lean into the uncomfortable spots. To breathe deeply, knowing that, yes, things were messy, maybe they always would be, and maybe that was okay.

My toes sank into the slush of the dewy turf, and I fell into a trembling child's pose. The sting of wet earth and sweat alive in my nostrils, I held still for a moment as the wayward animal of my breath came back to center. As chickens ran across the glistening sod in the distance, I began to whisper a small and hushed prayer: *I have been a fugitive from the void for too long. I have traveled too far to keep running away. If I am to love, let it be easy. If I am to find horror, let me wrap a ring of flowers around its neck.*

If I am to belong nowhere, let me belong everywhere.

ACKNOWLEDGMENTS

I'd be remiss if I didn't extend exactly 542 hugs and rambunctious expressions of thanks to both my agent at Janklow and Nesbit, Chad Luibl, and my editor at Little A Publishing, Laura Van der Veer, for taking a chance on this book when it was in its not-so-adorable infancy and for their countless hours spent reading and offering notes to help create the bundle of words you now hold.

Sincerest thanks to Hal Clifford, for providing additional editorial support and making sure that I got my species of woodpeckers straight. Thanks to Jacy Johnson for enduring my nitpicking long enough to draft the perfect adventure map of my yearlong journey, and to Kristin Lunghamer and Shara Alexander for their expert PR work. Huge thanks to Luke, for being my friend and book mentor; without you, none of this would have happened.

Massive thanks to both Abigail Wise and Mary Turner at *Outside* magazine for their incredible work shaping and editing my columns. Abby, you believed in this vision from day one; you've changed my life for the better in a million different ways, and I don't think I can ever overstate how grateful I am for that.

A thousand thanks to Itai, who shepherded me through the book-writing process (and the nausea, anxiety, terror, and joy contained therein) with the poise and good humor of a cheeky old monk, and for generally being one of the most kindhearted humans I've ever had the honor of knowing and loving. Life is more blissful with you in it.

Thanks to Brian, who gave me the courage I needed to flee the nest and the nudge I didn't know I needed to stay out of it forever. To Brandon for always offering the best (and most oblique) advice. To J.C. for occasionally joining the adventure and always texting me back late at night when it felt like the world was falling apart. To Julia for listening and understanding across the airwaves when it felt like no one else could. To Alex for being the very best kitten ninja witch a gremlin could ask for—you have saved my life more times than I can count. To Ave for holding my hand through two of the worst weeks of my life and for doing so with grace.

Thank you to Farry, Aryiel, Nick, Peggy, Onyx, Erika, Alison, Galen, Cameron, Maude, Jason, Brendan, Myra, Jacqui, Alleghany, and the dozens of others who either met up with me on the road, offered a driveway to sleep in, called me up on the phone, or helped brighten my spirits on a random trail. Thanks to Sister D for holding my hand spiritually when the light got dim. Thank you to Sean for making the leaving part easy and for setting me up for success, and thanks to the guides I hired along the way—your enthusiasm and wealth of knowledge added much-needed color and soul to what could have otherwise been a blurry year of wandering.

Huge gobs of thanks to my mother for being a great role model for strength, perseverance, independence, and resilience as I grew up. Your zest for travel and adventure is mirrored in my own. Thank you for fearlessly handling me as a headstrong teenager (and a headstrong adult) with more love than I even knew existed.

Thank-yous and bear hugs to Jim for being my chosen family and for catching me in your wings when I had none of my own—the risk to remain tight in a bud is nearly always more painful than the risk it takes to blossom. And thanks to Daniel for helping me to feel whole again after the world dragged me through its wreckage.

Lastly, enormous, soul-splitting, elephant-sized gratitude to Kate for her guidance, mischief, and bone-deep advice along the way. Whatever souls are made of, ours are the same.

ABOUT THE AUTHOR

Photo © 2022 Darren Eskandari

Emily Pennington is an adventurer, world traveler, and freelance writer. Apart from being a regular columnist at *Outside* magazine, she's had work published in the *New York Times*, *The Guardian*, *Condé Nast Traveler*, and *Backpacker* magazine, among others, as well on dozens of websites, including Lonely Planet, mindbodygreen, Adventure Journal, and REI Journal. Emily has also appeared on NPR and the podcasts *Women Who Travel*, *Anxiously*, *The Outdoor Renaissance*, *Of Mountains and Men*, and *Tough Girl Podcast*. Los Angeles is Emily's home base, but you can often find her sleeping in the dirt all over Sequoia, Yosemite, and the Eastern Sierra.